"*Unraveling Fairy Tales* invites its readers on a journey to personal tra... intimate relationship with God. The book is well-written and offers an opportunity for personal or group study. Each chapter provides five daily readings with prompts for personal reflection. Every day I found something I could ponder, reflect on, or a truth I could apply to my life. I recommend this book for new believers in Jesus as well as those who have walked in a relationship with Him for years. There are treasures hidden within for any reader."

 —Kristie Fredrickson, The Olive Branch Ministries

"I loved the Chicken Little chapter in Unraveling Fairy Tales, and I found value in every chapter. I appreciated Kim's willingness to be vulnerable in sharing her life experiences, which were believable and engaging. As a group leader, I enjoyed the questions at the end of each chapter and the page numbers provided to find the answers. The chapters promoted great authentic discussions. The group, many who didn't know each other very well, grew close because of it, which was fun to see. Now they light up when they see each other!"

 —Pam Haglund, Living Well Women's Coaching

"Kim's conversational writing style is engaging and encouraging. She points readers to God's love in a non-judgmental manner. She recognizes we are all in different places and shows us God meets us where we're at. I enjoyed her personal stories and appreciated her honest transparency. Anyone who truly wants to experience a new closeness to God would benefit from reading *Unraveling Fairy Tales*."

 —Pam Lagomarsino, Above The Pages Editorial Service

"I would recommend *Unraveling Fairy Tales* to any of my female friends who want to grow spiritually. Kim does an excellent job at intertwining fairy tales into our relationship with God—this book deserves your attention. A person should take her time with it, so that she can get the most from it. It really provided me more meaningful talks with God."

 —Judy Balluff, executive board member for Releasing Destiny World Wide

"*Unraveling Fairy Tales* offers a unique way to see who we really are in Christ against a backdrop of familiar fairy tales. The study awakens a spiritual desire within to know and love our Prince of Peace. Kim's stories are delightful and her illustrations are relatable, practical, and written in a loving way. Her authenticity helps group participants feel comfortable to be honest and open. It is a refreshing way to study Scripture and applicable to both young and old."

 —Marcie Lind

"I loved Kim's sense of humor and how her personal stories showed God at work in her life. She was real and transparent. Not at all preachy, but powerful. I found the fairy-tale elements engaging.

They did not detract from God's Word but helped illustrate biblical principles. I would recommend *Unraveling Fairy Tales* to any woman who wants to grow in her faith."

    —Nancy Bradley

"I highly recommend *Unraveling Fairy Tales* to any woman looking to grow in her faith. Weaving in fairy-tale elements is such a creative way to get faith lessons across! I wasn't sure what to expect, and I was genuinely surprised by each lesson. Kim shares personal, relatable stories and correlates fairy tales to everyday life and biblical principles. It was excellent!"

    —Donna Villiard

"For a closer relationship with God, let the Spirit work through this carefully researched, creative, uplifting, authentic Bible study."

    —Helen Allenson

Unraveling Fairy Tales

Learning to Live Happily Ever After

Kim A. Larson

Contents

Introduction

Life rarely happens as planned. My dream of marrying a hometown boy and living on a farm near my parents never came true. Nor did having half a dozen children or being a stay-at-home mom. And, unfortunately, I still live three hundred miles from my hometown—the place and people I never intended to leave. College pulled me away, and falling in love kept me there. Even after my first marriage fizzled like a Fourth of July sparkler, I stayed put so my two boys could grow up near their father.

Though few of my previous dreams have come true, I can look back at life's disappointments, failures, and traumatic events and be grateful—because God is faithful. I'm learning to trust he works all things for good—one secret to living *happily ever after*. In addition, I'm learning that his dreams far exceed any I could imagine.

The Lord longs to reveal his heart to you so you'll know without a doubt he loves you and has a wonderful plan for your life. More important, he wants you—all of you—just as you are. No words adequately describe the never-ending, sacrificial love God has for you. Yet reading about it and experiencing it are two different things. That is why it has been my continual prayer while writing this book that you'll *experience* God, for God is love. The expression of love requires a relationship, and God is all about relationships.

Unraveling Fairy Tales is meant to facilitate a deepening, intimate relationship with God, the one and only true God, who is crazy about you!

As we embark on this journey, each of us brings a story filled with drama, conflict, and complicated relationships. These entanglements keep us from living an abundant life until we allow them to serve a higher purpose: to draw us closer to the supreme Storyteller. God alone can unravel the messy parts of our lives, heal our wounds, bring truth to false beliefs, and set us free from bondages. Inner healing not only draws us to God, but it also removes what keeps us from experiencing love and intimacy with him.

Why fairy tales? Besides their familiarity, a rich symbolism exists. Like the voice of a heart expressing itself when words seem inadequate, universal themes lie within these stories, such as good versus evil, sacrifice versus selfishness, and freedom versus captivity. Our hearts recognize the familiar struggles, and we're drawn back to these memorable tales in search of a resolution. We want justice to prevail, life to have meaning, and happy endings to exist. Fairy tales offer more than a good story, they offer hope. Hope that fills the temporary G.A.P. between reality and our dream until that which is the **G**ood, **A**cceptable, and **P**erfect will of God becomes our reality and our dream (see Romans 12:2).

Also woven into the fabric of each story are longings. Longings to be loved and adored, to have a purpose, to belong, to be accepted—warts and all—and in more subtle ways, to be rescued from a task, circumstance, relationship, or something we dislike about ourselves. These longings summon our hearts in search of fulfillment, only to discover the quest is impossible when limited to the world's inadequate offerings. Fairy tales hint at what our hearts suspect: there is more to this life than what meets the eye.

Somewhere deep within, we know we belong to something greater: a kingdom; and to some *One* greater: a King. We sense a world beyond the tangible—a spiritual world where *happily ever after* is possible in the here-and-now. We connect with fairy tales because of the parallels between the magical and spiritual worlds where strange creatures exist: angels, demons, and an antagonist—Satan; and where an all-knowing, all-seeing, and all-powerful King rules, who happens to be our Creator and loving Father. We believe this because his love draws our hearts to this conclusion and satisfies our longings by his presence. "For in him we live and move and have our being" (Acts 17:28).

Each story in *Unraveling Fairy Tales* highlights a common problem with which many of us struggle and will no doubt recognize in ourselves. By dissecting the fairy tales, we'll gain insight into specific difficulties. We'll find solutions by applying God's principles and receiving truth from Scripture and the Holy Spirit. Our ultimate goal is to know, love, and trust God more because we've *experienced* him. Freedom is the byproduct of knowing God. Freedom to dream, to believe, to act, to choose, to trust, to love, to give, and to die—to ourselves.

Herein lies the secret to living happily ever after: *to live for him.*

About this Book

The first chapter in this book addresses foundational truths helpful to spiritual growth. The following nine chapters center on different fairy tales and their corresponding problems. I've broken each chapter into five days so you can use this book as a weekly devotional or group study. At the end of each day, you'll find questions, an exercise, or just something to ponder. I call this *yada time*. It's meant to help you engage with God in an experiential, intimate way. Don't skip or rush through it. God longs to spend time with you. You may want to use a journal and record your feelings, questions, and experiences so you can look back and see how God continually reveals himself to you.

I've also included questions at the end of each chapter for personal reflection or to aid discussion for those meeting weekly in groups. Hebrews 10:25 says, "[Let us] not [give] up meeting together, as some are in the habit of doing, but encouraging one another—and all the more as you see the Day approaching." Though the most important interaction will happen daily between you and God, you'll gain additional benefits from discussing this book with others. A spiritual synergy occurs when believers gather to encounter God together. As we risk being vulnerable, God honors our transparency. When we share our burdens with others, we lighten our load. By expressing our hurts, healing can begin. When we confess our struggles, we diminish Satan's power over us. As we gather in Jesus' name—faith, hope, and love increase exponentially.

To those leading a group, the questions provided will probably be more than you can get through, depending on your allotted time. Feel free to choose which questions you discuss, giving others an opportunity to share what touched them most. At the end, share prayer requests and allow time to pray for each other. This will strengthen your group's relationships.

Chapter 1
Elements of a Fairy Tale—Foundational Truths

Memory Verse:

Now to him who is able to do immeasurably more than all we ask or imagine,
according to his power that is at work within us, to him be glory in the church and
in Christ Jesus throughout all generations, for ever and ever! Amen.
Ephesians 3:20–21

Day 1: Suspend Disbelief—and Believe

Imagine that a man has tied a thousand colorful helium balloons to his house, lifting it off its foundation until it floats into the wild blue yonder. Hard to believe? What if the man is an animated Pixar movie character? Then anything is possible, right? Did you recognize the *Up* movie plot?

To enjoy a fantasy movie or even a fairy tale, we must choose to believe things that aren't possible in the natural world. Samuel Taylor Coleridge first coined the phrase "suspension of disbelief" in 1817. He suggested that a reader would suspend judgment or disbelief in a fantastic tale if the writer included enough elements of "human interest and a semblance of truth."[1]

With the plethora of fairy tales, novels, television shows, and movies, I assume you are quite proficient at suspending disbelief. So, I'm asking that you not only suspend disbelief as we delve into the lives of fairy-tale characters, but also as we explore the fantastic solutions God offers. Suspend all disbelief and simply *believe*, even if an answer seems too good to be true, because God's answers fall into that category.

What we believe about God is important, too. I believe that God is triune—three Persons in one: God the Father, Jesus his Son, and the Holy Spirit. If you're not sure *who* God is, that's okay. There will be opportunities for him to reveal himself to you, but it's important that you believe he exists. Consider: "For since the creation of the world God's invisible qualities—his eternal power and divine nature—have been clearly seen, being understood from what has been made, so that people are without excuse" (Romans 1:20).

It's also important to understand that in the Bible the word believe encompasses more than our English definition, which is to accept something as true. In the original New Testament language, the word believe in Greek is *pisteuo*. It's defined as "to have faith (in, upon, or with respect to, a person or thing), i.e. credit; by implication, to entrust (especially one's spiritual well-being to Christ)."[2]

James Dobson gave an illustration of faith many years ago on his radio talk show that left a lasting impression on me. Here's my version:

Imagine you're standing on the bank at the top of Niagara Falls with a crowd of people. A tightrope stretches above the falls and spans the length from side to side. The rushing water sprays your face as it violently descends. A young, muscular man appears. He's the reason you and the others have gathered. He pushes a wheelbarrow to the bank's edge where the tightrope begins, and he stops.

A camera person scans the crowd as a reporter addresses the audience. "Do you believe that this man can cross Niagara Falls on a tightrope while pushing a wheelbarrow?"

You've seen the advertisements and fully expect he can, so you shout with the others, "Yes, I believe!"

The reporter approaches the man with the wheelbarrow. "Do you have anything to say to your audience?"

The man locks eyes with you. "Get in! I'll push you across in the wheelbarrow."[3]

Would you get in? To say yes would take more than believing that he could do it; it would also take entrusting your life to him.

To a much lesser degree, we exercise faith daily when we flip a light switch, use a telephone, or turn the ignition key to start a vehicle. Faith doesn't require that we understand how something works; it only asks us to trust and act on our belief. But how would you feel if only half the time the lights came on when you flipped the switch? Or what if your car started only occasionally? My first car, a rusty 1978 Mercury Monarch, gave me little reason to have faith in it. Unreliability creates questionable faith and causes doubt. Thus, the object of our faith, in which we believe and place our trust, is of the utmost importance.

Neil Anderson, the author of *Victory over the Darkness*, writes about faith: "How much faith you have is dependent upon how well you know the object of your faith. When people struggle with their faith in God, it is not because their faith object has failed or is insufficient. It is because they don't have a true knowledge of God and His ways."[4]

For our faith (trust and belief) in God to grow, we need to know God—the person of our faith—better. Not just knowledge *about* him, but truly *know* him personally. In Hebrew, the Old Testament language, the word know is *yada*.[5] It can mean varying degrees of knowing, but the one I want to focus on is when it refers to *knowing God experientially and intimately through a covenant relationship*. The Bible tells us Adam knew (yada) Eve, and she conceived a child. Adam didn't know *about* Eve he *knew* her. They were in a covenant relationship, and their union created a new life. Likewise, encounters with God will create a new life in us because of our covenant relationship with God through Jesus.

As you come to know (yada) God better, your faith will increase. Why is faith such a big deal? Hebrews 11:6 tells us "And without faith it is impossible to please God, because anyone who comes to him must believe that he exists and that he rewards those who earnestly seek him."

Faith pleases God, and he promises to reward "those who earnestly seek him." These rewards include such things as indescribable peace, unconditional love, exuberant joy, abundant provision, and freedom from sin and condemnation, to name a few (see Philippians 4:7, Matthew 6:26, Nehemiah 8:10, Galatians 5:1, Romans 8:1). This sounds like a partial definition for living happily ever after to me.

The writer of Hebrews says faith is foundational: "Now faith is confidence in what we hope for and assurance about what we do not see" (Hebrews 11:1). In Greek, the word assurance is *hupostasis*. It means a substructure or foundation.[6] Therefore, believing and trusting God is the foundation to expecting that which you cannot see. In *Great Cloud of Witnesses,* E.W. Bullinger explains faith this way:

> We all hope for many things, but the question is, [w]hat foundation or ground have we for our hope? As to our hope for eternity, it all rests on the faithfulness of God's promise. If there be no God; or, if His promise be not true, then we have no foundation whatever for our hope; all is baseless. Everything, therefore, depends upon the fact that God has spoken, and that what He has said is true. Faith is hearing God and believing what He says.[7]

If you struggle to hear God, don't despair. Day three will cover the many ways God speaks to us and how we can experience and come to know him better. For now, believe that one way he speaks is through the Bible. Jesus said, "I came that they might have life, and might have it abundantly" (John 10:10, NASB). God sent his Son, Jesus, so we could live happily ever after *now*.

It is by God's gracious favor anyone believes and trusts in him, so faith is also a gift. If you struggle to believe or trust God, you can ask for his help, like the man who brought his demon-possessed son to Jesus. An evil spirit had robbed the man's son of speech and often threw him into fire or water, trying to kill him. In desperation, the father cried out to Jesus:

> "But if you can do anything, take pity on us and help us."
> "If you can?" said Jesus. "Everything is possible for one who believes."
> Immediately the boy's father exclaimed, "I do believe; help me overcome my unbelief!" (Mark 9:22–24)

Even though the father questioned Jesus' ability to help, Jesus cast out the deaf and mute spirit from the man's son. This gives me great hope. We don't have to possess an unshakable, super-sized faith to approach Jesus with our problems. He is compassionate, loving, and willing to answer prayers despite wobbly faith. When you find yourself in a situation that seems hopeless and impossible, cry out to God, "I do believe, Jesus; help me overcome my unbelief!"

Mary and Martha, two of Jesus' closest female friends, faced a different crisis. When their brother, Lazarus, was sick, they sent word to Jesus because they believed he could heal him. But Jesus took his time getting there, and Lazarus died. When Jesus finally arrived, Lazarus had been in the tomb four days! I'd have been more than a little upset with Jesus. Possibly the sisters were, too.

Although Mary and Martha met with Jesus individually, each said, "Lord, if you had been here, my brother would not have died" (John 11:21, 32). Was that their polite way of blaming Jesus for Lazarus' death? Did they believe Jesus would raise their brother from the dead?

Jesus said to [Martha], "'Your brother will rise again.' Martha answered, 'I know he will rise again in the resurrection at the last day'" (John 11:23–24). Martha didn't ask Jesus to raise her brother from the dead. The situation seemed too impossible—he'd been dead for four days! She probably didn't have the slightest hope that things could change. This mindset continued even after Jesus commanded that the stone be rolled away from Lazarus' tomb. Martha cautioned Jesus, "By this time there is a bad odor …" (John 11:39).

Don't you love Martha's honest response? She reacted like any of us might. Despite her doubt, Jesus raised Lazarus from the dead. When we can only think about how bad our situation stinks, Jesus still miraculously changes everything!

Though Martha couldn't believe in a miracle, she displayed remarkable faith—maybe even *great* faith. In a seemingly hopeless situation, she trusted Jesus and believed he was the promised Messiah. She didn't allow her sorrow or disappointment to distance her from him. She kept the line of communication open—and honest.

It's tempting to withdraw from God or blame him when solutions to problems appear to be taking too long. You may find yourself in this situation now: distant from God because of what you've been through. Faith isn't easy. It requires that we suspend disbelief—and believe, with an emphasis on trust—regardless of circumstances.

Living happily ever after is possible, but not apart from a relationship with Jesus. If you're struggling to trust him or your relationship feels distant, please don't give up. I believe God led you here and that your life is about to change for the better. But don't believe me, believe God, and seek him—because he rewards those who earnestly do. In Jeremiah 29:13, God said, "You will seek me and find me when you seek me with all your heart."

In the movie *Up*, Carl Fredricksen eventually found what he was looking for and reached his dream destination, Paradise Falls. God offers us an even greater destination: Paradise without the "fall" (of mankind). Heaven is real, and we can experience foretastes of heaven while living on earth. Ephesians 2:6 says, "And God raised us *up* with Christ and seated us with him in the heavenly realms in Christ Jesus" (emphasis added). We don't need a thousand helium balloons to reach Paradise—God gave us Jesus.

If you haven't begun a personal relationship with Jesus and would like to, you can turn to Appendix A for help in doing so.

Yada Time

Reflect on how well you *know* God. Think about the different times and ways you've experienced him. Don't hurry. Let the memories come.

How would you describe your relationship with him? Are you super close, distant, or somewhere in between? Regardless of your answer, in what ways would you like to know him better? Talk to him about this. What area in your life do you sense he wants you to believe and trust him more? With your spirit, listen to what he wants to tell you.

Day 2: Our Helper, the Holy Spirit

What would have happened had Cinderella's fairy godmother not shown up? It's doubtful she'd have met the Prince, let alone become his bride. Most likely she'd have continued to sweep fireplace cinders as a ridiculed servant to her abusive stepmother and ugly stepsisters for the rest of their lives.

What a difference a little help can make. Not just your ordinary, run-of-the-mill help, either, but supernatural help. Several other fairy-tale characters had influential sidekicks with special powers, too. Pinocchio had Jiminy Cricket. Aladdin had Genie. The Shoe Maker had magic elves. And Sleeping Beauty had christening fairies.

We're no exception. Our helper is the Holy Spirit. He is better than all the mythical, magical characters combined. For one thing, he's real—and magnificently powerful! The word dynamite comes from the Greek word *dunamis*, and the Bible uses it, among others, to describe him.[8]

How well do you know the Holy Spirit? To many, he's the least understood person of the triune Godhead and as mysterious as a fairy-tale character. He plays numerous roles, and without his help, it's impossible to live happily ever after. Though he's active in our lives, we don't always recognize his presence. At least that's been my experience, which I'll relate to you through this next story.

For Christmas one year, I bought my husband a fancy, automatic coffee maker. I considered the gift personal, given that coffee hasn't touched my lips since I mistakenly took a big, cold gulp of it as a child. The brewer's high-tech feature of percolating at a preset time sold me, along with guilt, because my husband left for work before I awoke. The coffee chamber was square, unlike our previous model's round compartment. Thus began my unsuccessful hunt for square coffee filters in the remaining days before Christmas.

After my husband had opened his gift, I explained I had searched diligently for square coffee filters and assured him I'd continue the quest. He simply asked, "Won't the round filters work?"

Sure enough, they did. I had searched for something I already possessed, much like my previous pursuit of the Holy Spirit, which I'll share more about in a minute.

In the Old Testament the Holy Spirit visited only certain people chosen by God, such as prophets and kings. But after Jesus rose from the dead and ascended to heaven, God sent the Holy Spirit to earth to dwell in all believers. The book of Acts tells the story of when this happened:

When the day of Pentecost came, [Jesus' disciples] were all together in one place. Suddenly a sound like the blowing of a violent wind came from heaven and filled the whole house where they were sitting. They saw what seemed to be tongues of fire that separated and came to rest on each of them. All of them were all filled with the Holy Spirit and began to speak in other [languages] as the Spirit enabled them. (Acts 2:1–4)

At age twelve, I asked Jesus to be my Lord and Savior. This was in 1975, during the peak of the Charismatic Movement. Crusades being held across the United States ushered in revival and a return to the days of the early church, manifested by the gifts and power of the Holy Spirit. Signs, wonders, miracles, healings, and speaking in tongues confirmed the Spirit's presence as he blew through communities and forever changed lives.

As with any movement, not everyone was moved—at least not in the same direction. The Holy Spirit, like the wind, distributed his gifts regardless of denominational beliefs, which polarized congregations and contributed to church splits. New denominations sprung up over differing beliefs, and to this day the subjects of the Holy Spirit, the baptism of the Spirit, and gifts of the Spirit elicit questions and, at times, controversy.

I share this brief history to encourage you not to let varying beliefs about the Holy Spirit cause division, especially if you are reading this book in a group. As a believer in Christ, you can be certain the Holy Spirit lives in you. Several experiences as a youth caused me to doubt this truth.

While growing up, I attended a small country church led by a Spirit-filled pastor. He and his wife belonged to the same fellowship group as my parents, which met weekly in our home's basement. I often listened from the top of our stairs, unseen, as they spoke in tongues, longing for such an experience.

Prior to being confirmed, the Pastor and his wife met privately with each student. During our meeting, they asked, "Would you like to receive the baptism of the Holy Spirit?" I answered, "Yes," and they laid their hands on my head and prayed for the Holy Spirit to fill me. Nothing spectacular, or even tangible, happened as I had anxiously anticipated. No violent wind blew through. No strange language gushed from my lips. I've often wondered if they had expected, as had I, something more to have happened.

A few years later, a Spirit-filled classmate invited me to attend her Bible study group. They spoke in tongues at their gatherings and on several occasions laid hands on me to receive the gift of tongues. To my repeated embarrassment and disappointment, nothing happened then either.

Finally, years later while reading the Bible, the words "All do not speak with tongues, do they?" (2 Corinthians 12:30, NASB) jumped off the page and into my heart. Speaking in tongues is a gift, a manifestation, not exclusive evidence of God's Spirit living in a person. Realizing that the Holy Spirit had conveyed this message, I chose by faith to believe I had received the Spirit just as I had received Jesus into my heart.

9

Ephesians 1:13 says, "And you were included in Christ when you heard the message of truth, the gospel of your salvation. When you believed, you were marked in him with a seal, the promised Holy Spirit."

Whether you believe the Holy Spirit is given at infant baptism, adult baptism, another baptism, confirmation, or when you received Christ as your Savior, *believe* the Holy Spirit lives in you. I lacked only the *assurance* of my possession, or, more accurately, his possession of me. We receive all God's gifts by faith: salvation, the Holy Spirit, the gifts and fruit of the Spirit, and God's wonderful promises.

The fairy godmother's assignment was to give Cinderella a makeover. Likewise, the Holy Spirit's task is to transform us. Let's face it—we're all a little messed up. The Holy Spirit works to clean us up from the inside out and transform us into our Savior's likeness. Granted, the Father accepts us regardless of our condition. Our acceptance is based on what Jesus did on the cross and not on anything we'll ever do. Yet the more we become like Jesus, the more we'll experience happily ever after.

So, let's look at the Holy Spirit's job description by reading the following verses. I have made keywords bold for emphasis.

- "The Spirit himself **testifies** with our spirit that we are God's children." (Romans 8:16)
- "These are the things God has **revealed** to us by his Spirit. The Spirit **searches** all things, even the deep things of God." (1 Corinthians 2:10)
- "The Spirit himself **intercedes** for us through wordless groans." (Romans 8:26)
- "God chose you as firstfruits to be saved through the **sanctifying work** of the Spirit and through belief in the truth." (2 Thessalonians 2:13)
- "But the fruit of the Spirit is love, joy, peace, forbearance, kindness, goodness, faithfulness, gentleness and self-control. Against such things there is no law." (Galatians 5:22–23)
- "Now to each one the **manifestation of** the Spirit is given for the common good. To one there is given [gifts] through the Spirit the message of wisdom … the message of knowledge … faith … gifts of healing … miraculous powers … prophecy … distinguishing between spirits … speaking in different kinds of tongues … the interpretation of tongues …" (1 Corinthians 12:7–10)

Before Jesus returned to heaven, he told his disciples:

"But the Advocate, the Holy Spirit, whom the Father will send in my name, will **teach** you all things and will **remind** you of everything I have said to you." (John 14:26) "He will **guide** you into all truth. He will not speak on his own; he will **speak**, and he will tell you what is yet to come. He will **glorify** me because it is from me that he will receive what he will **make known** to you." (John 16:13–14, emphasis added)

These verses explain why Jesus said it was for our benefit that he would leave (see John 16:7). He'd then send the Holy Spirit who teaches, reminds, guides, sanctifies, testifies, washes, renews, reveals, searches, speaks, comforts, counsels, empowers, intercedes, guides, gives glory and life and gifts, produces fruit in our lives, and more. Wow, talk about busy!

God is passionate about seeing us changed because he loves us too much to leave us in our present condition. He knows living happily ever after is impossible in our sinful state. Therefore, he gave us his Spirit—the same powerhouse Spirit who raised Jesus from the dead—which means we have resurrection power at work in us (see Romans 8:11, Ephesians 1:19–20).

Like a round coffee filter in a square coffee chamber, the Holy Spirit embodies our current shape and transforms us into Jesus' likeness. If he's the filter, then we're the beans. What does it take for beans to release their flavor? A lot of hot water—after they've first been ground! Brokenness and difficulties release Jesus' aroma in and through us. Yet, like coffee, we keep our own unique flavor because God is a coffee connoisseur. The Spirit not only transforms us, but he also equips us to transform the world. Therefore, I believe God would say, "I've given you the Holy Spirit, so let's get brewing!"

Yada Time

Reflect on the action words and gifts attributed to the Holy Spirit found on the previous pages. In what specific ways has the Holy Spirit been at work in your life? If you need help remembering, ask the Holy Spirit to remind you. Take a moment to record those stories in your journal, such as the time he orchestrated a divine encounter with someone, or when he helped you with a decision or gave you a greater understanding of something. How did these events draw you closer to God?

In what area of your life do you sense him now at work?

Thank the Holy Spirit for his previous and persistent involvement.

Day 3: Are You Talking to Me?

Can you imagine a fairy tale without dialogue? Bor-ring. In any story, characters should talk and have something worthwhile to say. Even silent movies weren't *silent*. Besides the mood-setting music, title cards appeared on-screen after an actor or actress spoke because they not only had to communicate with each other, they had to communicate with their audience.

In the movie *Cast Away*, the main character, Chuck, was stranded on a deserted island for four years. Did he talk? Certainly he did, and not only to himself. He drew a face on a volleyball named "Wilson" and talked to it—because God created us for relationships. For any relationship to be meaningful, it must include some form of two-way communication.

The various communication modes have advanced exponentially since I was young. Besides sharing a single, corded telephone with seven family members, we also shared one telephone line among neighbors—called a party line. Believe me, it was no party. Waiting for neighbors to end their conversations tested my patience and self-control. The temptation to eavesdrop persisted, since the only way to know if someone had finished their conversation was to pick up the receiver and listen.

Obviously, this was decades before the widespread availability of cell phones and the internet, back in the 70s when global communication seemed as likely as contacting an alien from another planet. Yet, we learned from the 1982 movie *E.T.* that even an extra-terrestrial will find a way to phone home. We think nothing of calling or video chatting with friends and family around the globe today. Improvements in communication continue to advance because we're relational at our core, with a God-given need to communicate.

To elicit interaction, we may ask questions such as "Mirror, mirror, on the wall, who's the fairest one of all?" or "Do these jeans make my butt look fat?" We don't always ask questions to receive a truthful answer. Now factor in nonverbal cues such as eye contact, facial expressions, and tone of voice. Like any learned skill, good communication takes practice—and good listening skills. James 1:19 says, "Everyone should be quick to listen, slow to speak and slow to become angry."

Communication with God is no different. It requires listening and, more importantly, believing God does and will speak to *you*. Unfortunately, some of us treat God like Chuck's volleyball; we talk to God and don't listen because we don't expect him to reply. What kind of relationship would we have if God didn't speak to us? Yet God rarely speaks in an audible voice, so it's imperative that we learn to recognize his voice and the ways he communicates.

Graciously, God has given us a hearing aid. "For who knows a person's thoughts except their own spirit within them? In the same way no one knows the thoughts of God except the Spirit of God" (1 Corinthians 2:11).

Like GPS navigation, the Holy Spirit is our communication link with God. He knows our exact coordinates, where we're headed, and everything else about us, including our thoughts before we think them. Even more amazing, God invites us to become as personally acquainted with him as he is with us. This intimate communication system gains us access to God's thoughts! Let's see someone invent something better than that.

God is Spirit. So when he speaks, he speaks to your spirit, sometimes referred to as your inner being or heart. It's where the Holy Spirit resides in every believer. His words may come as thoughts in your mind or impressions in your spirit. Some describe this communication as simply knowing something they can't attribute to originating from themselves. His voice can be heard through what we think, read, hear, sense, or see—like how highlighted words on a page grab our attention. God is extremely creative, and his choice of highlighter often varies in intensity, ranging from a still small voice, like Elijah's mountain-top experience, to a burning-bush encounter such as Moses had.

Jesus said, "My sheep hear My voice, and I know them, and they follow Me" (John 10:27, NASB).

If you think you've never heard God's voice, it's likely you have but just didn't recognize it as such. You definitely heard his voice when you realized your need for Jesus. The Holy Spirit called to you then, and he has never stopped talking to you. Have you ever felt the need to pray for or call a friend at the exact moment they needed you? That was the Holy Spirit's nudge. Has a specific song come on the radio right when you needed to hear the comforting or encouraging words? Again, God was speaking to you.

God communicates with us because he loves us and we're in a relationship with him—a relationship based on love, trust, and on him being in control. It isn't that he wants subjects to boss around; it's because he knows what's best for us. He communicates so we will know (yada) him better, as a friend. He wants to share his thoughts, ways, truths, purposes, and plans with us, which also reveal his heart.

Examples of how God speaks are many and diverse. He speaks through visions, dreams, nature, angels, Scripture, and prophets. Less obvious ways include open doors, circumstances, a still small voice, spiritual gifts, timing, peace, desires, counsel of others, songs, books, billboards, sermons, or clocks. The examples are endless. Whole books have been written about hearing God's voice. This one day's dedication to the subject is meant to create expectancy that you, too, will hear him. If recognizing his voice is new to you, don't despair. I've woven stories throughout this book as various examples of how God has spoken to me.

God often speaks loudest to me through the Bible, his written Word. It's as relevant today as when it was first scribed, and it should be the plumb line by which we measure everything we hear. God will never tell you something that contradicts what he's already said in his Word. He may bring new understanding or interpretation to a verse, but even then he will support it with other Scripture passages. Becoming familiar with what the Bible says will help you distinguish God's voice from your thoughts, worldly desires, and the enemy's voice.

But not every answer to a specific problem is found in the Bible. If it were, we wouldn't need to hear his voice or be in a relationship with him. We might even be tempted to elevate his written Word above God himself. He knows what each person needs to hear. Like a good parent, our heavenly Father speaks to us individually and in ways we can understand.

We often recognize God's voice best after the fact. We learn from experience, from hearing correctly and incorrectly. So, it's important that we continue to listen and learn. For example, when the Children's Ministry Director (CMD) position opened at our church, I applied, longing to be in full-time ministry. For several days, I poured out my heart to God. Then one evening while reading my Bible, a verse leaped off the page and brought excitement to my heart. "Eli answered, 'Go in peace, and may the God of Israel grant you what you have asked of him'" (1 Samuel 1:17). I interpreted this to mean that God had heard my prayer and I'd get the CMD job. From then on, I believed the job was mine. I even told the committee during my interview that I thought God wanted me to have the job. Imagine my disappointment and embarrassment when they hired someone else.

I learned several things from this experience. First, I could survive disappointment with God and still love him. Second, faith isn't a magic formula guaranteeing something will happen because a person believes strongly enough. Third, we don't always correctly interpret what we hear. God had said he'd heard my heart's cry. In all honesty, I'd have taken any job in ministry. A change in perspective helped me realize I don't need a title from a church to be about my Father's business. We're already in ministry if we're doing what he has called us to do, which includes working at anything.

Mistakes in hearing happen, partly because we hear and interpret through filters: mindsets, belief systems, prejudices, preconceived answers, etc. Mistakes are part of the learning curve. Yes, the fear of making a mistake can be frightening. But when we seek God for an answer, our trust should be in his ability to communicate and not in our ability to hear. So, relax and trust that he will make the answer clear to you. One verse I repeat to myself when waiting on God's answer is "Whether you turn to the right or to the left, your ears will hear a voice behind you, saying, 'This is the way; walk in it'" (Isaiah 30:21).

When an opportunity arose to change employers, I again sought God for direction. All signs indicated God was behind this change, but the decision was difficult because the risk was great. Leaving my current employer meant giving up the security of a base salary, great health and dental coverage, a 401K, and six weeks' paid vacation. The mortgage company pursuing me offered none of these. But because my income would be commission-based, I'd have the freedom to set my own hours and pursue writing during slow times.

As I contemplated this huge decision, I trusted that God would make his will clear. With my husband's support, I waited for God's answer. During a time of general prayer with friends, a woman sensed the Lord saying, "Cast your bread upon the waters." I opened my Bible and found the verse in Ecclesiastes 11:1. Curious as to its meaning, I read the notes in my *NASB Study Bible*, which says, "Be adventurous … accept the risks … Do not always play it safe."[9] In my spirit, I knew God had confirmed that I should change jobs.

God has more to say besides directing our paths. He longs to spend time with us and tell us how much he loves us. He works to remove our filters, so we can hear and accurately interpret his words. His voice reveals who he truly is—our happily ever after.

Yada Time

Reflect on the times you've heard God's voice. Write them in a journal if you haven't already. By documenting these times, you'll be more expectant and alert to hearing his voice. It will also provide encouragement when you look back and remember.

If you don't easily recognize his voice, ask the Lord for help. The prophet, Eli, counseled Samuel, a young boy, to say to the Lord, "Speak, for your servant is listening" (1 Samuel 3:10). Tell God you are listening, and, by faith, believe he will speak to you. Then pay attention—because it is by getting your attention God speaks. For example, notice when a question pops into your mind, and expect God to provide the answer.

More important, God wants you to know (yada) how much he loves and accepts you. Some words are best spoken through the heart. Be prepared for such an experience.

Day 4: Drama and Trauma

My niece Maggie is a drama princess. She's not a full-fledged queen yet because she's only nine, and her meltdowns and theatrics happen mostly when she's tired. But even in a good mood, she's a performer. She's the baby in her family and in our extended family, and when we're all together, she's the center of attention.

Be honest, have you ever created a little drama just for entertainment? I'm guilty, especially with Maggie. One weekend we taught her how to play the game Telephone. Hearing how muddled a message became provided our entertainment. Yet, this outcome infuriated my niece. Her drama enticed me even more to relay the next message imperfectly. Knowing a person's expectation and altering the outcome can create drama.

This type of drama is child's play, yet real-life drama in adult lives is anything but fun and games. Drama is what keeps us reading a story or watching a movie. It may be entertaining when it's happening to someone else, but who wants to be the queen of it? Drama infers conflict, serious storylines, and tragedies. These are the events, situations, and circumstances we hope to avoid. When they happen, we blame them as our reason for not living happily ever after.

Is happiness even possible in a drama-filled world?

The Bible tells us yes. Jesus said, "These things I have spoken to you, that in Me you may have peace. In the world you have tribulation, but take courage; I have overcome the world" (John 16:33, NASB).

Jesus spoke these words to his disciples the week of his crucifixion. Talk about drama! More than stating the indisputable fact that bad things happen, Jesus was preparing his friends. He knew how and when he would die, and he cared about what would happen to them afterward. He knew they would be persecuted along with others who professed him as Lord. Of the remaining eleven disciples, all except John were martyred. And they all lived joyous lives and died courageously because Jesus had given them the "how-to" answer: to live *in him*.

Yes, Jesus is the answer to all life's trials and problems, and only *in him* do we find true happiness and peace. This peace encompasses more than the absence of noise or strife, and his Jewish disciples would have understood the rich meaning of the Hebrew word for peace: *Shalom*.

It includes health, healing, harmony, prosperity, and overall well-being.[10] That sounds a lot like happily ever after to me.

Jesus also said, "Take courage," or, in other Bible versions, "Take comfort," or, "Be of good cheer." He was telling them to *choose* it, or to *take* it, because he had overcome (conquered) the world and they could too. He was confident that he had succeeded at his mission even before his death.

I promised not to tell you the answer without also giving you the how-to piece. So *how* do we live *in him*? We choose to walk, talk, and interact with God throughout our day, every day. The more we grow in our relationship with God, the better we'll understand how to live *in him*—with the Holy Spirit's help, of course. That means—change is coming!

In my senior year of college, I entered a fashion design contest and modeled my fitted, sleeveless blouse in a tropical print with matching cropped pants. To add pizzazz to the ensemble, I wound a band of the same colorful fabric around my head, turban style, forcing my shoulder-length hair to jet up and out the opening like a volcanic eruption. On the day of the contest, I felt nauseous and assumed it was nerves. After making it down the runway, then into a restroom (thankfully), I threw up. But my abdominal pain escalated. When I could no longer stand without doubling over, my fiancé drove me to the emergency room.

Imagine the pain level it took for me to leave my dorm room with my hair still standing at attention (though now out of its turban). I looked as if I'd been electrocuted. Even so, the hospital shouldn't have tried to send me home without helping me. Refusing to leave, I cried, "Make it stop hurting."

The next morning, a doctor removed my appendix during exploratory surgery. Afterward, he told me the incision was only an inch-or-two long and in a position where it wouldn't be seen while wearing a bikini. I couldn't have cared less, having only wanted the pain to stop.

Pain's positive side is that by its presence we know when we are hurt, sick, or something is wrong. It moves us to act. Yet, too often pain serves no purpose other than to hurt. Read any newspaper or turn on the television and see how senseless pain infiltrates lives. Many of us needn't look any further than our households for examples. Who doesn't view pain as an adversary to living happily ever after?

The source of pointless pain is never God. He doesn't cause us to get cancer, break a leg, or have a car accident. God is good. He *allows* bad things to happen because he's given us free will. Unfortunately, we often make poor choices, causing others and ourselves pain. This doesn't mean God leaves us to our own devices. On the contrary, to those who love him, he's made this promise: "And we know that in all things God works for the good of those who love him, who have been called according to his purpose" (Romans 8:28).

Trusting that God will bring about good from life's dramas and traumas is foundational to happiness.

Living happily isn't about avoiding or managing pain, it's about walking *through* it with God's help and allowing him to redeem (make something good from) your situation. This involves inner healing or trauma recovery, and to some degree, we're all in recovery. In *Living From the*

Heart Jesus Gave You, the authors state: "Recovery is about exceeding one's current potential, and reaching one's God-intended destiny."[11] This requires that we face the pain in our lives so we'll learn lessons, gain power, achieve maximum growth, and then help others do the same.

The authors separate trauma into two categories. Type A trauma is the absence of good things, and Type B trauma is the presence of bad things. To varying degrees, we've all experienced both forms.

God created us with needs. Type A traumas occur when those who are supposed to love and care for us withhold good things from us. Besides our basic necessities, examples include unconditional love, guidance, discipline, nurturing, protection, and a safe environment. They should encourage us to become the person God created us to be. But our parents and teachers aren't perfect, and living in this broken world causes many wounds from the absence of these good things.

It's easy to downplay Type A traumas because we often compare them to what we reason are worse things such as abuse, which falls under Type B trauma. Plus, we may feel disloyal to our parents, whom we love, by acknowledging these losses. They did the best they could, after all. But when we view Type A traumas as insignificant we remain confused about why we struggle in life. "It is important to remember that to discount 'lesser' trauma is to avoid the truth about how much it hurts, and thereby miss the chance for healing."[12]

Type B trauma is harmful by its existence, such as in verbal, physical, sexual, and emotional abuse. These are more easily recognized as trauma and they vary in degree of cruelty. The ramifications of these traumas tend to manifest themselves in more visible ways. Children and adults may act out, often perpetuating a cycle of abuse or victimization.

Trauma from abuse isn't always recognized by the person. The Lord created our brains with coping mechanisms that allow us to deny these traumas for self-preservation. It may feel threatening to your existence to address these wounds—if you can even access their memory. Yet the Lord knows what happened to you. Facing your past will take courage, and God will walk with you on this path to healing and freedom.

Unfinished trauma recovery makes it difficult to live happily ever after. When pain from our past isn't sufficiently dealt with, it won't stay in our past. Like an infected wound, it won't heal. It needs cleansing, which requires that we bring our wounds into God's presence. By God's grace we can deal with the infection (pain, hurt, trauma, lie, sin, guilt, anger, bitterness, etc.) so healing can begin.

Sometimes healing happens instantaneously, and other times it's a process. Yet trauma recovery is vital to living happily ever after. Therefore, I pray this book helps facilitate your healing through encounters with God, our Healer. Then we can replace our drama-queen crowns with the crowns he provides. We'll tell our drama-filled stories from a place of victory, sharing how God took what the enemy meant for evil and brought about our happy endings (see Genesis 50:20).

Yada Time

You might be tempted to dig up your past hurts all at once, but please don't. Let each one surface in God's timing. When they do, talk to God about them. Ask for his truth and healing touch. Give him your pain and follow the Holy Spirit's guidance. You may need to forgive someone, including yourself. If at any time a traumatic memory seems too difficult or painful to process, seek help from a friend or a professional familiar with inner healing.

We may never understand the *why* behind our traumas, but we can trust God to work all things for our good (see Romans 8:28). Meditate on this truth. Believe he will bring healing to your deepest wounds. End your time by thanking God in advance for what he is about to do in your life. Healing change is on its way!

Day 5: Happily Ever After

When God gave me the idea for this book in 1999, happily ever after seemed right around the corner—as did the Lord's return in the midst of the Y2K frenzy. That year, our circle of Christian friends expanded as my husband and I began hosting a fellowship group in our home. Together we experienced God. Physical healings occurred, like when the painful ganglion cyst on my wrist disappeared. Our group traveled to a Christian conference where mysterious gold dust sparkled on our skin. Deep, emotional inner healing also took place, such as when God replaced a lie I had believed for twenty-seven years with the truth and miraculously restored my relationship with my mom. I'll share more details about this in the next chapter. The Lord's presence was tangible during this season, and in his presence are the fullness of joy, freedom, and miracles.

It's easy to live happily ever after when experiencing the Lord's manifested presence. But what happens when the "glory cloud" seems to depart, when it's hard to hear the Lord's voice, or the answers to our prayers are delayed and miracles seem nonexistent? Is it possible even then to live happily ever after?

While writing this book, doubt crept in. I struggle some days to live above my circumstances, like when fibromyalgia pain keeps me from writing or doing anything else. How could I write this book and not make false promises or appear to be a hypocrite? As I explained this to the Lord, he repeatedly encouraged me to keep writing. At the height of my struggle, he led me to reread one of my favorite classics. In the preface to the allegory *Hinds' Feet on High Places*, the author, Hannah Hurnard, wrote, "The High Places and the hinds' feet do not refer to heavenly places after death, but are meant to be the glorious experience of God's children here and now—if they will follow the path he chooses for them."[13]

Maybe those words don't speak to you, but I heard God's voice clearly. We *can* live happily ever after on this side of heaven, so I'll do my best to lead you on a journey that will bring you closer to it, trusting God to accomplish his purposes through this book.

I'm convinced living happily ever after is possible, are you?

Even if you're not, you may secretly hope it is. Why else would you still be reading? Perhaps it's because God led you here. That has been my prayer, along with God richly blessing you. Living happily ever after isn't reserved for fairy tales or the afterlife—which, by the way, exists—and heaven will far exceed any happily ever after you could imagine.

It's for us today. Here and now.

First, we should probably establish what happily ever after looks like so we're on the same page. How would you define happily ever after? Grab your journal and take a few moments to describe what you're looking for or what you expect.

In fairy tales, the words *happily ever after* insinuate the story's drama is over. But the words *ever after* infer there is more life to be lived. Orson Welles said, "If you want a happy ending, that depends, of course, on where you stop your story."[14] Stories conclude when what follows would bore the socks off you. A perfectly happy life wouldn't keep anyone's attention. Is that what you're looking for?

Maybe we should start with the definition of happy. The words used to define happy are as similarly vague and abstract: pleasure, contentment, fortunate. A few synonyms include cheerful, joyful, jolly, and merry. Sounds like a description of Santa Claus, the character we often confuse with the real meaning of Christmas. But I digress.

Happiness is subjective. What makes one person happy doesn't always make the next person happy. Sure, we could probably agree on some basics, but let's aim higher than our needs. What would make you happy—really happy? Grab your journal again and take another moment to access your mental list of if-only wishes to happiness. Think hard.

How long would those things make you happy? Are you sure? We're talking ever after, after all, which is a long time. Are you mentally adding a few additional things to your list?

Beyond the basics, we all need loving people in our lives and loving relationships to help fulfill our need to belong. We also need a sense of purpose. Whatever your list includes, whatever you think will make you happy, if it doesn't include an intimate relationship with Jesus then we aren't on the same page—yet.

God knows all your needs because he hardwired them in you. He knows your heart's desires, and he wants to give them to you. He only asks you to put him first in your life, and that's because only *in him* will all your wants, needs, desires, and more be fulfilled. You knew I'd end up here, right?

Any path other than the one leading to Jesus is a happily-ever-after counterfeit. Worldly happiness promises one thing and delivers another because our sin nature will demand more. That could be why the word *content* is one word used to define happy.

Long before the movie character Jerry Maguire said "You complete me" to the love of his life, the Apostle Paul stated the same thing about Jesus to the church at Colossae. "For in Him all the fullness of Deity dwells in bodily form, and in Him you have been made complete" (Colossians 2:9–10, NASB). Jesus completes us, and he provides the true meaning of happily ever after—love story included.

Isn't romance at the heart of happily ever after? The three small words preceding it say yes: "and *they* lived …" It's seldom written singularly, such as "he or she" lived happily ever after. Fairy tales conclude when two characters find each other and love redeems them. Was love included on your happiness list? Maybe you couldn't even dream of romantic love as an option. Finding a soulmate won't complete you. You're a spiritual being, and nothing on this earth—no other person or thing—can, or will, fill the *complete-me* void within you. The completion you long for is only found *in him*, Jesus.

The answer may be simple, yet the "how to" is easier said than done. You may already know this if you're at all acquainted with Jesus' teachings. For example, "Then he called the crowd to him along with his disciples and said: 'Whoever wants to be my disciple must deny themselves and take up their cross and follow me. For whoever wants to save their life will lose it, but whoever loses their life for me and for the gospel will save it'" (Mark 8:34–35).

Was Jesus serious? Take up a cross? Isn't dying the opposite of living happily ever after here on earth? No, it's still the answer. Before you toss this book across the room, think about how living for yourself has worked so far. Isn't that how most of our messes get started? Jesus offers a way out of an unhappy, unfulfilling, unacceptable life. "Follow me," he says. Lose all rights to your life by surrendering it to him.

When a rich, young ruler asked Jesus what he must do to receive eternal life, Jesus answered, "If you wish to be complete, go and sell your possessions and give to the poor, and you shall have treasure in heaven; and come, follow Me" (Matthew 19:21, NASB).

Jesus didn't tell him he had to sell all his possessions to be saved. He addressed the rich young ruler's real question: How does one live happily ever after? Or, more accurately, how is one made complete? Isn't this where most of us get stuck? We've accepted Jesus as Savior and know we're going to heaven, yet we feel incomplete, like something is still missing.

The Greek word used here for complete is *teleios*. In English, this word is translated elsewhere in the Bible as perfect. It means "to end, complete, consecrate, finish, fulfill … in various applications of labor, growth, mental and moral character."[15]

It's used in Matthew 5:48: "Be perfect, therefore, as your heavenly Father is perfect." Sound impossible? Would Jesus command us to do what isn't possible? No. In him, we *were* made perfect—complete. That's how God already sees us because he operates outside of time. He sees the beginning from the end. The process of *becoming* how God sees us is called sanctification. So, we *were* made complete, and we *are being* made complete—both through a relationship with Jesus as we abide (live) in him.

Like the concept of living happily ever after, living "in and for him" may seem abstract, subjective, and difficult to obtain. What would that entail? And wouldn't it look different for each person? If you're willing to find out, the rest of this book will answer those questions and show you how—because happily ever after is only found in a personal relationship with Jesus. God isn't concerned with religion, he's concerned with relationships. He wants you to know him intimately.

Jesus' answer to the rich young ruler was to "sell your possessions and give to the poor, and you will have treasure in heaven. Then come, follow me" (Matthew 19:21). We aren't told whether the young man did so, but we are told "he went away sad, because he had great wealth" (Matthew 19:22).

Jesus said, "Where your treasure is, there your heart will be also" (Matthew 6:21). It doesn't matter if your treasure is your money, spouse, house, children, career, social status, or—you fill in the blank. Whatever, or whoever, has first place in your heart is your treasure. If it isn't God, happily ever after will continue to slip through your fingers no matter how hard you try to grab hold of it.

God wants to be your treasure so much that he creates and allows circumstances to help turn your heart toward him. He also tries to capture your heart by romancing you. Have you ever thought about being romanced by God? I hadn't until it spilled out of my heart in prayer one day. I was really saying, "God, please remind me of how much you love me. I need to experience your love."

God's love is audacious, indescribable, irresistible, and unconditional. Once you've experienced it, you can't help but fall madly in love with him and give yourself completely to him. Isn't that what happily ever after is all about, spending your life with the One you love? The One who completes you?

Then get ready to be swept off your feet!

Yada Time

Dare to ask God to romance you. If you're unsure of what that will look like when he does, trust me, you'll know when it happens. Maybe you'll awaken to a song playing in your mind. The words will be God singing to you. Or you'll witness a majestic act in nature, such as a meteor shower, a falling star, or a soaring eagle. I feel romanced whenever I see double digits on a clock—11:11, for example—which reminds me of God's double portion of love. Whatever it is, it will be something special to you.

If you haven't asked him to romance you yet, what are you waiting for? Go ahead, ask. Then stay **A**lert, **W**atch, and **E**xpect to be romanced—and you'll be in AWE of what God does!

Chapter 1
Elements of a Fairy Tale—Foundational Truths
Questions for Reflection or Discussion

Day 1: Suspend Disbelief—and Believe

1. Define faith in your own words and why it is important. (p. 5)

2. Share a time when you heard from God and how your faith grew.

3. Define yada and how it relates to faith. (p. 5)

4. In what area would you like to know God better?

Day 2: Our Helper, the Holy Spirit

1. Did you ever have any misconceptions about the Holy Spirit?

2. Like a fairy godmother, what major role does the Holy Spirit play in our lives? (p. 10)

3. Discuss the Holy Spirit's "job descriptions." (p. 10–11)

4. Share stories that demonstrate how the Holy Spirit is active in our lives.

5. What word best describes how the Holy Spirit is currently at work in your life?

6. Share any experience you have with journaling.

Day 3: Are You Talking to Me?

1. How does God communicate with us? Share examples. (pp. 12–13)

2. Share a time when you recognized God's voice and acted on it.

3. If you've ever misinterpreted what God said, what did you learn from it?

4. How can we position ourselves to listen for God's voice more intentionally?

5. Share a Bible verse God used to answer a question or encourage you in the past.

6. How did God speak to you this week?

Day 4: Drama and Trauma

1. What does it mean to live in Jesus, and why should this be our goal? (p. 16)

2. Discuss the differences between type A and type B traumas. (p. 17)

3. Why do people downplay type A traumas? (p. 17)

4. If you feel comfortable, briefly share how God redeemed a trauma you experienced.

5. Have you experienced a trauma you'd like prayer for? Consider sharing your request during your group's prayer time.

Day 5: Happily Ever After

1. Did your definition of happily ever after change? If so, in what way?

2. People often think, "If only I had …, or if only … was different, I'd be happy. Discuss where you've looked for happiness and what you've learned.

3. Had you ever thought about God romancing you? (p. 21)

4. Share how God romanced you this week.

5. Is there anything else in this chapter you want to discuss?

Like Mary and Martha whose brother had been dead for four days, we face situations that really stink—and require a miracle from Jesus. Share prayer requests and pray for each other. Let's believe for a miracle together.

Chapter 2
Cinderella—Embracing Your True Identity

Memory Verse:

See what great love the Father has lavished on us, that we should be called
children of God! And that is what we are!
1 John 3:1

Day 1: Princess Incognito

When someone describes a movie as a Cinderella story, we're all familiar with the rags-to-riches plot. Despite its familiarity, there's something endearing that draws us into watching another variation, such as *Ever After, Ella Enchanted, A Cinderella Story, Pretty Woman,* or *Caddyshack.*

In the movie *Caddyshack,* Bill Murray plays Carl Spackler, a lowly country club groundskeeper. Pretending to be a finalist in the Masters Golf tournament, he says about himself, "What an incredible Cinderella story," as he beheads carnations, one by one, with his golf club. He continues, "A former greenskeeper, and now, about to become the Masters Champion." He swings and steps back. "It looks like a mirac— it's in the hole! It's in the hole!"[1]

Who doesn't root for the underdog? We cheer when the have-nots triumph over those who have. Is it because we can easily relate? We know how it feels *not* to be top dog. It hurts to be overlooked and underappreciated. Our lives may seem ordinary, but they're not. As the King's daughters, we are anything but ordinary.

We are princesses!

Still, I struggle to embrace my true identity. Too often I feel more like a cook or a cleaning woman than a princess. On a super bad day, I may even be mistaken for an ugly stepsister. I don't always look, act, or feel like a princess when I allow people, circumstances, or emotions to influence how I see myself.

It's easy to forget or choose not to identify with being the King's daughter. You're a princess, you know, if you've asked Jesus to be your Lord and Savior. That's all it took and— BAM! You were rescued from the kingdom of darkness and brought into his marvelous kingdom of light, forever to be God's beloved daughter (see Colossians 1:12–13).

Do you realize what a big deal that is? The benefits are out of this world, literally. It's also the prerequisite to living happily ever after. Does your life reflect the life of a princess? If you answered no, you're not alone. Most of us fail to embrace our true identities and live up to our potential. We live less-than-ordinary lives, like Cinderella's pre-palace days, with our true identities concealed.

We live incognito.

I love saying the word *incognito*. As the syllables roll off my tongue, it feels as if I've finally mastered a foreign language. The word sounds mysterious and evokes images from old detective movies, such as Humphry Bogart wearing a trench coat lurking in the shadows. His wide-brimmed fedora slants over his forehead and rests on dark glasses while he searches for a mysterious, veiled woman.

We may not physically hide, but emotionally and spiritually we conceal our true selves from others. Perhaps it's out of guilt, shame, or the fear of not being accepted. Or maybe we simply don't know who we are—because we fail to remember *whose* we are.

God says you are special, significant, chosen, greatly loved, and that he has an amazing plan for your life. There is no other princess like you. Until you believe you are everything God says you are, you will live incognito—and forfeit living happily ever after before heaven. Are you ready to embrace your true identity? Let's begin by learning to *LAF* like a true princess.

Go ahead, laugh.

Most people would benefit from laughing more often; however, the LAF I'm referring to is an acronym for the words: Look, Act, and Feel. It's difficult to embrace our royalty when bombarded with misconceptions about our LAF (looks, actions, and feelings). Like the glass slipper on the ugly stepsister's foot, we think our LAF doesn't fit. So, let's unravel the LAF of a fairy-tale princess to embrace our true identities.

What images surface when you envision a princess? Take a moment to imagine what she looks like.

Whether you imagined one of the many Disney princesses or the real-life Princess Kate Middleton, she's gorgeous, right? The princess I envision has long flowing hair, a clear, vibrant complexion, and a Jennifer Lopez figure. She may not be perfect, but she's closer to a "ten" in my mind than I'll ever be. She dresses exquisitely on every occasion, with just the right shoes, purse, and jewelry to match her designer outfit. Ugh! Who can compare?

Imagine how this princess acts.

Perfectly, you say? She could teach Miss Manners a thing or two. You won't catch her committing a faux pas for the tabloids to print. She efficiently accomplishes all she sets out to do without self-doubt or grumbling.

Bear with me one moment longer and consider a princess' temperament.

With Mary Poppins' disposition, she awakens every morning with a song in her heart and its lyrics on her perfectly plump lips. Words like depressed, lonely, afraid, or angry aren't in her vocabulary. She's energetic and feels as if she could conquer the world, and I expect her to. After all, she's a princess living happily ever after.

Okay, you get my point. There is no way our LAFs (looks, actions, and feelings) will ever measure up to such an idealistic image. Nor should we insist they do. We know this perfect woman doesn't exist even if magazines and the media try to convince us otherwise. Besides, we're a different type of princess. We're a Christian princess. We aren't supposed to LAF like a worldly or fairy-tale princess. We have our own beautiful LAF—one that's more … spiritual?

We can even become disheartened by trying to LAF like a super-Christian princess—one who's several spiritual women rolled into one. First, she's ambitious like the Proverbs 31 woman who even wove the cloth she used to sew her family's clothing while buying and selling real estate. *Whew! I'm already exhausted.* Boy, can this godly princess worship! Like Mary, she spends hours sitting at Jesus' feet. She also has the heart of Mother Teresa. In her spare time, she volunteers at a soup kitchen, makes blankets for the homeless, and fills hundreds of shoe boxes for Operation Christmas Child.

You may not have envisioned these specific women, but I suspect you've tried to LAF (look, act, and feel) like someone other than yourself. Perhaps your ideal is a fairy-tale princess combined with a super-Christian princess—some beautiful creature whose LAF is in the world but not of it. Maybe you've met women who appear to be this hybrid type, but they're the last women on earth you'd ever want to LAF like—because they seldom *laugh*.

Perhaps the *princess* title seems too worn-out, generic, feminine, or too idealistic to you. Or, you'd rather be a queen! If this rings true for you, please indulge me a bit longer as we look at how the Bible describes a Christian princess' LAF.

She dresses modestly, and her beauty doesn't come from outward adornments such as braided hair or wearing gold jewelry and fine clothing. Instead, she radiates inner beauty with a gentle and quiet spirit (see 1 Peter 3:3–4). She's considerate, caring, and gives generously to all in need. She spends her time productively, worshipfully, and sacrificially (Proverbs 31). Shame, guilt, and remorse have no place in her life. She's overjoyed because she's overcome fear, anger, jealousy, resentment, and the need to control. It doesn't bother her if she doesn't fit in at work or social gatherings. Not fitting into her favorite jeans doesn't even cause her a meltdown. She's not depressed, lonely, or anxious. She feels special because her heavenly Father has told her she is.

This biblical princess may also seem like a fairy tale. But there's genuineness in her LAF (looks, actions, and feelings), and if we're honest, deep inside we want to LAF like this. We dream of becoming her because we know she's truly happy. Soon, you can be too when you learn to LAF like the beautiful, unique princess God created you to be.

Isn't it time to stop living incognito and embrace your true identity? What do you have to lose—except an inaccurate self-image?

Yada Time

In what areas would you like to see yourself more positively? Talk with God about those struggles. Let him know you want to LAF more like him, and you want to see yourself as he sees you. Imagine sitting on his lap and placing your head against his chest. Can you hear his heart beating for you? Listen to what he says to you. Write down what you hear/sense.

Day 2: Jesus' LAFTER

Attending the Royal Ball must have felt like a dream to Cinderella—and dancing with the Prince was the icing on her royal cake. "Who, me?" she may have stammered. "How could this be?" Perhaps the crowd wondered the same thing. Where had she come from? Who was this beauty capturing the Prince's attention, winning his heart? As the two glided across the dance floor, I imagine a playful interchange occurred. "Did it hurt when you fell from heaven?" he asked. Not only was he charming, but also witty. She notably blushed, and his gaze deepened. "There must be something wrong with my eyes. I can't take them off you."

Oh, to be madly in love.

I fell for my current husband at a singles' dance, where the dreary atmosphere was far from dreamy. We went as friends, just friends, as dating was prohibited while attending *Beginning Experience* (BE), a recovery group for those grieving a relationship loss. We had met at BE and became instant friends. Chuck's selfless acts and generosity revealed a kind heart. Because he is nineteen years my senior, I hadn't considered him romantically—until that fateful evening when he swept me off my feet.

After our first dance, we wouldn't dance with anyone else. Others tried to cut in unsuccessfully. This created a stir among our BE friends, giving the impression we were dating. How could I be falling for someone so soon and so quickly? I was too broken, too untrusting. Just hearing his voice filled me with great joy. We talked on the telephone into the wee hours of the morning. Despite our age difference, I fell hard and fast. Nothing else matters when you're falling in love.

Can you remember how it feels to fall in love? How your stomach flip-flops at the sound of their voice, the touch of their hand, or just the thought of them? Time seems nonexistent when you're with the one you love and like an eternity when you're apart. You require less sleep, less food, less of everything except caffeine the next morning. When passion jumps into the driver's seat, hang on, everything else flies out the window, including logic.

Even if it's been awhile since you've experienced romantic love, it shouldn't be difficult to stir up the emotion. God created us in his image, to love and be loved. God *is* love. This could be why defining love is massively complex. It's like trying to define God. The Greek language uses at least four different words for love in comparison to our one English word. Love isn't a concrete or tangible object either, such as a car or an elephant. It's abstract and subjective, meaning how each person defines love may vary. For now, I want you to imagine fairy-tale love—the passionate kind that drove the Prince never to stop searching for Cinderella until he found her.

That, dear friend, is the love God has for *you*.

Jesus told several stories to demonstrate God's love and passionate pursuit of us. One is about a shepherd who left his ninety-nine sheep to search for one lost sheep until he found it (see Luke 15:4–7). Another is about a prodigal son who left home and squandered his inheritance. When he returned, his father ran to him and welcomed him back by throwing a party (see Luke 15:11–31). Bible verses are sprinkled throughout this book describing God's love for you. Maybe you know this one by heart: "For God so loved the world that he gave his one and only Son, that whoever believes in him shall not perish but have eternal life" (John 3:16).

But reading or hearing about God's love isn't the same as experiencing it. It's the intimate encounter with love that changes lives. That's what *yada* is all about. It's experiencing God's love not only in your head but also in your heart. You are precious to him because he's crazy about you. He loves you so much he died for *you*.

If you struggle to believe or receive God's love, hang in there. God is strong enough, bold enough, and persistent enough to break through whatever is keeping you from experiencing his love. Past hurts and lies once stood in my way, but God never gave up on me, and he never gives up on anyone.

I went to BE that January because I'd finally accepted that my marriage was over. The previous January my husband had moved out. Jesse was only eight months old, and Jordan was three-and-a-half. To his credit, my ex-husband has stayed active in our boys' lives. Five months later, he divorced me. He once said he may have been the one who left, but my footprint was on his rear end.

My ex-husband had been right. I was angry, bitter, and initially relieved at his departure. Nonetheless, I had hoped we'd work things out. Divorce destroys families. The devastation is widespread; it's emotional, physical, financial, and often includes losing mutual friends and your spouse's family. It was a heart-wrenching period, but God used it to draw me to himself. I clung to the Lord as never before, stumbling through each day. He comforted and carried me through this painful season—and he turned it into one of the sweetest.

It was there in my Savior's arms I experienced his LAFTER, his Love, Adoration, Favor, Truth, and Extravagant Riches. The journey of discovering who he is, and who I am, deepened. His LAFTER taught me how to LAF (look, act, and feel) like a princess. It transformed me, and it continues to transform me. That's what love does. It brings out the best in us. It reveals who we are in him and sets us on the path to happily ever after.

Jesus' LAFTER is transforming—and contagious.

When my son Jesse was younger, he loved to mimic my mom's deep staccato laugh. It sounds like how one might laugh in a doctor's office with their mouth open wide—ah, ah, ah, ah, ah—like the Count's laugh on Sesame Street. Jesse mastered the right tone and inflection by spending time with his grandmother, and she laughs with him knowing that imitation is the sincerest form of flattery.

Paul tells the church at Corinth, "Be imitators of me, just as I also am of Christ" (1 Corinthians 11:1, NASB).

We learn to imitate by spending time with a person. This answer may tire you, but it applies to almost all spiritual how-to questions: spend time with Jesus. It's how you'll experience his LAFTER. The opportunities to enjoy his company are endless because he lives in you. Wherever you go, he goes. But so do your toenails, and I doubt that you spend much time thinking about them.

God is Spirit, so you connect with him by your spirit. It's the part that senses things, the real or eternal you. Your options aren't limited to going to church, reading the Bible, or singing praises to God. You can spend time with Jesus whenever and wherever by turning your affection toward him. You don't even have to be doing anything spiritual. Washing the dishes or taking out the trash will do.

God is a real person with whom you're in a love relationship. Let that be your guide. Better yet, let God guide the time you spend with him. Let's face it: we fall short when we treat God like he's just another relationship. We struggle to love others well the way it is. Even if we didn't have the best examples while growing up, we can learn by following God's example. He continually draws us to himself, wanting us to include him in all we do. But *quantity* doesn't trump *quality,* or vice versa, regarding spending time with God. He wants both. As in human relationships, both matter. My son Jesse taught me this.

When Jesse was in first grade, he stayed home from school one day with a headache. I treasured our time together and doted on him the whole day. That evening as I went to leave his room after bedtime prayers, he grabbed onto my shirt, pleading, "Mommy, please don't go. You haven't spent enough time with me."

I had never spent more time with him, so I reminded him of our activities. "We watched cartoons and the movie *James and the Giant Peach*. We played Go Fish and Trouble. We colored, and you helped me make the best-ever chocolate chip cookies."

He looked at me with sad, blue eyes. "But Mommy, we haven't had snuggle time yet." Quite often we ended our days snuggling, and a day full of other activities couldn't replace such closeness.

No matter how old we get or how long we've known the Lord, we will always need snuggle time with God. Nothing compares to resting in his loving arms and experiencing his LAFTER, his love, adoration, favor, truth, and extravagant riches toward us. His LAFTER will cause you to LAF (look, act, and feel) like his beloved princess.

Yada Time

Find a comfortable, quiet location and spend time with Jesus. Play worship music if you'd like, and think about how much God loves you. He died on the cross for *you*. Thank him for all he's done in your life. Psalm 100:4 says, "Enter his gates with thanksgiving and his courts with praise." Giving thanks and praise ushers us into God's presence.

For some, this may be difficult. God may seem too distant. If that's you, tell him how you feel, and if you can, tell him you want to experience his love. Be still and listen for his response. He loves you. He really does.

Day 3: Identity Identified

For a brief yet glorious moment, Cinderella had become someone else. She'd held her head high, danced with the Prince, and even LAFed like a true princess. Then midnight struck—and she ran. She had to. Otherwise, she'd face utter embarrassment. Everyone would see who she truly was or who she *thought* she was. Before her dress turned back to rags, she ran, leaving a lone glass slipper as the only proof of her existence.

In our *un*redeemed state, we were much like Cinderella's incognito days. Isaiah 64:6 says, "All of us have become like one who is unclean, and all our righteous acts are like filthy rags." Too often we forget that this verse describes our condition *before* accepting Jesus as Lord and Savior. Through Isaiah, God said, "Come now, and let us reason together … Though your sins are as scarlet, they will be as white as snow; though they are red like crimson, they shall be like wool" (Isaiah 1:18, NASB).

Once we are born again, Jesus replaces our filthy rags with his robe of righteousness (see Isaiah 61:10). Galatians 3:27 says, "For all of you who were baptized into Christ have clothed yourselves with Christ." Better than any ballroom gown, Christ's magnificent robe of righteousness adorns you. Nothing else compares to its beauty—now your beauty. It doesn't matter what sins you've committed in the past or even what sins you'll commit in the future. Those who are in Christ are forgiven (see Matthew 26:28). You've been made perfect, without stain or blemish.

In God's eyes, you could never look more radiant. Is that hard for you to wrap your head around? How about your heart? Both need to be convinced. The only way to do this is to allow God to tell you who you are, to show you how he sees you. Unlike popular opinion or your assessment, your identity in Christ is unchangeable because Jesus never changes (see Hebrews 13:8).

Obtaining our identities from anything other than God makes them fluid. They'll be determined by whatever we're identifying with at the moment. Concentrate on our sins, and we'll see ourselves as sinners. Dwell on past failures, and we'll believe we're failures. Even our work can produce an identity determined by how well we're doing—or not doing—at the time.

Too many things influence how we see ourselves: people, the world, the devil, past mistakes, emotions, attitudes, wounds, lies, etc. When we give in to these influences, our identities become like an ever-moving target. They change quicker than a clock striking midnight. Just ask Cinderella. One minute she's the belle of the ball, the next she's racing off in fear of being exposed as an imposter.

It's a battle to obtain and keep our true identities as the King's daughters. We have an enemy, the devil, who strives to keep us from knowing who we truly are. He bombards us with lies and accusations. He tells us who *he* wants us to be, hoping we'll believe him instead of God. He strives to keep us from knowing and embracing our true identities because when we do we become a threat to him. Christ defeated him, and we are *in Christ*.

The following verses describe who we are in Christ:

Praise be to the God and Father of our Lord Jesus Christ, who has **blessed** us in the heavenly realms ***with every spiritual blessing*** in Christ. For he ***chose us*** in him before the creation of the world to be ***holy and blameless*** in his sight. In love he ***predestined*** us for **adoption to sonship** through Jesus Christ … In him we have ***redemption*** through his blood, ***the forgiveness of sins***, in accordance with the riches of God's grace. (Ephesians 1:3–7, emphasis added)

Your relationship with God is secure because he chose you (see Ephesians 1:11). He purchased you with his life, and you belong to him. You are God's temple (see 1 Corinthians 3:16), the salt of the earth (see Matthew 5:13), and the light of the world (see Matthew 5:14). In Christ you are more than a conqueror (see Romans 8:37) and nothing can separate you from his love (see Romans 8:38–39). You are God's workmanship (see Ephesians 2:10), his precious princess, the one he died for.

Listen. Did you hear Jesus' LAFTER (love, adoration, favor, truth, and extravagant riches)?

Replacing your identity with Christ's identity takes practice. You may have to put him on repeatedly even though you don't remember taking him off. At first, it may seem as though his identity doesn't fit you well. Most likely that's because you're still wearing some of your old clothes. It's easy to put certain pieces back on because they're more comfortable than new ones. Believing who God says you are may take time, so keep putting Christ on daily and find your identity in him. Eventually, you'll LAF like he does.

Until then, God loves you just as you are. He sees Jesus' righteousness on you—while you keep your uniqueness. God doesn't want clones, so he gives everyone distinct personalities and characteristics. No one else is like you. God created you to be matchless, an incomparable jewel.

I believe this, although I'm frequently mistaken for someone else. Recently a woman pulled a picture from her purse to show me who she thought I was. "I have one of those faces," is usually my response. That evening I laughed, imagining God trying to keep billions of us straight. As my blessings flitted through my mind, gratitude and humility rose in my spirit. Playfully, I questioned God. Had he mistaken me for someone else? Maybe he intended my blessings for someone I merely looked like.

Surprisingly, I sensed God agreed. But he assured me it was no mistake. When God looks at us, he sees Jesus. All our spiritual blessings are because of him. God chose us in Christ before he created the world (see Ephesians 1:11). You won't comprehend your significance, how special you are, until you realize God chose *you*.

Too many times in life we've not been chosen, such as in grade school when captains picked teammates for playing dodgeball, or our class voted on student council representatives or the homecoming queen. Maybe we didn't get the lead in a play. As adults, perhaps someone else got the job we wanted, the promotion we were more qualified to receive, or the baby we couldn't conceive.

When we're rejected, we assume there's something wrong with us. We compare ourselves to others to see how we measure up. When people act cruelly to us, like Cinderella's stepmom did to her, we wonder why. Was it something we did? Is there something wrong with us? I imagine Cinderella wondered these same things. She probably compared herself more than once to her stepsisters and believed she didn't belong.

We learned the skill of comparing in kindergarten. Remember the worksheets showing pictures of three similar items such as a brush, a comb, a barrette, and one odd item, like a fork? We were to figure out which item was different and didn't belong. Unfortunately, we got too good at this elementary skill—as did others. If we missed discovering our uniqueness, others quickly pointed it out. Like the ugly duckling, we too may have believed that we didn't belong.

As a youth, my overbite and large front teeth provided an opportunity for others to tease me. When my son Jordan got braces in junior high, I contemplated getting them myself. Though my friends told me my teeth looked fine, I didn't believe them. I still felt the stinging words and saw the faces of those who had mimicked my overbite.

As Jordan sat on the stage at his band concert waiting for his grade's turn to play, his smile exuded a zest for life despite his braces. I smiled, filled with the joy he brought me. Soon my eyes rimmed with tears and my heart overflowed with love.

Then God turned the tables on me. I sensed him say he loved to see me smile. He wished I'd smile more often because I had a beautiful smile, and I brought him great joy. His words changed my concern about getting braces and caused me to smile more often.

Shouldn't God's opinion be all that matters to us?

Let's not be like Cinderella, who by running away gave little credit to the Prince's character when she assumed he was only interested in her appearance or social status. That's how we act when we doubt God's love and acceptance after we've sinned. The Bible says, "But God demonstrates his own love for us in this: While we were still sinners, Christ died for us" (Romans 5:8). Jesus paid a great price for us while we were in an ugly condition. Why would he hold sin against us after he's welcomed us into his family?

We were saved by grace through faith. Jesus paid the penalty for our sin. We did nothing to become right with God except believe in Jesus and receive his gift. We weren't good enough. We weren't remorseful enough. We didn't say enough right words. We simply believed and received God's gift of salvation. It was a done deal. On the cross, Jesus said, "It is finished!" (John 19:30) and he meant it.

That's how you should approach learning to LAF (look, act, and feel) like a true princess, by believing and receiving. Remember, you aren't alone in this. The Holy Spirit led you to Christ, and he will teach you to LAF like him too. He facilitates your transformation and enables you to reflect how God already sees you, which is perfect. When you mess up, no heavenly clock is going to strike midnight and replace your righteous robe with rags. Nothing can separate you from God's love in Christ Jesus (see Romans 8:38–39). Nothing!

Yada Time

Meditate on who you are in Christ as found on page 31. Allow these truths to sink deep into your inner being. Listen for Jesus' LAFTER. Zephaniah 3:17 says, "[God] will take delight in you with gladness. With his love, he will calm all your fears. He will rejoice over you with joyful songs" (NLT). Can you hear the love song he's singing to you? Don't be surprised if you awaken to a song in your heart or one pops into your mind during the day. Pay attention and believe it is God singing over you. Many songs that express our love for him can also apply to his love for us.

Day 4: Rescued

I understand why Cinderella ran. Running felt safer. As did hiding. How could she have known the Prince loved her so much that he'd never stop searching until he found her?

Referring to God, King David wrote, "Where can I go from your Spirit? Where can I flee from your presence? If I go up to the heavens, you are there; if I make my bed in the depths, you are there" (Psalm 139:7–8).

It's impossible to hide from God and even silly to try. It's like how my granddaughter played Hide and Seek when she was young. She'd bury her face on the floor in a corner, her tiny tush sticking up in plain sight. Because she couldn't see me, she thought I couldn't see her. Though we can't hide from God, we can act as if we are by withholding from him. We withhold our affection, trust, resources, time, talent, treasures, etc. We may not mean to, but we do for many reasons.

In her ragged condition, Cinderella thought she had nothing to offer the Prince. She never imagined he delighted in her just as she was. Why else would he have searched far and wide and never given up until he found her? His passion propelled him. Had he known about her circumstances and why she was hiding, it would have stirred him even more—to rescue her.

Do you need rescuing?

Jesus delights in you so much that he died on the cross to rescue you from sin, death, and the devil's influence. Jesus' death paid the price for everything we'll ever need. Our part is to "work out [our] salvation with fear and trembling" (Philippians 2:12).

Soteria is the Greek word for salvation.[2] It's a noun. The active or verb form of the word is *sozo*. Its rich meaning includes words such as saved, delivered, rescued, healed, and forgiven.[3] It includes past, present, and future tenses. You *were* saved when you placed your trust in Jesus as your savior. You *are being* saved as your life is transformed by walking with Jesus on earth. You *will be* saved when you die and meet him face to face in heaven.

Salvation in any tense is a gift. There is nothing you can or need to do but receive it. Perhaps you remember the exact moment you placed your trust in Jesus and invited him into your heart. Maybe you grew up trusting him, and you don't remember a specific day. If you're unsure of having ever made this commitment, turn to Appendix A and settle the matter. God wants you as his daughter.

Though salvation is a gift, Paul tells us to "work out" our salvation. The words "work out" come from the Greek word *katergazomai* (kat-er-gad'-zom-ahee), which means "do work fully, i.e. accomplish; by implication, to finish, fashion"[5] Pastor Mark Adams of Redland Baptist Church explains:

> This same Greek word was used in Paul's day to refer to a farmer working out his field in order to reap the greatest harvest possible. The seeds had already been planted. The crop was already growing. Now it was time to go out and harvest the crop. The farmer WORKED OUT his field so he could gather a maximum harvest.[4]

Our part in "working out" is to appropriate (take and apply) all that Jesus' death provides for us. We can accomplish this by believing for a "maximum harvest" in our lives. To lay hold of it, we need to comprehend and contend for what God promises us as his daughters.

Let's use Cinderella's life as an example. The Prince rescued her and brought her to his home. She will forever live with him, and he accepts her just as she is. He won't treat her like a servant. Though at times she may act like one, wanting to serve from heartfelt gratitude. She won't have to beg for food or scrounge for leftovers; she'll dine with the Prince. She'll no longer wear rags because he'll clothe her with beautiful tailor-made garments. She won't sleep outdoors or on the floor; she'll lie next to him in his bed.

Would the Prince *make* her do any of these things?

No, he loves her too much to force her to do anything. She must choose to embrace her new identity and choose to accept the Prince's provision. He understands how the transition might not be easy. She may not always look, act, or feel like his beloved. She'll need to renew her mind and receive the Prince's love and favor before fully embracing her true identity. By spending time with him, she'll grow to trust him. He'll heal her wounds and speak truth to the lies she's believed. Eventually, she'll see herself as the Prince sees her.

"Work out" implies a process. Paul states we are to do it with "fear and trembling" (Philippians 2:12). We should not do this because we're afraid of God but because we're in awe of him and what he's done. Fearing God means to give him the respect and honor he deserves. We should tremble at his magnificence. Likewise, contemplating what God has done for us should evoke as great a response. We've been rescued, saved, healed, and forgiven! That should make us want to sing, dance, shout for joy, and in the presence of our rescuer, bow down in awe, honor, gratitude, and reverence.

The next verse gives an additional reason to be awestruck: "for it is God who works in you to will and to act in order to fulfill his good purpose" (Philippians 2:13). Praise the Lord! He not only saves us, he "works in" us the ability and desire to "work out" our salvation and see it manifested. For me, this process involved healing the childhood wound I mentioned in chapter one.

I grew up in an old, cold two-bedroom farmhouse. A wall heater in the living room provided heat to the kids' bedroom above through a grated hole in the ceiling/floor. At age nine, I liked to rearrange the metal twin-sized beds in our room, but I was told not to. Disobeying orders, I scooted my bed across the room until one of its legs slipped into the grated hole in the floor and got stuck. From downstairs, my mom screamed, "The ceiling's falling in!" I imagined the entire ceiling crumbling to the living room floor below.

She came charging up the stairs, and I knew I was in huge trouble. "Do you know what I could do to you?" she asked. I was terrified and answered, "You could kill me?" She ran to her room crying, and I cried in mine. We never spoke of this incident for over twenty-seven years.

I believed the lie my mom wanted to kill me, and it became the lens through which I saw our relationship. I felt unloved and tried to earn her love. I also thought I had to earn God's love and became fearful of ever making a mistake. If only I could be good enough, smart enough, or helpful enough to receive love. But nothing is ever enough when seeing through a faulty lens.

My experience may be minor compared to what you've gone through, but I know that God can rescue you, too. He wants to free us because wounds and lies hurt us and affect our relationship with him and others.

One night while praying with a friend, the Holy Spirit brought to my memory the time when I thought my mom wanted to kill me. The healing-prayer technique we were learning invites God to expose the lie attached to a painful memory. When God's truth replaces a lie, it also releases the pain. Miraculously, this happened. God filled me with his peace, and I knew my mom hadn't wanted to kill me and that she loved me. I was rescued from the pain inflicted by a lie, yet the story's best part was still to come.

This prayer ministry was being taught at our church in two weeks, and my parents happened to be coming for a visit. I shared what I knew about this prayer technique with my mom, expressing a desire to learn more, and asked her to attend the class with me. I never mentioned the painful memory I'd received healing from because I didn't want to hurt her.

We attended the class together, and during a break, she surprised me in the restroom. She placed her hands on my shoulders, and with teary eyes, she looked into mine and said, "God told me there's a nine-year-old girl who thought her mom wanted to kill her. That's not true. I love you." Then she asked my forgiveness, and we hugged and cried.

God rescued my mom, too. He worked salvation (healing) in us both, freeing us from the pain and lies of a past event so we could "work out" our relationship with each other. God is all about relationships, redemption, restoration—and rescuing us!

Yada Time

Whenever a painful memory comes to mind, ask God for truth. Tell him how you feel and what you believe about the past event. You may think it was your fault or believe you deserved what happened. A lie will feel like the truth, so ask the Lord to expose the lie and reveal *his* truth. Listen with your heart. Whether there's a lie or not, your pain is real, and God wants to take it from you. Can you release it to him? He longs to rescue you.

Day 5: The Shoe Fits

What were your dreams as a child? What did you want to become when you grew up? Was there a cute boy you hoped to marry? Cinderella probably had similar hopes and dreams, longing for the freedom to make choices herself. The death of her parents surely impacted those dreams, as would have being raised by a wicked stepmother. What got her through each day? Was it a dream? Hope for a better future?

Dreams are like drinking from a perpetual well of hope. They get us through the tough times and encourage us to persevere through the disappointments and daily drudgeries. I'm not talking about wishful-thinking dreams, such as "I wish I'd win the lottery." Those dreams are as elusive as the gold-filled pot at the end of a rainbow and provide no lasting satisfaction. The dreams I'm talking about are God-given dreams, those placed in your heart by God.

If you're afraid God hasn't given you any dreams, rest assured, he gives dreams to everyone. We may not recognize them or realize they're from him, but they're there, planted in seed form. Like a good story, God's dreams unfold one page at a time. In *The Dream Giver*, the author, Bruce Wilkinson, says, "God has put a driving passion in you to do something special. Why wouldn't He? You are created in His image—the only person exactly like you in the universe. No one else can do your dream."[6]

A dream fulfilled provides happiness, contentment, satisfaction, a sense of accomplishment, and more. It overflows with God's goodness spilling onto others. Yet, reaching this point often involves hard work and taking risks—like when Cinderella faced trying on the glass slipper.

What if Cinderella had refused? What if when faced with her dream she'd let fear, timidity, low self-worth, or her family's ridicule keep her incognito? Would she have ever made it to the palace? Trying on the glass slipper would expose her as the princess imposter who had crashed the royal ball. She had no guarantee the Prince would respond positively to her. Though he'd stated his intentions, he could still change his mind. After all, her dishmop dress wasn't magically going to become an evening gown again, and her cinder-smudged face wasn't going to glow radiantly with makeup. Her perpetual bad hair day was reason enough to stay hidden. And anyone would think twice about extending a foot as calloused as hers.

Becoming a princess carried risks. Did Cinderella contemplate the lifestyle changes she'd have to make? Living in the palace would be overwhelmingly different. She'd be thrust into the limelight, exposed to a new crowd. Would they accept her? The reasons to be leery were many, and yet her dream propelled her onward. She replaced timidity with boldness and gave fear the boot—trying on faith *and* the slipper. She chose not to remain incognito and risked becoming who God destined her to be.

Trying on God's dream for your life may raise similar concerns. There are risks associated with following a dream. People may laugh at you or question your ability to achieve grandeur. They may get jealous, angry, or envious. The Bible tells about a dreamer named Joseph. Though his was also a literal dream, he understood it meant one day his brothers would bow down to him. In hindsight, he probably wished he hadn't told them about his dream. Joseph was their father's favorite son, and his brothers were already jealous of him. Only because the brothers couldn't agree to kill him did they sell him as a slave to foreigners (see Genesis 37).

Sometimes the path from our dream to the palace isn't what we expect. We hit roadblocks, detours, and even a few potholes. To Joseph, it may have seemed like he'd stepped on a landmine had there been any back then. After being falsely accused of putting the moves on his boss' wife, Joseph landed in prison. Could his dream have seemed any further from becoming a reality?

During what seemed like setbacks, God was building Joseph's character and preparing him to save Egypt and his brothers from starvation. We'll look further at our character maturing process when studying Chicken Little's story. God is as concerned with molding us into his image as he is with us fulfilling our dreams. That's why we often have to grow into our dreams, for our good and the good of others. Our dreams can also be the vehicle God uses to mature us. They force us out of our comfort zones and increase our dependency on God.

When I was younger, I mistakenly believed God's dreams required such stretching as being sent to Africa as a missionary. I thought he only gave sacred service dreams, not realizing the desires of our hearts can be God-given. In *The Pursuit of God,* A.W. Tozer said: "Let every man abide in the calling wherein he is called and his work will be as sacred as the work of the ministry."[7] God gives dreams to influence the world, whether it's being a parent, a business person, an artist, a scientist, or whatever you are called to do. God doesn't designate some dreams as sacred and others as secular. Ephesians 2:10 says, "For we are God's handiwork, created in Christ Jesus to do good works, which God prepared in advance for us to do." We can do anything and everything for God's glory.

Prince Jesus holds in his hand a glass slipper tailored specifically to fit your foot. No other princess can fill your shoes because no one else LAFs (looks, acts, and feels) like you, and God loves your LAF. He loves everything about you. Do you recognize the dream God has placed in your heart? Have you extended your foot to him?

I'll never forget how awkward I felt wearing mint green polyester pants and dress shoes when entering the seventh grade. Both were at least one size too big for me. My parents couldn't afford replacements any time soon, so they anticipated I'd grow into them. Worse yet, my parents wouldn't allow me to wear jeans and tennis shoes to school like most of my classmates.

Though God's shoes (dreams) are made specifically for your feet, they may feel too big at first, like my pants and shoes did. Or they may seem so different from everyone else's that you feel awkward in them. Or they may feel restrictive and need to be broken in. You'll have to practice walking in them before you're comfortable wearing them. But if you allow fear, timidity, discomfort, self-consciousness, or anything else stop you from wearing them, you'll remain incognito.

The Bible says, "For God has not given us a spirit of timidity, but of power and love and discipline" (2 Timothy 1:7, NASB). Other versions use the word *fear* instead of timidity. God doesn't want us to have either. We should be bold and filled with faith, love, and power because that's what God gave us. Boldness replaces timidity when you learn to trust God. When you believe God is in control and has a great plan for your life, you can accomplish anything. It feels safe to stop hiding when you trust that the one searching for you loves you unconditionally. Jesus proved his love by dying on the cross. Are you willing to try on the shoe he's extending to you?

I hope so, because the world needs you. No one else can fulfill the dreams God placed in your heart. In your unique way, you represent Jesus on earth. That makes you God's ambassador (see 2 Corinthians 5:20). We all are. In everything we do, we represent our King in this foreign land, for "our citizenship is in heaven …" (Philippians 3:20).

Therefore, we should strive to represent him well as we fulfill our dreams. Jesus illustrated a life well lived. Colossians 1:15 says Jesus "is the image of the invisible God." Through Jesus' example we come to know God's nature and character. We learn he is a loving father. Jesus said anyone who had seen him had seen the Father (see John 14:9). His life answered the question of what God is like. As his children and ambassadors, shouldn't our lives answer the same question? Many in the world are still asking, seeking to know the one true God. We have the opportunity and responsibility to fulfill our dreams so others will encounter God through us.

For others to encounter God through us, we must love and serve like Jesus: "Who, being in very nature God, did not consider equality with God something to be used to his own advantage; rather, he made himself nothing by taking the very nature of a servant …" (Philippians 2:6–7). Bill Johnson, Senior Leader of Bethel Church in Redding, California, said, "Royalty is my identity. Servanthood is my assignment. Intimacy with God is my life source."[8] Everything we do should flow from our love relationship with God.

By gazing into God's loving eyes and embracing the image reflected in them, you'll discover your identity. You'll believe the dreams stirring in your heart are from him, and you'll find strength to accomplish them in him. Your heart will sync with his, and you'll serve others with love and compassion. You'll stop living incognito because he chose you, he loves you, and he empowers you to fulfill your dreams and truly live—for him.

Yada Time

Talk with God about your dreams. Tell him your heart's desires. What does your shoe look like? Allow yourself to dream with him even further. Ask questions that pop into your head and listen for the answers. Is there another shoe he's holding out for you? Will you agree to try it on?

Chapter 2
Cinderella—Embracing Your True Identity
Questions for Reflection or Discussion

Day 1: Princess Incognito

1. In what way could you relate to wanting to LAF (look, act, feel) like someone else?

2. What things keep us from embracing our identity as a princess? (p. 24)

3. Why might someone conceal their true self from others? (p. 25)

4. What does God say about who we are? (p. 25)

5. What steps can you take to stop living incognito?

Day 2: Jesus' LAFTER

1. Reflecting on God's love (E.g. forgiving, unconditional, passionate, never stops searching for you, protective, etc.), what aspect of it touches you the most and why?

2. Tell about a time you clung to the Lord and how it changed you.

3. What does experiencing Jesus' LAFTER (Love, Adoration, Favor, Truth, and Extravagant Riches) do for us? (p. 28)

4. How can we include Jesus more throughout the day?

5. If you spent snuggle time with God this week, how did it impact you?

Day 3: Identity Identified

1. How do you get your identity from God? (p. 30)

2. What happens when we get our identity from other things? (p. 30)

3. What things influence how we see ourselves if we allow them to? (p. 30)

4. Describe who God says we are. (p. 31)

5. In what areas do you struggle not to compare yourself with others?

6. If you heard God sing over you this week, what song did he sing?

Day 4: Rescued

1. What has God rescued us from and how did he do it? (p. 33)

2. What does it mean to "work out" our salvation? (p. 34)

3. Why are we to do it with "fear and trembling"? (p. 34)

4. How does God help us "work out"? (Philippians 2:13, p. 34)

5. Share a story about when God rescued you.

Day 5: The Shoe Fits

1. What risks keep people from pursuing their dreams? (p. 37)

2. The path to our dreams isn't always a straight route because God is also concerned with what? (p. 37)

3. What dream or dreams are you pursuing?

4. What can stop people from pursuing their dreams? (pp. 37–38)

5. What dreams has God already fulfilled in your life?

6. Is there anything else in this chapter you want to discuss?

Share prayer requests and pray for each other. Let's believe God will fulfill our dreams!

Chapter 3
Little Red Riding Hood—Spiritual Warfare

Memory Verse:

The weapons we fight with are not the weapons of the world.
On the contrary, they have divine power to demolish strongholds.
2 Corinthians 10:4

Day 1: Through the Woods

Doesn't it seem odd that before setting off to Grandmother's house Little Red Riding Hood's mother never warned her about the wolf lurking in the woods? Her mom had to know he lived there and had a ferocious appetite. Did she assume her daughter already knew about him? Or did she not mention him to avoid scaring Little Red? Maybe she believed her daughter would be safe as long as she stayed on the designated path. That was her only warning, "Do not stray from the path."

Though good advice, the *path* was exactly where Little Red encountered the wolf. When he appeared, she cheerfully chatted with this curious creature. She had no reason to fear him because she had no knowledge of him. God said in Hosea 4:6: "My people are destroyed from lack of knowledge."

Knowing a wolf lives in the woods is crucial information if you're passing through. Had she known, Little Red could have strategized. She might not have drawn so much attention to herself by wearing her signature red cape. Or she might have chosen to wear it—to conceal a shotgun. Not knowing she had an enemy put her at a greater risk.

Like Little Red Riding Hood, we too have a crafty, dangerous enemy. He "prowls around like a roaring lion looking for someone to devour" (1 Peter 5:8). No doubt you've heard of him. He goes by several names such as Satan, Lucifer, the devil, deceiver, accuser, and Father of Lies. He's the antagonist in every story. While referring to him, Jesus said, "The thief comes only to steal and kill and destroy" (John 10:10).

Our history with the devil goes back as far as the Garden of Eden. Eve was as naïve about her enemy as Little Red was about the wolf. We don't know if God warned Eve about the devil. Yet we do know God said, "But you must not eat from the tree of the knowledge of good and evil, for when you eat from it you will certainly die" (Genesis 2:17).

If God didn't warn Eve about the devil, it was probably because she'd be safe as long as she obeyed God. Even if he had warned her, would she have understood? She had no context for evil because she hadn't eaten from the tree of the knowledge of good and evil yet. Unless the devil could get Eve to disobey God, he couldn't hurt her. Obedience wards off the enemy, which sounds simple: obey God. Yet, we all know obeying God is easier said than done.

Our enemy is crafty. He's a schemer. He finds our weaknesses and uses them to his advantage. He twists God's words, instills doubts and fears, and entices us to pursue the lusts of our flesh—he wants us to disobey God. Without God's help, we are doomed. The Old Testament documents our inability to keep the law and obey God.

Thankfully, we now live under the New Covenant of grace. This promise doesn't make sinning and disobeying God okay, but the New Covenant provides the answer to overcoming sin: abide in Christ and harness the power of his Spirit living in us. We entered into this New Covenant when we accepted Jesus Christ as Lord and Savior. This monumental act transferred us from the devil's dark domain into God's kingdom of light. It also began the process of our transformation.

Remaining in the light—God's presence—is the essence of living happily ever after. Psalm 16:11 says, "You make known to me the path of life; you will fill me with joy in your presence, with eternal pleasures at your right hand." Doesn't that sound like what you're looking for: the path of life, the fullness of joy, and eternal pleasures? God hardwired our hearts with these desires. As spiritual beings, we need God's presence because this is where we experience true love, joy, peace, hope, goodness, etc.

Second Corinthians 3:18 says, "But we all, with unveiled face, beholding as in a mirror the glory of the Lord, are being transformed into the same image from glory to glory, just as from the Lord, the Spirit" (NASB). *The Biblical Illustrator* commentary explains these verses: "The idea, then, is that they who are much in Christ's presence become mirrors to Him, reflecting more and more permanently His image until they themselves perfectly resemble Him."[1]

What we behold—what we fix our hearts and minds on—changes us. Like to how baby animals and children take on their parents' mannerisms and characteristics by being around them, we obtain Christ's likeness by beholding and spending time with him. Whatever we behold will grow in us like a planted seed. The opposite is also true. If we decline to nurture a seed by refusing to give it water, sunshine, and food, the seed will die. This is good news when we withhold life-giving support from the negative habits and vices entangling us, and it is bad news when we neglect to spend time with God.

Our best defense against the enemy is to become like Jesus. On his way to the cross, Jesus said of the devil, "He has no hold over me" (John 14:30). The devil will have no hold over us either when we become like Jesus. Therefore, Hebrews 12:2 instructs us to "[fix] our eyes on Jesus, the pioneer and perfecter of faith." When I fix my eyes on Jesus, they aren't on me, the devil, or worldly enticements. Plus, I'm transformed in his presence. What we gaze on greatly affects us.

When my boys were young, I limited my television viewing to three weekly sitcoms until I eventually quit cold turkey. I stopped because watching television stole my attention and robbed me of what precious time I had with my boys. To this day, they still tease me about becoming unresponsive while watching TV.

Have you ever been so engrossed in something that everything else around you seemed to fade away? You ignored your children or spouse, their voices not even heard. Time became nonexistent as the movie you were watching, the book you were reading, or the craft you were making captivated you for hours. Nothing else mattered except what you were beholding.

The real war is for our attention, affection, and adoration. What we love and adore can become an idol—even a television show. Our enemy wants us to worship him or anything other than God. In addition, the world and our flesh also compete for our worship.

First John 2:16 says, "For everything in the world—the lust of the flesh, the lust of the eyes, and the pride of life—comes not from the Father but from the world." We're not only warring against the devil, but we're also up against our sinful flesh and worldliness. It's no wonder living happily isn't as simple as trying to avoid the wolf in the woods. Who hasn't experienced their flesh being their worst enemy at one time or another? This is why we should put our sin nature to death. Galatians 5:24 says, "Those who belong to Christ Jesus have crucified the flesh with its passions and desires."

Notice how Paul used the past-tense phrase "have crucified." Those who belong to Christ are to associate with his death. Here's how one commentary explains the previous verse:

> This does not mean that their sin nature is then eradicated or even rendered inactive but that it has been judged, a fact believers should reckon to be true (cf. Rom 6:11–12). Victory over the sinful nature's passions and desires has been provided by Christ in His death. Faith must continually lay hold of this truth or a believer will be tempted to try to secure victory by self-effort.[2]

Identifying with Christ's death brings victory. But there's one small problem: we have an aversion to crucifying our sin nature. It can be painful! Experience tells me it's a process to identify with Jesus' death. It feels similar to blowing out trick candles on a birthday cake. When I've huffed and puffed and blown out one burning passion, a fleshly flickering flame reignites elsewhere. To succeed, we also need to identify with Christ's resurrection and elicit powerhouse help from the Holy Spirit who raised Jesus from the dead (see Romans 8:11).

One of the Holy Spirit's names in Hebrew is *Ruwach* (roo'-akh), meaning "wind; by resemblance breath, i.e. a sensible (or even violent) exhalation."[3] Imagine the Holy Spirit attacking your problem like the violent wind on the day of Pentecost. Poof! Goodbye, fleshly trick candles. The Holy Spirit is our greatest weapon of warfare—and he lives in every believer of Christ. Galatians 5:16 tells us to "walk by the Spirit, and you will not gratify the desires of the flesh."

Living happily ever after requires that we learn to live by the Spirit while being transformed into Christ's image. The two go hand in hand. We can't identify with Christ's death or resurrection apart from the Spirit's help. Nor can we recognize our enemy and his tactics, which we'll learn more about tomorrow, without the Spirit's help. Even obeying God is impossible without his help. Therefore, we must learn to depend on the Holy Spirit for everything.

I've purposely placed this chapter on spiritual warfare near the beginning because the following chapters will in many ways be a continuation. Engaging in spiritual warfare has several facets, including drawing closer to God. Though we must battle for happily ever after, we do not fight alone; God's resurrection power lives in us.

Yada Time

This week, practice fixing your eyes on Jesus. Notice him in creation's beauty and in those around you. Meditate on his goodness, his compassion, and the pleasure he finds in you because he greatly loves you. Be conscious of where you set your gaze and affection. When tempted to sin, turn to the Lord and identify with his death by drawing on the Holy Spirit's resurrection power within you.

Day 2: Follow the Yellow Brick Road

Little Red's first mistake wasn't straying from the path; it was conversing with her enemy. Granted, she didn't know who he was at the time. The devil is evil, but he's no dummy. He doesn't appear as some scary creature with fiery red eyes, horns sprouting from his head, and a trident clutched in his fist. He's a master of disguise and deception. It wouldn't have surprised me if he had worn a red cape to show solidarity with Little Red.

Second Corinthians 11:14 says, "Satan himself masquerades as an angel of light."

How do we fight someone so diabolical and deceptive?

We can discover his tactics from the Bible. While talking to Eve, the devil's first words were: "Did God really say, 'You must not eat from any tree in the garden'?" (Genesis 3:1). His main strategy is to *deceive*, and one way he does this is by *distorting* God's words. "'You will not certainly die,' the serpent said to the woman. 'For God knows that when you eat from it your eyes will be opened, and you will be like God, knowing good and evil'" (Genesis 3:4–5).

Not only did the devil deceive Eve, but he also caused her to doubt God's words and goodness. Thinking God was holding out on her, Eve gave in to another enemy, fleshly desire, and ate from the forbidden tree, *disobeying* God—our enemy's ultimate goal.

The Latin prefix "dis" means to have an opposite or reversing effect. In modern slang, it's used as a put-down, and the devil works overtime to "dis" us. When we feel *dis*appointed, *dis*connected, *dis*couraged, *dis*approved, *dis*illusioned, *dis*satisfied, or *dis*contented we can be sure the devil is behind the negativity because "dis" is contrary to God's nature. God appoints, approves, connects, encourages, and satisfies.

In Little Red's story, we find additional enemy strategies. First, he engaged her in pleasant conversation to *distract* her from her mission. He suggested she pick flowers for her grandmother, which seemed innocent enough except flowers don't grow on well-traveled paths. By tempting Little Red to leave her designated route, the wolf successfully caused her to take a *detour*, which bought himself time.

Like Little Red, we won't always recognize our enemy's subtle ploys. He's a sweet talker, and his words often sound logical. When I refer to the enemy talking, I don't mean in an audible, poltergeist way. He's too smooth for that. His words infiltrate our thoughts, sounding like ours. The Bible tells us to take our thoughts captive for a good reason. Second Corinthians 10:5 says, "We demolish arguments and every pretension that sets itself up against the knowledge of God, and we take captive every thought to make it obedient to Christ."

Books such as *Battlefield of the Mind* by Joyce Meyer bring to the forefront the importance of monitoring our thought life. Spiritual battles begin and are fought in the mind. Thoughts not aligning with God, his character, and ways need to be demolished. Removing these wrong thoughts can be a daunting task. Researchers state we have anywhere from twenty-thousand to seventy-thousand thoughts a day! Even using the more conservative number—which equates to one thought every three seconds while awake—you can understand how taking our thoughts captive may seem overwhelming. Yet, we aren't to do this alone. We can't. We need the Holy Spirit's help to win this epic battle.

We must also *choose* to fight. We're called to participate in this war actively, and our first mission is to enlist the Holy Spirit's help. Because we have free will, God likes to be asked. Why not pause now and do that. Ask him to alert you to any negative, harmful, nonproductive, or destructive thoughts when they occur. Then stay alert—because the Holy Spirit's nudge is often subtle. Some describe it as a prompt, a check in their spirit, or a quiet knowing. Any new awareness should cause us to pause. We'll be faced with a choice, often requiring a quick decision, which will govern what happens next.

The Holy Spirit doesn't make thoughts disappear. That's your job. You determine a thought's lifespan. You choose whether to capture a thought or let it roll on and on. That's not to say the Holy Spirit won't help. When asked, he'll encourage, strengthen, and enable you to make the right choice in all matters, at all times. The more you submit your will to God, the more help you'll receive.

Anytime we've been complacent about taking our thoughts captive we can repent and ask God again to bring to our attention all non-life-giving thoughts. I find it helpful to pinpoint one area to work on at a time so I don't feel overwhelmed. The categories are many. We battle critical or judgmental thoughts about ourselves and others. Worry and fear are two more big ones. Then there's pride, jealousy, envy, and taking offense.

If we neglect our assignment, our thoughts will take *us* captive. They will grow in size and intensity until we're carried away by them. They'll enslave us. Have you ever *not* been able to stop thinking about something? If so, you know what it's like to be in bondage. In this war, we are told to take no prisoners.

Obedience factors in to how long the Holy Spirit will alert us to wrong thinking. Why would he continue if we aren't doing our part? Thankfully, God is patient. He realizes his gentle nudge can be easily missed, dismissed, or ignored. Even if we don't act on every prompting, he provides many opportunities to prove our sincerity. He knows our hearts and in what area the battle is fiercest.

While Saul was King of Israel, God commanded him to destroy all the Amalekites and their possessions. After Saul had defeated them, the prophet Samuel visited him. Saul told Samuel he had carried out the Lord's instructions. But Samuel knew he hadn't. He said to Saul, "What then is this bleating of sheep in my ears? What is this lowing of cattle that I hear?" (1 Samuel 15:14).

Saul's excuse for disobeying God was he had kept the choicest animals to sacrifice to the Lord. "But Samuel replied: 'Does the Lord delight in burnt offerings and sacrifices as much as in obeying the Lord? To obey is better than sacrifice, and to heed is better than the fat of rams.'" (1 Samuel 15:22).

Likewise, the Bible tells us to destroy "speculations and every lofty thing raised up against the knowledge of God" (2 Corinthians 10:5 NAS). We are to destroy all thoughts, arguments, and pretense contrary to the knowledge of God.

We destroy, not ignore.

We destroy, not catch and release.

We destroy—period.

Not doing so invariably keeps wrong mindsets alive. Like the relentless bleating of sheep, they'll beg for our attention. But thoughts in opposition to God are far from innocent sheep; they're wolves in sheep's clothing.

When the Israelites were about to enter the Promised Land, Moses instructed them: "Destroy completely all the places on the high mountains, on the hills and under every spreading tree, where the nations you are dispossessing worship their gods" (Deuteronomy 12:2). Their enemies dedicated these lofty or high places to worshiping false gods. If not destroyed, God knew the Israelites would be tempted to worship idols, and he had commanded, "You shall have no other gods before me" (Exodus 20:3).

Without a doubt, the Apostle Paul knew these passages when he instructed the Corinthian church to destroy any "lofty thing raised up" as mentioned above. Thoughts contrary to the knowledge of God, his nature, or his ways can cause us to believe and trust in something other than God. It's as if we serve and worship false beliefs when we give them power and prominence in our lives. They become idols.

For example, when we allow worry or fear to flourish, it reveals that we trust more in the enemy's ability to cause harm than in God's ability to save. Critical thoughts about ourselves or others reveal that we don't share God's heart or his perspective about people. These attacks show us the areas in which we don't fully trust God or have his mindset. Capturing these thoughts is more than a positive mental-health activity; it's pledging our allegiance to God and making him Lord in all areas of our lives.

The Israelites possessed the Promised Land by dispossessing their enemy and demolishing its high places. To live happily ever after, this should be our objective too. We must take our thoughts captive and destroy those in opposition to God's character and ways so we will recognize the enemy's tactics and not stray from God's path. By replacing each lie or each wrong thought pattern with God's truth, we renew our minds—a process we'll explore tomorrow.

Yada Time

If you haven't asked the Holy Spirit for his help yet, do so now. It's impossible to win this war on your own. Talk with God about your thought life. Which negative thoughts run more rampant than others? Which blatantly mock God? Discuss what area you and he would like to work on together first. Then commit to capturing all thoughts God brings to your attention. Stay alert to the Holy Spirit's nudges, and when you've taken a thought captive, ask the Lord for his truth to destroy it.

Day 3: Renew Your Mind

Little Red Riding Hood stared at the wolf lying in her grandmother's bed, dressed in her nightcap and gown. "What big ears you have!" she said.

"The better to hear you with," he replied.

"What big eyes you have!" She gasped, continuing to assess what must have been an alarming sight.

"The better to see you with," he said, ready with an answer.

"What big teeth you have!"

Run, Little Red! Run!

Our fight-or-flight response serves a valuable purpose when facing life-threatening situations. I'm grateful that the odds of being attacked by a furious animal today are almost nonexistent. Yet we face other threats to our survival. You may be compiling a mental list right now. The media delivers proof daily these dangers exist. Bad things happen. This world can seem scary at times. Though, sometimes a scarier place to be is in our minds.

Mark Twain is often attributed to having said, "I've had a lot of worries in my life, most of which never happened."[4] Worry is but one inroad the enemy uses in his psychological warfare against our minds. Romans 12:2 says, "Do not conform to the pattern of this world, but be transformed by the renewing of your mind. Then you will be able to test and approve what God's will is—his good, pleasing and perfect will."

The word renew in Greek is *anakainosis*. It means to renovate, such as with an old house.[5] Renewing our minds is more like a renovation project than a new build because our minds aren't a clean slate. Over the years, thoughts accumulated that never aligned with God's truth. Lies and wounds produce a faulty belief system, which require walls to be torn down and faulty wiring replaced.

A renovation project usually begins by tearing down everything to the studs, but our mind's renewal is less systematic and more piecemeal than that. We knock out one wrong thought at a time by pummeling it with God's truth. Renewal also happens when we fill our minds with God's Word and safeguard it from enemy infiltration. Using this three-prong approach, we renew our minds by demolishing, building, and protecting.

Yesterday I shared about capturing and destroying thoughts contrary to God's character and ways. These lies, fears, past hurts, and strongholds keep us from knowing, loving, and trusting God. Staying with the renovation analogy, we use God's truth as a hammer or crowbar to demolish wrong thoughts. If a thought isn't embedded too deeply, applying the appropriate Bible verse will destroy it.

For example, when I catch a negative thought about myself, I say, "That's not true. God says …" and I fill in the blank with God's truth. If I've told myself I'm a bad person, I may say, "False. God says I'm righteous in Christ Jesus." If I've done something wrong, I ask God to forgive me, and I believe I'm forgiven. If I need to make amends with someone because of my actions or words, I do so and move on. By speaking truth to myself, I stop the negative mind chatter condemning or belittling me.

It's easiest to access the right demolition verse when it's already on your tool belt. If you're unfamiliar with God's Word, a topical concordance can help you find the verse needed. Or you can search on the internet, entering "What does God say about …" Or ask God directly. He wants us to know what he thinks about everything because his truth renews our minds.

God speaks in numerous ways, and whatever we hear from him should agree with what he's already said in the Bible. God won't contradict himself, so it's important that we know Scripture. Yet, some thoughts won't crumble no matter how many Bible verses we clobber them with. They gained staying power each time we thought them. That's what repeatedly thinking about something does. It reinforces the thought, like how additional nails pounded into a board will attach it more securely.

We established many of our thought patterns in childhood, providing years of fortification. Tougher yet to demolish are the thoughts secured by an emotion. Emotions act like super glue in our minds, affixing memories in place. An example of this is when I falsely believed my mom didn't love me. The emotions attached to the lie made it impossible to believe differently—until an encounter with the Lord's dunamis (dynamite) power. Once I was healed of my emotional pain, I could receive truth and demolish the lie.

Another example is the panic I felt as an adult whenever I lost something. My heart would race as I frantically searched for whatever I couldn't find. To calm myself, I recited Bible verses, but nothing helped. Finally, after losing three items in one day, I had a meltdown. I lost a button to my suit jacket and later an earring, both at work. That evening, while gathering my family's tennis shoes to be washed, I couldn't find a shoe I had just seen. Added to the day's earlier losses, my usual panic escalated to near madness, and I ran to my room crying.

Logically, I knew I was overreacting. But why? What caused anxiety and irrational behavior whenever I lost something? After addressing my question to God, a memory surfaced of a ride home from a birthday party I'd attended as a kindergartener. While my friend's father drove, he repeatedly asked if anything along the countryside looked familiar. As a six-year-old, every gravel road looked the same and every farmhouse unfamiliar. My little heart raced with anxiety. Would I ever find my way home?

As an adult, whenever I lost something those same anxious feelings surfaced and fueled my present-day panic attacks. God not only answered my question, but he also removed the anxiety attached to the memory and brought healing. Afterward, I laughed—a victorious laugh—because the enemy's stronghold in my life had been demolished. Reveling in my freedom, I searched for the missing shoe and found it between the steps. The lost button and earring also appeared on my desk the next morning.

The transformation occurred when I renewed my mind. By aligning our thoughts with God's, we become like him. This makes renewing our minds a battle because our enemy doesn't want us becoming like God. So, we must fight to know God's truth, spend time with him, and read his Word. And when we have meltdowns, we ask God for answers.

We talk to God—not our enemy, as Little Red did. That may seem like a no-brainer, but sometimes we get deceived. We forget that most thoughts sound like ours no matter their origin. Is it possible the negative conversations playing in your mind aren't only with yourself after all? What about the derogatory questions you ask, such as "What's wrong with me?" or "Why doesn't anyone love me?" Could Satan be planting these questions in your mind?

The enemy isn't lying in your grandmother's bed; he's whispering falsehoods in your head. Lie-based thoughts originate from the enemy, and he is waiting to swallow you whole. Though he seldom says aloud "The better to eat you with, my dear!" that's his intent. Kill. Steal. Destroy.

Reciting God's Word demolishes the enemy's influence the best. That's what Jesus did when Satan tempted him. Jesus said, "It is written ..." and quoted Scripture to refute his enemy's words (see Matthew 4:4–10). In Ephesians 6:17, Paul referred to God's Word as the "sword of the Spirit."

If nagging thoughts persist after wielding your sword, inner healing may be needed. Bring your questions to God in heartfelt communication. Tell him how you feel, such as "I feel nobody loves me." Listen for his response and continue the dialogue. Maybe you'll be brought to a memory and realize a lie you've believed, or maybe he'll bring to mind all those who do love you. Or he may overwhelm you with a huge dose of his love or peace. If nothing happens immediately, trust that God is at work and dive into Scripture. Search for God's truth and keep fighting.

Besides demolishing wrong thought patterns and building strong truth structures, an important aspect of renewing your mind includes guarding it. A popular children's song, "O Be Careful Little Eyes What You See," emphasizes this. It encourages children to be selective and protective in what they see, hear, say, and do because their heavenly Father, in love, is watching from above.[6] If we guard what goes into our minds, we'll have less to battle later. The music we listen to, the television shows we watch, the books we read, and the company we keep all influence our mental and spiritual health.

My husband and I received a video streaming service as a Christmas gift one year. After browsing through the movies and television shows one evening, I selected a sitcom starring a comedic actress I enjoy. Though the language was terrible, I continued watching it in hopes the humor would eclipse the profanity. My husband wandered in and out of the room several times, repeatedly asking what I was watching. Finally, he settled into the chair next to mine. After hearing a few colorful words, he again asked, "What's this show called?"

This time I spewed the title at him. My reaction surprised even me, and I immediately turned off the show and apologized. The characters' coarse language and chaotic, disrespectful behavior had somehow infiltrated my psyche. What we allow into our minds from improper boundaries affects more than our thoughts. Proverbs 23:7 says, "For as he thinks within himself, so he is" (NASB). If the devil can influence our thoughts, he's succeeded at influencing our behavior.

Boundaries often shift subtly, so it's important that we guard them. One glance at something we shouldn't view and we may look longer the next time. Lyrics from music can get stuck in our heads, and mood-altering melodies can cause melancholy or worse. One provocative romance novel can lead to others and create marital dissatisfaction. All seem harmless in the beginning, and that is exactly what our enemy wants us to believe. Instead, we must aggressively guard what we allow into our minds.

One helpful gauge to establish boundaries is Philippians 4:8: "Finally, brothers and sisters, whatever is true, whatever is noble, whatever is right, whatever is pure, whatever is lovely, whatever is admirable—if anything is excellent or praiseworthy—think about such things." Protecting our minds and building them up with God's Word will lessen our need for future demolition.

Yada Time

Yesterday, you and God pinpointed an area of thought you'd work on capturing together. Your mission today, and going forward, is to find Scripture to destroy those thoughts. Use a concordance, search on the internet, or ask a friend for help. Write these verses in your journal or on note cards and meditate on them until they are fully affixed to your tool belt.

Don't wait until a meltdown before talking to God about haunting thoughts. Tell him how you feel and learn what emotion has super glued those thoughts in place. Ask God for his dunamis power and truth to destroy all lies and bring inner peace and healing.

Day 4: Cover Girl

Don't put on anything you don't want to take off. These words interrupted my thoughts as I contemplated wearing mascara again while putting on my makeup. I had quit wearing mascara six months earlier partly because I despised taking it off. No matter how hard I scrubbed, I still woke the next morning with black flecks beneath my eyes.

While still considering the idea of not putting on anything I didn't want to take off, a greater spiritual application arose in my spirit. As a Christian, there are worse things I shouldn't put on, sins such as jealousy, anger, bitterness, greed, envy, worry, and pride. When I do put one on, I know I'll need to take it off as soon as possible. The longer we wear sin, the more it becomes a part of us. Like glue, sin is easiest to unstick before it sets—before it adheres to us. Then, until we become broken over our sin, it won't come off.

Hebrews 12:1 tells us to "throw off everything that hinders and the sin that so easily entangles. And let us run with perseverance the race marked out for us." If you've ever watched a marathon race, I imagine you've seen some scantily clothed runners. Their attire reflects how we're to live life, running spiritually free and unencumbered because we've refused to put on anything that could slow us down.

Besides slowing us down, sin causes us to stumble, become sidetracked, and it has the power to trap us. Opportunities to sin abound, so we must rely on the Spirit. The Spirit provides the means to resist gratifying our sin nature's cravings and lusts (see Galatians 5:16). Still, living by the Spirit and refusing to put on sin is a huge battle.

We may know the right thing to do or not do, but we're tempted to do the opposite. The Bible tells us to forgive, yet when someone offends us, we want to put on the offense. We call a friend and say, "Do you know what so-and-so did to me?" Our conversation secures the last button on our offense, and now we're wearing it.

Whenever it's a fight to do what's right, a weak area has been exposed. We learn where we're vulnerable and likely to be attacked again. Reinforcements are needed, so it's time to call in the Holy Spirit cavalry. First Corinthians 10:13 says, "No temptation has overtaken you except what is common to mankind. And God is faithful; he will not let you be tempted beyond what you can bear. But when you are tempted, he will also provide a way out so that you can endure it."

That's a wonderful promise, but you still may feel discouraged because the issue of sin is huge and we easily slip into it. Who doesn't have at least one sin they struggle not to wear? The enemy loves it when we feel defeated because then we'll stop fighting. We'll give up and keep wearing sin. Turning to God who provides a way of escape and staying engaged in this battle is crucial. We're not going to be perfect overnight, so let's not beat ourselves up when we put on something we shouldn't. Instead, let's make every effort to confess sin, throw it off as soon as possible, and receive God's forgiveness while remembering to forgive ourselves.

First John 1:9 says, "If we confess our sins, he is faithful and just and will forgive us our sins and purify us from all unrighteousness." We must believe we're forgiven so we don't disengage from God or the battle. When struggling with sin, it's easy to shame, blame, and condemn ourselves, which is never the right response. Confess sin and move on. Fight the enemy, not yourself. Romans 8:1 says, "Therefore, there is now no condemnation for those who are in Christ Jesus." God dealt with our sin at the cross, so he no longer holds it against us. He loves us. He doesn't want us to sin because sin's consequences keep us from living the abundant life he offers. Plus, sin is contrary to God's nature, and we're to be conformed to Jesus.

One way not to put on sin is to "clothe yourselves with the Lord Jesus Christ, and do not think about how to gratify the desires of the flesh" (Romans 13:14). "Put on the new self, which is being renewed in knowledge in the image of its Creator" (Colossians 3:10).

In a passage on spiritual warfare, Paul instructed his readers to *put on* the full armor of God, which he compared to a Roman soldier's attire.

Stand firm then, with the belt of *truth* buckled around your waist, with the breastplate of *righteousness* in place, and with your feet fitted with the readiness that comes from the gospel of *peace*. In addition to all this, take up the shield of *faith*, with which you can extinguish all the flaming arrows of the evil one. Take the helmet of *salvation* and the *sword of the Spirit*, which is the *word of God*. (Ephesian 6:14–17, emphasis added)

Essentially, when dressing with Paul's battle armament, we are putting on the Lord Jesus Christ, who is Truth, Righteousness, Peace, Salvation, the Perfecter of Faith, and the Incarnate Word. Many find it helpful to put on these armor pieces symbolically when under attack. But if we fail to embrace Christ as the embodiment of our spiritual weaponry, this becomes an exercise of our imaginations. Likewise, if we don't reflect Christ by speaking truthfully and doing what is right, living peacefully with our neighbors and sharing the good news of peace, walking by faith, embracing all salvation offers, and spending time with God and in his Word, we aren't fully dressed with Christ.

In keeping with Paul's theme of readying for battle, I've applied his analogy to something more familiar to women: putting on makeup. While getting ready for the day, we can meditate on these verses and clothe ourselves with Christ.

- While applying your foundation, remember Christ Jesus is the cornerstone of our faith. "Built on the foundation of the apostles and prophets, with Christ Jesus himself as the chief cornerstone." (Ephesians 2:20)

- Concealer may hide imperfections, but "love *covers over* a multitude of sins." (1 Peter 4:8, emphasis added)

- Adding blush to your cheeks, remind yourself to "clothe [yourself] with humility toward one another, because, 'God opposes the proud but shows favor to the humble.'" (1 Peter 5:5)

- While sealing your makeup with powder, call to mind "when you believed, you were marked in him with a seal, the promised Holy Spirit." (Ephesians 1:13)

- In addition to makeup, while brushing your teeth, pray, "Set a guard over my mouth, Lord; keep watch over the door of my lips." (Psalm 141:3)

- Mouthwash is a surface cleaner, so ask God for heart-level purity. "What you say flows from what is in your heart." (Luke 6:45, NLT)

- After applying lipstick, confess and praise Jesus' name. "Through Jesus, therefore, let us continually offer to God a sacrifice of praise—the fruit of lips that openly profess his name." (Hebrews 13:15)

- A final spritz of perfume can remind you that God "uses us to spread the knowledge of Christ everywhere, like a sweet perfume." (2 Corinthians 2:14, NLT)

In the Old Testament, priests were required to wear cotton garments to keep from perspiring. First Peter 2:9 states we are a "royal priesthood," and as priests, we're not to sweat. Antiperspirant helps, but better yet, "Cast all your anxiety on [Christ] because he cares for you" (1 Peter 5:7).

Colossians 3:12 and 14 tells us to "clothe yourselves with compassion, kindness, humility, gentleness and patience. And over all these virtues put on love, which binds them all together in perfect unity."

No outfit is complete without earrings. In biblical times, when a slave was set free, if he loved his master and wanted to continue serving him, they pierced his ear. It signified being bonded by love to a master for life (see Deuteronomy 15:16–17). Christ was pierced for our transgression, setting us free from slavery to sin. In love and gratitude, we choose to serve him, our Master, and become bondservants.

Instead of being concerned about the latest fashions, let us become fashionistas of Christ and learn to wear him well. Then we won't want to put on sin because we're already fully dressed—with him.

Yada Time

In what areas do you struggle to wear Christ? Ask God to show you one small change you can make in this area and commit to making this change. Try putting on Christ while getting ready for the day by meditating on Bible verses. Which verse impacted you the most and why?

Day 5: What *Not* to Wear

In my wardrobe, comfort rules. I found my favorite piece years ago on a clearance rack at K-Mart for only four dollars. It's a loose-fitting red fleece jacket, boys' size 14/16, displaying gray racing stripes down its sleeves. It's ridiculously ugly but the perfect weight. Its front zipper makes it easy to whip off when overwhelmed by heat. Though my daytime hot flashes are gone, I still wear it indoors, most days. I'm surprised my family and friends haven't signed a petition, taken up a collection, or alerted the fashion police about me.

Not even Little Red could have enjoyed her riding cape as much as I enjoy my red jacket. Then again, maybe she didn't even like her cape. If it was made from scratchy wool, it might have been itchy. As a young girl, Little Red probably tried to sneak outdoors without wearing it more than once. Can't you hear her mother calling, "Wear your cape, young lady, or you'll catch a cold." Before heading off to Grandmother's house, her mother might have glanced up from washing dishes and noticed Little Red wearing dirty play clothes. "For heaven's sake, child," she might have said, "you can't go to Grandma's looking like a ragamuffin."

Most moms are like that, telling their kids what to wear or not wear. If they didn't, a child might wear mismatched clothing fit for an altogether different season. Oh, the horror! If only I could show you a photo of me as a child wearing striped pants and a floral shirt, their psychedelic colors clashing. It was the '70s, and I lived on a farm. Play clothes didn't have to match.

When we were children, adults determined what we wore. Parents bought our clothes with or without our consent, and schools enforced dress codes. Eventually, peers influenced our choices. In the fourth grade, I wore a yellow sleeveless sundress several days in a row—until a classmate made fun of me, suggesting I rotate outfits. As if I had several choices. In the seventh grade, I painfully relearned this lesson with a favored T-shirt.

Who would imagine I received a college degree in fashion design? Yes, that's me, the woman typing in a boy's red fleece jacket. At some point, a person needs to quit caring what others think—and not only with respect to clothing. As adults, we get to choose what we wear.

Unfortunately, many of us are still wearing things placed on us as children. Perhaps it's a word, phrase, or an event—something stupid we (or others) did or said—causing shame or embarrassment. It could be a moniker we've since outgrown but haven't taken off. Having worn it for so long, we don't realize it's there. It feels a part of us, maybe as comfortable as my red fleece jacket.

Our enemy has worked overtime to keep us clad in combustibles—garments that easily ignite, inflict pain, and cause us to stop, drop, and roll toward whatever mind-numbing activity we use for coping. As children, we might not have noticed when these pieces were added. They came underhandedly, like a kick-me sign placed on our backs. Even if these hurtful things weren't told to us outright, we comprehended their meaning. Messages such as "You're not good enough," "You're a mistake," or "You never do anything right."

What are you still wearing that you or others put on you?

Across from our family's farm is a two-acre wooded area. As a child, this was an ominous, fearful place. If going to Grandmother's house had meant going through those woods, my grandma wouldn't have had a visit from me, not by myself, anyway. Dad had taught us that children would easily get lost in the woods. Lost? Gulp! I never went into the woods alone.

Dad hadn't meant to place fear in me all those times he warned me not to do things, such as *not* run with hard candy in my mouth, *not* ride my bike on the tarred road, or *not* cross the streets in town without him. As parents, we caution our children to be careful because we love them, but we're also telling them to be "full of care." I gleaned my dad's perspective and viewed the world as a scary place. Sometimes just being close to someone, or something, causes things to stick to us—like the prickers found in the woods.

No matter how careful I was when venturing into the woods with others, I came out with prickers stuck to me. That's what I call the pesky, prickly burs from burdock and cocklebur plants. Better than Velcro, they stick to anything and everything, including heads of hair. What a tedious process it is to get de-prickered, but oh how necessary.

The world is a sticky, prickly place, and many of us are still wearing things caught, taught, or placed on us as children. Like prickers, these labels, fears, and derogatory words need to be removed. We aren't meant to wear anything but Christ, so we must learn how to get de-prickered and keep things from sticking to us in the future.

In Max Lucado's children's book *You are Special*, wooden people called Wemmicks placed stickers on each other based on appearance, abilities, accomplishments, or lack thereof. Wemmicks received either gray dot stickers for acts of failure and not measuring up or gold star stickers for being beautiful and demonstrating remarkable talent.[7] Sadly, it parallels our society too well.

We know what it's like to receive stickers. We also know they are seldom handed out in equal proportion. Even if they were, gray dots seem to overpower gold stars. It takes several stars to cancel one gray dot's negative effects. Gold stars don't seem to last as long as gray dots either, so the desire for more stars keeps us performing.

Satan loves all aspects of the sticker system. He doesn't even mind if we wear gold stars. He likes it when we're puffed up. He knows pride precedes a fall (see Proverbs 16:18). The more gold stickers we wear, the greater our chance of yielding to pride. Gray dots aren't any better. They keep us downtrodden and unable to fulfill our dreams.

The only solution is to live sticker free.

A Wemmick named Lucia discovered how to keep gray dots and gold stars from sticking. Her creator explained, "Because she has decided that what I think is more important than what they think. The stickers only stick if you let them."[8]

Who wouldn't want to be like Lucia, where the words and opinions of others don't stick? She achieved a sticker-free life by spending time with her creator. In his presence, she experienced how special she was, which caused her to care only about what her creator thought.

In God's presence, things attached to us will fall off. It may not happen instantaneously or everything all at once, but it will happen, layer by layer. Enveloped in his love, childhood hurts and labels lose their stickiness. Guilt and shame wash away in the flood of his acceptance. The world's prickers don't stick anymore because we won't let them.

Caring only about what our Creator thinks is the goal of renewing our minds. It's how transformation occurs, in addition to being in God's presence. With our eyes fixed on Jesus, we become like the One we're beholding. We'll be less tempted to put on sin when we're already wearing Christ.

Through his death, Jesus defeated the devil. He accomplished everything we need to live happily ever after. Therefore, we fight from a place of victory to obtain what's already ours. We possess these promises by dispossessing the enemy's influence in our lives. That is what spiritual warfare is about: dispossessing the enemy to advance God's kingdom within us.

The ways we accomplish this are many, so additional strategies such as praise, thanksgiving, and the power of Jesus' name will be introduced in future chapters. As you continue through this book renewing your mind and drawing closer to God, warfare will inadvertently happen. Knowing you have an enemy is important, but the better you know (yada) God, the easier it will be not to wear anything but Christ.

Never forget, God goes with you. He fights for you.

"Hear, Israel: Today you are going into battle against your enemies. Do not be fainthearted or afraid; do not panic or be terrified by them. For the Lord your God is the one who goes with you to fight for you against your enemies to give you victory." (Deuteronomy 20:3–4)

Yada Time

What labels or gray dots are you wearing? If the list is long, don't despair. Offer them to God, and you'll soon be rid of them. How about gold stars? What did you do to get them? What keeps you performing? Offer them to God as well. Stars belong in the sky, not on us.

Knowing how special you are will release all dots and break performance cycles.

Now spend time with God. Listen to Christian music, read your Bible, sit quietly in his presence. Pursue an encounter with Love—and expect one. Ask to know how special you are and listen for God's answer. If you don't hear him right away, stay alert. He'll get his message through because he loves you—and you truly are special to him.

Chapter 3
Little Red Riding Hood—Spiritual Warfare
Questions for Reflection or Discussion

Day 1: Through the Woods

1. How can we overcome sin? (p. 42)

2. What is the essence of living happily ever after? (p. 42)

3. What is the real war over? (p. 43)

4. What three forces come against us to sin? (p. 43) Share an example of each.

5. What must we do not to gratify the desires of the sin nature? (Galatians 5:24, p. 43)

6. How do we crucify our sin nature?

Day 2: Follow the Yellow Brick Road

1. What is Satan's main strategy? (p. 44)

2. Discuss his other strategies. (p. 44)

3. According to 2 Corinthians 10:5, what must we do with our thoughts? (p. 45)

4. Who determines a thought's lifespan? (p. 45)

5. Why must we destroy all thoughts in opposition to God? (p. 46)

6. How can a false belief become an idol? (p. 46)

Day 3: Renew Your Mind

1. What should we use to knock out a wrong thought? (p. 48)

2. Describe the process of renewing your mind. What is the 3-prong approach? (p. 48)

3. How do we stop negative word chatter? (p. 48)

4. What Bible verse did you add to your tool belt to demolish a wrong thought pattern?

5. Did you discover you need to guard your mind better?

Day 4: Cover Girl

1. What things shouldn't we put on and why? (p. 51)

2. How do we take off something we shouldn't have put on? (p. 51)

3. When putting on the armor of God, what are we actually putting on? (p. 52)

4. What else does the Bible tell us to wear? (pp. 52–53)

5. Did you become a fashionista of Christ this week and wear him well?

Day 5: What Not to Wear

1. List some things that get placed on us as children.

2. Discuss the Wemmicks' sticker system as it relates to our society. (p. 55)

3. Why shouldn't we wear gold stars? (p. 55)

4. How do we get rid of the things people place on us? (p. 55)

5. If you've taken off something placed on you, share how you did it.

6. What is spiritual warfare about? (p. 56)

Share prayer requests and pray for each other. Let's displace the enemy's influence in our lives.

Chapter 4
Sleeping Beauty—Awakened by the Lord

Memory Verse:

One thing I ask from the Lord, this only do I seek:
that I may dwell in the house of the Lord all the days of my life,
to gaze on the beauty of the Lord and to seek him in his temple.
Psalm 27:4

Day 1: A Beautiful New Day

Most, if not all, fairy-tale princesses were innocent victims. They did nothing to deserve the evil waged against them, and Sleeping Beauty was no exception. Her parents, the King and Queen, tried for many years to conceive a child, so when their beloved princess was born, they rejoiced by throwing a party for the entire kingdom. The guest list also included seven fairies, chosen to be the child's godmothers.

At the celebration, the fairies blessed the princess with attributes such as goodness, happiness, beauty, a quick mind, dancing feet, and a lovely voice. But one old, grumpy, and *uninvited* fairy crashed the party and cursed the princess. She foretold that the princess would prick her finger on a spinning wheel on her sixteenth birthday and die. Shortly after, the seventh fairy, a much younger and more timid fairy, came out of hiding to bless the princess. Though the fairy lacked the power to reverse the curse, she could alter it. She declared, "Instead of dying from the finger prick, the princess will fall into a deep sleep and be awakened by a prince's kiss."

Just as Sleeping Beauty couldn't avoid the grumpy fairy's curse, we too fell under sin's curse, and there was nothing we could do to avoid it. Heaven knows Sleeping Beauty's parents tried to prevent the curse from happening. Immediately after the pronouncement, they destroyed all the spinning wheels throughout the entire kingdom. Despite her parents' diligence, sixteen years later, Sleeping Beauty happened upon a spinning wheel. The old woman sitting at the wheel encouraged her to try spinning. When the princess did, she pricked her finger as foretold and fell into a deep sleep.

For thousands of years our world lay under sin's curse, waiting for our Prince's kiss to break sin's power and awaken us to new life. Jesus accomplished this—Praise the Lord!—when more than two thousand years ago he gave his life on the cross. "Christ redeemed us from the curse of the Law, having become a curse for us—for it is written, 'Cursed is everyone who hangs on a tree'" (Galatians 3:13, NASB).

The law brings a curse because no one can obey the law perfectly. Romans 3:23 says, "For all have sinned and fall short of the glory of God." In our unredeemed state, it's impossible not to sin because we were born sinners. That doesn't make us evil; it makes us in need of a savior. Without Jesus, we are as hopeless as my niece Maggie trying to behave while shopping.

As a child, Maggie loved to shop with her mom. But this didn't happen often because Maggie couldn't behave in stores. One day at Target, after my sister had given Maggie multiple warnings about her conduct, my sister carried her out the store in a football hold with Maggie flailing her arms and legs, screaming, "But I want to be good! I want to be good!"

We may want to be good, but even after becoming saved we frequently don't behave as we should. Some sins seem so deeply rooted they feel a part of us, like how other family traits such as eye and hair color get passed along. These sinful habits or characteristics seem like they're inherited, and maybe they are. Maggie's mom, my youngest sister, was a strong-willed child. When she didn't get her way as a baby, she held her breath until she turned purple and passed out. Being strong-willed isn't a sin, but certain traits may bend us toward particular sins.

I've also noticed how sin can repeat itself in family generations. Without casting blame or judgment, you may recognize these family patterns: a pregnant teenager has a child who later becomes a teen mom, or multiple generations produce alcoholics, gossips, liars, or unfaithful spouses. Things not considered sinful also get handed down, such as poverty, depression, obesity, or the inability to keep a job. Can you identify a pattern in your family line?

Learning about one's ancestry is increasing in popularity. With a few drops of blood, genealogical DNA testing can discover your ethnicity. Besides being interesting, it can be useful for biological reasons because some ethnicities are more prone to specific health risks. Similarly, some families are more prone to certain sins. It's like their spiritual DNA predisposes them toward it. Did anyone in your family alert you to a sin you might easily yield to?

No one had to tell me my mom had a temper. I saw firsthand how she controlled through anger—until she received deliverance. Some might say I learned this behavior, but I hope by sharing my story you'll see otherwise. I was turning thirty and in a failing marriage when I recognized how angry I was. Though I thought my situation was causing the anger, I knew as a Christian my circumstances shouldn't determine my behavior. I read books on overcoming anger, but I couldn't rise above it.

After my divorce, the anger toward my ex-husband ceased when I forgave him, but I still had bouts of uncontrollable anger toward my boys. When these outbursts happened, my heart broke, and I felt shame and remorse. I never physically harmed my sons, but my behavior scared them. Like an alcoholic, I'd ask their forgiveness and promise never to get that angry again. I'd also ask God's forgiveness and beg him to take away my anger.

Galatians 5:24 says, "Those who belong to Christ Jesus have crucified the flesh with its passions and desires." In *They Shall Expel Demons,* the author, Derek Prince, states:

The remedy for the flesh is crucifixion. By Jesus' sacrificial death on the cross, He cancelled the claim sin has on our fleshly nature. It is a remedy each of us needs to apply personally. The remedy for demons, on the other hand—as often demonstrated in the ministry of Jesus—is to cast them out. These two remedies are not interchangeable. It is not possible to cast out the flesh, and it is not possible to crucify a demon.[1]

Many Christians believe it's impossible for a Christian to have a demon. I once thought that, too. It's true that demons can't possess a Christian, because a Christian belongs to Christ. But Christians can succumb to demonic influences, especially those passed from one generation to the next. If we can't obtain victory over sin by crucifying the flesh, it's possible a demon is behind the behavior.

Luke 10:19 states we have authority to "overcome all the power of the enemy." Jesus also said, "And these signs will accompany those who believe: In my name they will drive out demons …" (Mark 16:17).

After a few years of ministering through inner-healing prayer, the friends who introduced it to our fellowship group asked God for additional ways to help those who needed more than inner healing. Eventually, my friends connected with a deliverance ministry who provided training and hands-on experience. Among friends, I found the courage to attend a deliverance session.

To my relief, nothing like in the movie *The Exorcist* happened. I confessed my sin, forgave everyone God brought to mind, and believed God delivered me from anger through Jesus' finished work.

When my son, Jesse, was a teenager, he could push my anger button like no one else. He didn't try to; he had inherited the generational anger demon. Shortly after my deliverance session, a conflict arose between us, but this time I didn't get angry. For the first time, it felt as though I had a choice, and I chose not to get angry. The deliverance session also broke generational anger from my children, and the change in Jesse proved it had worked.

Demons will try to return (see Luke 11:26), so the battle isn't over once they leave. We must fill ourselves with God's truth and stand firm in our new freedom. James 4:7 says, "Submit yourselves, then, to God. Resist the devil, and he will flee from you." This becomes possible once the demon is expelled, and then it's our job to stay free.

Sinful acts or habits, generational or not, can open the door to demons, as can word curses, such as the one spoken by the angry fairy over Sleeping Beauty. Word curses are real and all too common. In the heat of the moment, a parent might speak one over her child: "You're so dumb!" or "You'll never amount to anything." We speak them over friends and family, too. "Your worrying will give you a heart attack." We even speak them to ourselves. "I'm sick and tired …" The phrase I'm working to keep from my lips is "I feel bad …" It's what I used to say when I couldn't comply with a person's request, but I no longer curse myself by that declaration.

Derek Prince also said, "Words concerning death are particularly dangerous. Many times people say, 'I nearly died laughing,' or, 'You'll die when you hear this one!' Death is a dark, evil power, and we are foolish to treat it lightly."[2] Words have power, so we should be careful what we speak.

Sleeping Beauty was an innocent victim and had no choice in accepting her curse, but as Christians, we can refuse a word curse. We aren't doomed to fulfill the words spoken over us. We can tell the devil we don't receive them. We might say, "In Jesus' name and by the power of his shed blood, I refuse …" then name what was spoken over you to cause harm. Forgive the person who cursed you and ask God to bless them as the Bible tells us to do (see Luke 6:28).

Yada Time

Recall any word curses spoken over you as a child. Ask the Holy Spirit to remind you if you can't remember any. Declare the curse broken in Jesus' name and confess the opposite to be true about yourself according to God's promises. Pay attention to the words others speak, and refuse to receive all word curses. Ask the Holy Spirit to point out when you say things that curse others or yourself.

Day 2: Beauty Defined

The author of *Sleeping Beauty*, Charles Perrault, never described the princess' physical appearance, but we know she received beauty as an attribute from one of her fairy godmothers. Beauty can be difficult to describe, although we recognize beauty when we see it. A general definition is "the quality present in a thing or person that gives intense pleasure or deep satisfaction to the mind, whether arising from sensory manifestations (as shape, color, sound, etc.), a meaningful design or pattern, or something else (as a personality in which high spiritual qualities are manifest)."[3]

King David declared the Lord beautiful when he penned, "One thing I ask from the Lord, this only do I seek: that I may dwell in the house of the Lord all the days of my life, to *gaze on the beauty of the Lord* and to seek him in his temple" (Psalm 27:4, emphasis added).

Undoubtedly, David found "intense pleasure or deep satisfaction" from gazing on the Lord. He desired nothing more than to abide in God's presence and experience his beauty. No wonder God declared David a man after his own heart (see Acts 13:22).

Because God is invisible, have you ever questioned what David saw? Or how he knew the Lord is beautiful? What does the Lord's beauty look like?

I pondered these questions a few years ago while attending a prayer group with older, beautiful Christian women. Their passion for the Lord matched David's, and they expressed their love for the Lord unashamedly. "You are beautiful, Lord," they proclaimed, "beautiful beyond description." At first, witnessing such intimate discourse made me uncomfortable, but curiosity and envy urged me to pursue what they were experiencing. Clearly, they were gazing on the Lord's beauty and enjoying his presence. But try as I may, I could not *see* the Lord or comprehend his beauty.

Week after week, I struggled. Then one evening, as I prayed again to see his beauty, the Lord brought to my mind the times I had experienced him. Beginning when I was a child, the memories of God's love, his protection, provision, and answered prayers played in my mind like a film trailer of my life's highlights. As I reflected on the times God had revealed himself to me, he opened my spiritual eyes, and I saw the Lord as beautiful. I didn't see him in a vision or picture in my mind but with my heart, and he was as real as if physically present. The Lord's beauty is who he is—it's his heart, his character, his beautiful attributes—his very existence.

Because the word splendor defines both beauty and glory,[4] Moses made a similar request when he asked to see God's glory. God responded in a dramatic fashion:

> Then the Lord came down in the cloud and stood there with [Moses] and proclaimed his name, the Lord. And he passed in front of Moses, proclaiming, "The Lord, the Lord, the compassionate and gracious God, slow to anger, abounding in love and faithfulness, maintaining love to thousands, and forgiving wickedness, rebellion and sin …." (Exodus 34:5–7)

After meeting with the Lord, Moses' face radiated God's glory. Moses' face glowed, and the people feared to come near him (see Exodus 34:29–30). So, after Moses communicated the Lord's words to the people, he put a veil over his face. "But whenever he entered the Lord's presence to speak with him, he removed the veil until he came out" (Exodus 34:34). The people could see Moses had been in the Lord's presence because the Lord's glory had changed his appearance.

Wouldn't it be wonderful if others could tell we've been with the Lord because our words, actions, and attitudes reflect him?

In the last chapter, I explained how we become like what we behold. Second Corinthians 3:18 bears repeating: "But we all, with unveiled face, beholding as in a mirror the glory of the Lord, are being transformed into the same image from glory to glory, just as from the Lord, the Spirit" (NASB). Other versions say we're transformed "from glory to glory," or from "beautiful to more beautiful."

Being changed by beholding is like lying in the sun. We don't work to become tan; we position ourselves in the sun, and we're changed. But we won't get a tan if we lie in the sun with a blanket over us. Paul said, "But whenever anyone turns to the Lord, the veil is taken away" (2 Corinthians 3:16). Like Moses, we must approach God without a veil by turning to the Lord. Jesus provides the only way into God's presence (see John 14:6).

In biblical times, a thick veil hung in the temple and kept the people from the Holy of Holies, where God dwelled. Only the high priest entered this sacred place once a year on the Day of Atonement.[5] On the cross, when Jesus breathed his last breath, "At that moment the curtain of the temple was torn in two from top to bottom. The earth shook, the rocks split" (Matthew 27:51). Jesus' death removed the veil separating us from God the Father.

The law can't make anyone holy, so Jesus did for us what the law couldn't. He made us holy, sinless, and beautiful in God's sight. Our goal now is to reflect outwardly how God already sees us. Though we can't become beautiful or sinless by our efforts, we can speed up our transformation by spending time in the Son's radiance. As a bonus, God's presence not only makes us beautiful, it convinces our heart we are beautiful because our head won't argue with what our heart experiences.

In Psalm 27:8, David wrote: "My heart says of you, 'Seek his face!' Your face, Lord, I will seek." Like his glory, the Lord's face represents who he is. God is Spirit, so we experience him with our spirit, sometimes referred to as our heart or inner being. Don't get hung up on trying to visualize the Lord's face as I mistakenly did. Seek God who said, "You will seek me and find me when you seek me with all your heart" (Jeremiah 29:13).

To help turn our attention to the Lord, I created an acronym for FACE. These four pathways can help us experience the Lord's beauty.

- **F – *Faith*.** Hebrews 11:6 says, "And without faith it is impossible to please God, because anyone who comes to him must believe that he exists and that he rewards those who earnestly seek him." By faith, we believe God exists, and he is always present. We begin with this mindset, believing and trusting we will experience God. The Greek word for earnestly seek is "*ekzeteo*" (ek-zay-teh'-o). It means "to search out, i.e. (figuratively) investigate, crave, demand, (by Hebraism) worship."[6] Ekzeteo describes something more than a mere wish. It infers a hunger and passion for God's presence and a determination to go after it. If you pursue intimate experiences with God, he will reward you—you *will* experience him!

- **A – *Attributes*.** The Lord is beautiful because of who he is. He is love, joy, peace, patience, kindness, mercy, holy, just, etc. We can meditate on an attribute by pondering it in our hearts and minds as we go through each day. We can also demonstrate that attribute in our actions and words, and we can watch how others display it in their words and actions. When we demonstrate or witness God's attributes, we can experience his presence. Jesus exhibited God's attributes when he lived as a man. Colossians 1:15 says, "He [Jesus] is the image of the invisible God." We can know what God is like by studying Jesus' life. By imagining ourselves in the Bible stories as we read them, we can encounter Jesus. As we meditate on his attributes, God will fill us with gratitude and thanksgiving for him and what he's done. "Psalm 100:4 says, "Enter his gates with thanksgiving and his courts with praise." Meditating on Jesus' attributes will stir up this worshipful response.

- **C – *Creation*.** Psalm 19:1 says, "The heavens declare the glory of God." We can see his invisible qualities, eternal power, and divine nature in what he's made (see Romans 1:20). I am drawn to his beauty when I take the time to marvel at his creation. A hummingbird or flower, a beautiful sunset or vibrant rainbow, or a star-filled night reveals his majestic beauty. More miraculous yet is a baby's birth and the love bond formed between parents and child. Creation invites us to experience God's beauty through his handiwork.

- **E – *Experiences*.** I finally recognized the Lord's beauty when I recalled the times I had previously experienced him. Keeping a journal helps preserve these encounters and enables us to draw from them when needed. Your history with God serves as an access code to experience him again. When you need his love, joy, peace, or comfort, you can recall when you've experienced him in any of those ways and receive what you need. If your experiences with him are few, tell him you want more and then pursue him.

When you earnestly seek his FACE—Faith, Attributes, Creation, Experiences—he promises you will find him. Many more paths exist to experiencing God, such as through art, music, reading the Bible, prayer, fasting, or other spiritual disciplines. A.W. Tozer said, "You can see God from anywhere if your mind is set to love and obey Him."[7]

We find true happiness in God's presence, and when we behold Jesus, he changes us from glory to glory—or from beautiful to more beautiful—and we become like him. Not only do we become beautiful in his presence, but we also become convinced we are beautiful. This mindset enables us to transform the world's ugliness by demonstrating our beauty to the world that desperately needs us.

Yada Time

Practice entering into God's presence now and throughout the day by using the acronym FACE. Unlike sunbathing, you don't have to be lying still to catch God's radiance. The Son shines all around and through you, so being changed by God's presence is like getting a tan while gardening, riding a bike, boating, etc. Turn your heart toward God and you'll experience his beauty.

Day 3: Beauty Rest

We don't know how long Sleeping Beauty slept under the curse, but when the prince found her, she was as beautiful as on the day she'd pricked her finger. Possibly that's where we get the expression of needing our beauty sleep. Sleepless nights are torture—just ask any new parent or menopausal woman with night sweats. Our bodies require sleep to rejuvenate and stay healthy.

Besides sleep, we also need time to unwind after a day's work. Rest is important to our well-being. God established patterns of night and day, work and rest, as far back as "In the beginning." As our example, God labored six days creating every awesome thing before resting on the seventh day, the Sabbath.

God introduced the Sabbath to the Israelites while daily feeding them manna from heaven in the wilderness. At the Lord's command, Moses said, "Tomorrow is to be a day of sabbath rest, a holy sabbath to the Lord. So bake what you want to bake and boil what you want to boil. Save whatever is left and keep it until morning" (Exodus 16:23). Normally, if they kept the manna overnight it would spoil, so they only gathered what they could eat each day (see Exodus 16:21). God wanted them to trust him for their daily provision. Now God said they should gather twice as much on the sixth day and rest on the seventh day, and miraculously the manna stayed fresh.

The word Sabbath next occurs in the Bible as the fourth commandment: "Remember the Sabbath day by keeping it holy" (Exodus 20:8). God instructed the Jews, "There are six days when you may work, but the seventh day is a sabbath of rest, a day of sacred assembly. You are not to do any work; wherever you live, it is a sabbath to the Lord" (Leviticus 23:3). Numbers 15:32–36 tells an unforgettable story about what happened to a man who gathered firewood on the Sabbath: he was stoned to death. It's a frightening story at any age, especially for those who think the law can save them.

Devout Jews today still observe the Sabbath from sunset on the sixth day, Friday, until sunset on the seventh day, Saturday, in which they do no work. It's called *Shabbat* in Hebrew. "The word 'Shabbat' comes from the root Shin-Beit-Tav, meaning to cease, to end, or to rest."[8] How and when the Sabbath changed from Saturday to Sunday for many Christians isn't our focus. God never intended the Sabbath to be solely a religious obligation. While the Sabbath provided a time for physical rest, it also held a symbolic meaning that foreshadowed Jesus, through whom we gain true Sabbath rest.

Much has changed since biblical times. In the last sixty years alone, church attendance has declined drastically, and other activities now fill our Sundays.[9] Growing up in the 70s, my family, like many others, observed Sunday as a day of rest. We attended church wearing our Sunday-best outfits and refrained from work. Most businesses closed but some retail stores waited until the afternoon to open. Christian farmers stayed out of their fields on Sundays—even during planting and harvest seasons. Yet women still prepared meals and washed dishes. Washing clothes rarely happened at our house unless you proved you had nothing clean to wear. As a young person, my family's Sabbath rules weren't as clear-cut or as strict as those described in the Bible.

Obeying God's commandments won't save anyone eternally because no one can fully keep them. We receive salvation only by trusting in Jesus. Yet God still wants us not to break his commandments, since they are for our benefit. So why wouldn't that include the Sabbath? I wondered what it might look like to keep the Sabbath in our modern age. How would someone keep the Sabbath today? Was God asking me to do this?

I first pondered whether I should continue observing the Sabbath on Sunday or switch to its original Friday sunset/Saturday time frame. Next, I contemplated what work, if any, was acceptable on God's holy day. For a season, I refrained from all unnecessary work on Sundays. I even stopped going out to eat, shopping, or doing anything that would cause others to work. Through online research, I learned modern Sabbath restrictions include writing, shopping, driving or riding in a car, talking on the telephone, and more.[10]

Christ died to set us free, and adding new rules didn't feel like freedom. While searching the Scriptures for truth about the Sabbath, I found Paul's instructions to the Colossae church, "Therefore do not let anyone judge you by what you eat or drink, or with regard to a religious festival, a New Moon celebration or a Sabbath day" (Colossians 2:16). The reason: "These are a shadow of the things that were to come; the reality, however, is found in Christ" (Colossians 2:17).

Imagine the diversity of the first Christians, Jews and Gentiles, with various cultural and religious backgrounds, embracing the New Covenant together. After becoming saved, the Jews continued with their rules and rituals, such as Sabbath keeping, and they tried to convince the Gentiles to do likewise. Paul instructed the Jews not to insist the Gentiles adhere to their religious activities because they were "a shadow of the things that were to come." The Jewish festivals and holy days were a prelude to the real show, Jesus, in whom we find true Sabbath rest. We can do nothing to get peace and favor with God apart from trusting in Jesus. Therefore, we can stop striving to earn God's approval by works and freely receive his grace. Rest comes when we embrace all Jesus provides, which includes carrying *all* our burdens.

Besides rest for our souls, the Sabbath foreshadowed additional blessings obtained through Jesus. God decreed resting times for the land, and every seventh year the land went unseeded. Not planting a crop meant no harvest, so the people would have to trust God to provide. In Leviticus 25:21–22, God said, "I will send you such a blessing in the sixth year that the land will yield enough for three years. While you plant during the eighth year, you will eat from the old crop and will continue to eat from it until the harvest of the ninth year comes in."

To those who had sold themselves, the seventh year held great significance. "If you buy a Hebrew servant, he is to serve you for six years. But in the seventh year, he shall go free, without paying anything" (Exodus 21:2). That is, unless the Year of Jubilee happened first, which occurred every fifty years when the Israelites canceled all debts and refrained from work. Even the land reverted to its original owner that year. The seventh year and the Year of Jubilee foreshadowed the freedom we find in Christ when he forgives all our debts (sin).

The Sabbath also signified a covenant—a promise God made to his chosen people. "The Israelites are to observe the Sabbath, celebrating it for the generations to come as a lasting covenant" (Exodus 31:16). God made a covenant with Abraham that continued with Isaac, then Jacob, and so on as each generation entered into that covenant by faith. God promised Abraham that he would bless the whole world through Abraham's seed. That seed is Jesus, and God invites us into that same covenant relationship today.

Verse 17 continues, "It [the Sabbath] will be a sign between me and the Israelites forever." The Jews transacted business at their cities' gates, and all their gates closed on the Sabbath. Resting set the Jews apart from other nations. Other outward observances, celebrations, and rituals also demonstrated their devotion to God and dedication to his ways. Today, our ability to love others becomes a sign to the world. Jesus said, "By this everyone will know that you are my disciples, if you love one another" (John 13:35).

As foreshadowed in the Sabbath, our covenant with God through Jesus grants us rest, restoration, freedom, forgiveness, abundant provision, and more—totaling the abundant life Jesus came to give us (see John 10:10).

Hebrews 4:9–11 says, "There remains, then, a Sabbath-rest for the people of God; for anyone who enters God's rest also rests from their works, just as God did from his. Let us, therefore, make every effort to enter that rest, so that no one will perish by following their example of disobedience."

We keep the Sabbath holy by entering into God's rest by faith. We cease from our labor and trust God for everything by embracing all Jesus did on our behalf. Isn't that great news? We can enjoy Sabbath rest every day if we abide in Jesus. Resting doesn't mean we don't work; it means we include Jesus in everything we do. We don't stress; we rest—in him—and become spiritually refreshed.

Yada Time

Burdens provide opportunities to rest in Jesus and to know and trust him more. What burdens do you need to release to him today? Is it an addiction, financial stress, relationship issue, or something else? Whatever your burden, come to Jesus and release them all. Find your rest in him, and whenever you take your burden back, return to Jesus and leave it again. Repeat the process as needed to enter into God's rest. Thank Jesus for providing Sabbath rest.

Day 4: Beautiful Savior

Falling asleep at an inappropriate time or place can be embarrassing. In my first year of menopause, I woke up many times a night from profuse sweating. This lack of sleep caused daytime drowsiness, and every Sunday I nodded off at least once at church—usually during the sermon. Though embarrassing, it wasn't deadly like the poor guy who fell asleep during the Apostle Paul's sermon. "Seated in a window was a young man named Eutychus, who was sinking into a deep sleep as Paul talked on and on. When he was sound asleep, he fell to the ground from the third story and was picked up dead" (Acts 20:9). Spoiler alert: Paul brought him back to life.

A pastor once said, "If I've been boring for twenty minutes and haven't struck oil, it's time to quit." I'm not inferring my pastor was boring, and in case he caught me nodding off, I told him about my sleepless nights. Staying physically awake can be challenging at times—as can staying spiritually awake.

How spiritually awake are you? Rate yourself on a scale of one to ten—ten being the most alive and one being the Mayor of Snoozeville. What number did you give yourself? Having walked with the Lord for over forty years, I've experienced every number on that scale—faith-filled and fully awake at times and spiritually dry and lethargic at others. No one wants to zone out on the Lord completely because when you snooze, you lose. You might miss out on God's gifts, callings, promises, and purpose for your life. I said *might* because God has a way of getting our attention, waking us up.

A wake-up call is a near-miss tragedy that motivates a person to make a positive change. A health scare, such as a heart attack, may prompt a person to stop smoking, lose weight, or start an exercise program. A DUI might convince a person to join AA. Near-death experiences have caused many to reevaluate their priorities, cherish loved ones more, and live each day more fully.

Though wake-up calls are positive, God doesn't instigate the negative situations that create them. He *allows* bad things to happen, yes, because he's given us free will. But God is good. Besides, we're quite capable of creating a crisis without his help. If anything, God intervenes so tragedies don't happen. He gives second chances, and he takes what was meant to hurt us and uses it for our good (see Genesis 50:20 and Romans 8:28). God allows these trials to gain our attention and awaken us to a closer walk with him. Even tragic events, such as a loved one's death or a divorce, can be likened to a kiss from the Lord when it awakens us to a closer relationship with him.

When did God first awaken you to your need for Jesus? Was there an event such as I described with my divorce that drew you closer to him? The Lord's wake-up kisses aren't limited to traumatic or painful experiences. God first kissed me while I said bedtime prayers as a child. God overwhelmed me with his love, and I knew he was real.

Take a moment to recall the times God has kissed you.

Besides wake-up calls, God quietly kisses us throughout the day with his presence, provision, and people who love us. His most memorable kisses surprise and change us. He continues to kiss us even after we're awake because he wants us to stay awake. The Bible tells us to "be ready in season and out of season" (2 Timothy 4:2, NASB). Jesus told the parable of ten virgins to show the importance of being awake and ready. I've partially paraphrased the parable found in Matthew 25:1–10:

While waiting for the bridegroom "who was a long time in coming," the virgins fell asleep. "At midnight the cry rang out: 'Here's the bridegroom! Come out to meet him!' Then all the virgins woke up and trimmed their lamps." However, the foolish ones hadn't brought extra lamp oil and were running out. They said to the wise, "Give us some of your oil; our lamps are going out." But they didn't have extra for them. While the foolish virgins were buying oil, the bridegroom arrived. "The virgins who were ready went in with him to the wedding banquet. And the door was shut."

It's a sobering thought to miss the bridegroom's appearance and the wedding feast, but let's not limit the story's application to Christ's second coming and whether we'll be prepared for it. The story teaches us to be ready at a moment's notice to do whatever God calls us to do. Jesus also said, "Be dressed ready for service and keep your lamps burning" (Luke 12:35). The lamps in biblical times burned oil. In the Scriptures, oil refers to the Holy Spirit. Staying filled with the Holy Spirit will keep us burning bright for God.

The ten virgins fell asleep because the bridegroom "was a long time in coming." They had been waiting for hours. It was late. Sleep was a natural response to their situation. Who hasn't experienced a time when it felt as if the Lord was slow in coming—slow to answer their prayers? It's easy to get discouraged and disappointed when our timetable doesn't coincide with God's. When it seems like he's taking too long, we can also become depressed or disgruntled and pull away from him. We might let our oil run out and take a spiritual siesta on purpose.

The disciples slept in the Garden of Gethsemane when Jesus had asked them to stay awake and pray. "When [Jesus] rose from prayer and went back to the disciples, he found them asleep, exhausted from sorrow" (Luke 22:45). Loss of a loved one through divorce or death, dreams unfilled or out of reach, and hopelessness of what could have been all create sorrow.

Sorrow overcame Sleeping Beauty's parents when their daughter fell asleep under the curse. A sympathetic fairy, seeing their distress and knowing there was nothing anyone could do, cast another spell and put Sleeping Beauty's parents to sleep as well.

In Matthew 11:28–30, Jesus said, "Come to me, all you who are weary and burdened, and I will give you rest. Take my yoke upon you and learn from me, for I am gentle and humble in heart, and you will find rest for your souls. For my yoke is easy and my burden is light."

A.W. Tozer explained these verses as follows:

The burden borne by mankind is a heavy and a crushing thing. The word Jesus used means "a load carried or toil borne to the point of exhaustion." Rest is simply release from that burden. It is not something we do; it is what comes to us when we cease to do. His own meekness, that is the rest.[11]

If you've experienced deep, life-altering sorrow, you know how it empties a person. It causes one to sleepwalk through life for a season or longer. If we turn away from and not toward the Lord during this time, our lamps will soon empty. Sorrow devours oil quickly. Being consumed by sorrow doesn't mean we're not saved. But without fuel, it's unlikely we're spiritually awake, dressed, and ready for service.

To refuel, we need the Holy Spirit. Rarely does the Spirit's oil penetrate someone whose fuel lines are plugged with anger, self-pity, resentment, or an unwillingness to forgive. Unhealed sorrow can cause great damage, but it's not irreversible. Remember, Jesus told us to come to him, and he didn't say we had to clean ourselves up first. In fact, he encourages us to come messed-up, burdened, and needing his help. He only requires that we come to him.

My come-to-Jesus moment came when I was separated from my husband as sorrow threatened to crush me. I cried out to Jesus more times than I can recount and found peace and comfort amidst my tears. He carried my burdens, and he carried me. One time it felt as if he'd physically put his arm around me. God didn't change my situation; he changed me. I learned to depend on him for strength and comfort.

Jesus can comfort us because he's personally familiar with suffering. The prophet Isaiah called him "a man of sorrows." The Hebrew word for sorrow is *mak'ob*. It means physical or mental pain, anguish, grief, or affliction.[12] Isaiah foresaw Jesus' suffering and sorrow:

> He was despised and rejected by mankind, a man of suffering, and familiar with pain … Surely he took up our pain and bore our suffering … He was pierced for our transgressions, he was crushed for our iniquities; the punishment that brought us peace was on him, and by his wounds we are healed. (Isaiah 53:3–5).

Isaiah also knew the reason for Jesus' suffering. On the cross, Jesus took on himself our sin, sickness, sorrow, and other burdens. When we come to him, we receive peace with God, healing, salvation, Sabbath rest, and everything we need.

I'll admit, though, not always does God fix everything this side of heaven. He hasn't taken fibromyalgia from my body yet, and I still struggle emotionally with insecurity and other issues. He's healed me physically, emotionally, and in so many other ways. Why not in all areas? Some things we may never understand. But when answers evade us, we must turn to God and not from him because no rest exists apart from God.

Sorrow, pain, and unanswered questions can keep us from coming to Jesus even though we know we should. Those plugged Holy Spirit fuel lines seem to create a Catch-22 scenario. We need the lines unplugged to receive the Holy Spirit's oil, but we can't unplug the lines without the Holy Spirit. God, help us! And he does—when we come to him. Come even if you're unwilling to release your anger, sorrow, self-pity, resentment, or an offense, and ask to be made willing. Cry out, "Lord, help me to be willing! I'm willing to be made willing."

By seeking God, we can wake up spiritually. When we receive the Holy Spirit's oil, we remain alert and avoid spiritual drowsiness. God has so much for us, and we receive it best when we are spiritually awake!

Yada Time

Has deep sorrow kept you from waking spiritually? Do you feel as though God hasn't heard your prayers? Sometimes our anger and resentment can be toward God. If this rings true for you, tell God how you feel. It's okay to tell him how much you're hurting and how upset you are with him. But don't stop there. Listen for his response, then release your judgments against God (forgive him). Give him all your negative emotions, hurts, and frustrations. Be willing to live without all the answers. If you're not able to do any of this, ask God to make you willing.

Day 5: A Beautiful Passion

One passionate kiss from the Prince and Sleeping Beauty awoke to her true love. Passion is that powerful. It not only awakens us, but it also keeps us awake. Passion fuels many late-night conversations between couples falling in love. My husband jokingly says he proposed so quickly because our courtship was exhausting him.

Passion may keep us awake, but over time it's difficult to maintain the same intensity of passion for anything or anyone—including God. Life happens. We grow weary. The world entices us toward other passions. Jesus said the most important commandment is to "Love the Lord your God with all your heart and with all your soul and with all your mind and with all your strength" (Mark 12:30). God wants to be first place in our hearts, but sometimes our passion for him grows cold. Like the ten virgins, we forget to keep oil in our lamps. We become more vulnerable to other passions, even God-given passions, and replace him as our first love. This happened to me while designing our last home.

Blueprints ignite a passion in me—dreaming, drawing, tweaking, and staring at quarter-inch-to-scale grid-lined paper. I designed the four homes we've built, but they aren't fancy as I value efficiency over aesthetics. Designing homes is neither my profession nor a hobby since more than a decade can span between building them. It's more like an investment. We reduce the building costs by contracting the construction ourselves—meaning we hire all the subcontractors and oversee the process. We learned this through trial, error, and much prayer. It's amazing what risks we'll take for passion's sake.

The lines between passion, obsession, and addiction can quickly blur. As I strived for perfection in every detail when creating my blueprints, the hours turned into days, then weeks, and months before I finalized my design. While poring over every square inch, I spent more time imagining my next house than caring for my family and the home I lived in.

A passion gone rogue can consume every waking thought and action, stealing our devotion to God while producing guilt, shame, and remorse. Even if you've never battled an addiction, you can probably imagine the emotional parasites that suck the life from a person in bondage.

I have never felt weaker than when unable to resist looking at or thinking about my blueprints. I have also never felt less worthy of God's love. Somehow my blueprints had hijacked my passion for God. When something takes God's place in our hearts, or when we look to someone other than him to meet a need, it becomes sin.

If you're like me, you try to manage sin by sheer willpower, and you create a few rules for yourself in an attempt to fix things. I limited, or tried to limit, how long I could stare at my blueprints. Even if I only viewed them for an hour a day, I could dwell on them anytime and anywhere I pleased because they were etched in my mind. I knew that house's every nook and cranny by *heart*, which was the real problem. Rules can't change a behavior when it's a heart issue.

The cycle of guilt, shame, remorse, and determining to change through self-discipline plays havoc on a person's self-esteem. Who can comprehend our bondage? Oh, happy day! God can and did when he sent Jesus to liberate us from our misplaced passions.

With heartfelt repentance, I asked God to forgive me for not placing him first in my heart. His response caught me off guard. He asked me to feel the passion I felt when looking at my blueprints. Then he said this is how he feels about me—and about you. God is passionate about us. Trusting I'm hearing God, and not my thoughts, isn't always easy, but in this case, I had expected God to reprimand me—not overwhelm me with his love. My head may have known God loves me, but my heart needed convincing. How about you? Does your heart know how passionate God is for you?

This encounter helped me understand three things. First, God no longer sees our sins. Jesus' blood covered them all—past, present, and future—when we trusted in him as Savior.

Second, God not only sees us as righteous and forgiven, he sees us as complete. He sees the person we're destined to become as if we're already that person. Just as I'm able to look at my blueprints and envision the finished house, our Master Architect sees us as his finished masterpieces.

Third, experiencing God's passion for me created a deeper, more abiding passion for him. First John 4:19 says, "We love because he first loved us." If human passion can awaken someone as listless as Sleeping Beauty lying in her glass casket, imagine what experiencing God's passion can do. He gives wake-up kisses and passionate encounters because there's nothing more important to him than us staying awake and loving him with our whole heart.

In the book of Revelation, Jesus told the Ephesian church to return to their first love. He initially praised them for persevering, enduring hardships for his name, and for not growing weary (see Revelation 2:3). But then in verse four, he admonished them: "Yet I hold this against you: You have forsaken your first love." The Bible doesn't tell us how or why they lost their first love, but it's easy to imagine it happening. In verse five, Jesus told them how to regain their first love. He said, "Remember the height from which you have fallen! Repent and do the things you did at first."

Jesus instructed them to: remember, recognize, repent, and repeat.

My siblings and I love to reminisce whenever we're together. We tell stories about our childhood and the events that created our love bonds. It renews our love for each other. To regain their first love, Jesus told the Ephesians to remember the passion they once had for God. Then he said to recognize how far they'd fallen. If we don't acknowledge what we've lost, we'll have no desire to get it back.

Next, Jesus told them to repent. The Greek word for repent is *metanoeo*, which means "to think differently or afterwards, i.e. reconsider (morally, feel compunction):"[13] Remorse and tears often accompany heartfelt repentance, but they aren't mandatory. We repent by changing how we think about something and then demonstrating this change by our actions.

Lastly, Jesus instructed them to repeat the things they had first done after giving their lives to him. What things did you first do after becoming a Christian? You probably spent as much time as you could with God, talking to him all day and not just at bedtime. Perhaps you met frequently with others who love him. No doubt you got your hands on a Bible and read to learn what pleases God. With heartfelt gratitude, you may have even shared the good news about Jesus with others.

In Acts 2:44–46 we learn what the first Christians did:

> All the believers were together and had everything in common. They sold property and possessions to give to anyone who had need. Every day they continued to meet together in the temple courts. They broke bread in their homes and ate together with glad and sincere hearts.

Experiencing God in community creates an unmatchable synergy. But I'm not referring to spending an hour in a church pew—unless your church is more interactive than mine. We need intentional, God-centered fellowship with other believers on a personal level. I've never been more spiritually awake than the years we hosted a fellowship group in our home. Like the early church, we shared life together. We ate meals, worshiped, traveled to conferences, and studied God's Word together. We supported each other emotionally and even financially when needed. As wonderful as those years were, we eventually disbanded. I now realize our group's passion for God and each other was a gift. James 1:17 says, "Every good and perfect gift is from above."

More and more I'm discovering how dependent we are on God for everything, including (or especially in) spiritual matters. God pursued us first; we didn't seek him. We love because he first loved us. Apart from Jesus, we can do nothing. We can't drum up Holy Spirit oil or ignite a passion for God on our own. It's impossible to live an abundant life without his help. Therefore, we must trust God to provide the passion needed to keep him as our first love.

That's not a free pass to do nothing—unless you like wake-up calls.

Even without passion, we can *choose* to do the things we did at first—the spiritual disciplines of prayer, fasting, fellowship, giving, meditation, good works, studying God's Word, etc. But we shouldn't view these activities as some spiritual-duties checklist needing completion. These spiritual disciplines position us before God to receive from and experience him. When we choose to obey and do them with the right attitude, the King will meet us more than halfway and awaken us with a passion to live for him—our true love. We don't have to be Sleeping Beauty, forever waiting for the Prince.

Yada Time

Has God slipped from first place in your heart? Are you struggling with a misplaced passion? If you could ask God for anything (and you can), what would it be? What's your greatest need? Talk to God about it and ask for it.

If you didn't ask for passion, ask for that now, and pray Ephesians 1:17, "I keep asking that the God of our Lord Jesus Christ, the glorious Father, may give you the Spirit of wisdom and revelation, so that you may know him better." Seek his FACE (faith, attributes, creation, or experience), do the things you did at first, and ask to experience his passion for you.

Chapter 4
Sleeping Beauty—Awakened by the Lord
Questions for Reflection or Discussion

Day 1: A Beautiful New Day

1. Why is it impossible for us to never sin? (p. 60)

2. Could you identify a generational pattern in your family?

3. Did anyone in your family alert you to a sin you might easily yield to?

4. Why might an older family member not warn the younger generation of family sins?

5. If you broke off any word curses spoken over you, share how that's affected you.

Day 2: Beauty Defined

1. Describe or define the Lord's beauty? (p. 63)

2. How can we help speed up our transformation? (2 Corinthians 3:18, p. 63)

3. List the four pathways to experiencing God's beauty (FACE). (pp. 64–65)

4. Share examples of each.

Day 3: Beauty Rest

1. Did your family have Sabbath restrictions when growing up?

2. What is true Sabbath rest and how do we get it? (p. 67)

3. What Sabbath blessings did Jesus fulfill by his death? (p. 67–68)

4. How does honoring the Sabbath teach us to trust God? (p. 68)

5. What should set us apart from the world? (John 13:35, p. 68)

6. How do we keep the Sabbath? (p. 68)

Day 4: Beautiful Savior

1. How spiritually awake did you rate yourself?

2. Define a kiss from God and give an example. (p. 69)

3. Share a time when God kissed you.

4. Have you experienced a sorrow so deep it depleted you?

5. What must we do to find rest in Jesus? (Matthew 11:28, p. 70)

6. What can keep us from coming to him? (p. 71)

Day 5: A Beautiful Passion

1. Has a passion for something ever replaced God as your first love?

2. How do people try to *manage* sin or addiction? (p. 73)

3. Since God doesn't see our sin, how do we look to him? (p. 73)

4. What four things can we do to return to our first love? (p. 73)

5. Share the things you first did after becoming a new Christian.

6. If you've lost your first love, what will you do to regain it?

7. Is there anything else in this chapter you want to discuss?

Share prayer requests and pray for each other. Let's reignite our first-love passion for God.

Chapter 5
Little Red Hen—Work and Worship

Memory Verse:

For we are God's handiwork, created in Christ Jesus to do good works,
which God prepared in advance for us to do.
Ephesians 2:10

Day 1: Sowing Greater Rewards

Like many women, Little Red Hen was one busy, hard-working chick. When she happened upon some wheat kernels, she resisted the urge to eat them and instead prepared to plant them. Wishing to share her good fortune with her friends Cat, Pig, and Duck, she asked, "Who will help me plant these seeds?"

With words every mother has heard more than once, they answered, "Not I."

Had I been Little Red Hen, I may have changed my mind and eaten the seeds rather than planted them. How about you? Foresight helped Little Red Hen persevere. She replied, "Then I'll do it myself." And she did. She delayed gratification, anticipating a greater reward from planting rather than eating the seeds.

In the 1960s, psychologist Walter Mischel and his graduate students studied delayed gratification among children. They gave preschoolers a treat, such as a marshmallow or a pretzel, and promised them another if they would wait before eating it. Some children covered the treat with their hands or covered their eyes to resist the temptation. Others did calisthenics, tugged on their hair, or distracted themselves in other ways. Only one-third of the children waited the full fifteen minutes.[1]

The study followed the children into adulthood, and they noticed the ability to delay gratification contributed to greater success later in life, such as higher SAT scores, lower body mass index (BMI), and lower substance abuse rates.[2] Don't despair if you would have eaten the marshmallow right away. We can learn delayed gratification by trusting our Reward Giver.

Recently, an updated study showed how building trust between a child and their researcher increased the child's ability to delay gratification four times longer than a child conditioned not to trust their researcher. The researchers built trust with the children beforehand by telling them they would do certain things and did them. They created mistrust by not doing the things they said they would.[3]

Were you conditioned as a child to trust or not to trust? Our experiences influence our ability or inability to trust, which can impact our spiritual lives. Overcoming trust barriers is important because if we are to live happily ever after we must have complete trust in God. In human relationships, trust should be earned. God tells us to give certain things freely, such as forgiveness, grace, and mercy, but he doesn't tell us to trust freely. We *give* our trust only to God because he alone is perfect and trustworthy. He is Truth, so he cannot lie, and he will faithfully fulfill his word. As we come to know him better, our trust in him will increase.

God doesn't expect us to trust him blindly. He reveals himself through his creation and the Bible, and he speaks to us personally. But he doesn't provide every answer. Life's unknowns require us to exercise faith, and faith pleases God. Plus, God wants us to seek him so he can reward us as promised in Hebrews 11:6.

We receive rewards on earth, but many more await us in eternity. Life here is but a blink compared to the endless days we'll spend in heaven. God created us as eternal beings. Ecclesiastes 3:11 tells us God placed eternity in our hearts, so we know God created us for more than just living happily here on earth. Our actions have eternal consequences.

In Matthew 16:27, Jesus said, "For the Son of Man is going to come in his Father's glory with his angels, and then he will reward each person according to what he has done." Good deeds done on earth can provide eternal rewards. Mistakenly, though, some people do good things as a way to get to heaven. They believe they can earn their entrance ticket, but the Bible says no one can. "For it is by grace you have been saved, through faith—and this not from yourselves, it is the gift of God—not by works, so that no one can boast" (Ephesians 2:8–9).

God will reward good works when done for the right reason.

Jesus said, "But love your enemies, do good to them, and lend to them without expecting to get anything back. Then your reward will be great" (Luke 6:35). He said we should give to the needy in secret. "Then your Father, who sees what is done in secret, will reward you" (Matthew 6:4). He also said, "Be careful not to do your 'acts of righteousness' before men, to be seen by them. If you do, you will have no reward from your Father in heaven" (Matthew 6:1).

Our love for God should be our motivation to do good works. When we do something to gain praise, honor, or recognition, God says we've already received our reward. By doing good deeds in secret, we defer a reward now for a greater reward later in heaven.

It's natural to desire gratitude, admiration, acknowledgment, etc., so it's difficult to do good works secretly. It helps to keep our endgame in sight by remembering delayed gratification equals an eternal reward. I've learned to play "I've Got a Secret" with God. I talk to *him* about what I'm doing so I'm not tempted to tell others.

My grandmother enjoyed making and giving things to people. She sewed a quilt for my husband and had enough fabric for matching pillowcases, but she hadn't started them before coming to visit us. On arrival, she asked me to make the pillowcases before Chuck got home. I sewed them together quickly, and she gave the quilt and pillowcases to him with great joy.

It's silly, but when she didn't tell him I had made the pillowcases, I wanted to. Something inside me craved the credit for what I'd done. Sure, I could have told my husband in private.

Instead, I seized the opportunity to practice doing a good deed in secret and allowed someone else to receive all the praise.

Developing a delayed-gratification lifestyle isn't optional to living happily here and now; it's a part of the how-to equation. Colossians 3:1–2 tells us to set our hearts and minds on things above. We're to acquire a heavenly, kingdom mindset. Jesus said, "Seek first his kingdom and his righteousness, and all these things will be given to you as well" (Matthew 6:33). God promises to provide all we need when we seek him first.

Our time, talents, and treasures are like seeds, and each day we determine where they're sown by the choices we make. Will we sow them into God's kingdom, the worldly realm, or Satan's domain? Hearing testimonies of changed lives or seeing situations improve because we planted seeds encourages us. But we may not know the fruit our seeds produce until we get to heaven. Some seeds take longer to mature. Other times we won't see the fruit because we planted in secret. We aren't rewarded for the outcome but for our obedience.

Jesus told his disciples, "You are the light of the world. A city on a hill cannot be hidden" (Matthew 5:14). Though God rewards things done in secret, Jesus also said, "Let your light shine before men in such a way that they may see your good works, and glorify your Father who is in heaven" (Matthew 5:16, NASB).

Shining our light before others may seem to contradict doing good works in secret, but both are appropriate at different times. It's our motivation that concerns God. Do we want to receive the glory ourselves, or do we want God to receive it? We should do everything for God's glory (see 1 Corinthians 10:31). Martin Luther said, "Man's chief end is to glorify God, and to enjoy him forever."[4]

In Sally Lloyd-Jones' children's book *Thoughts to Make Your Heart Sing*, she explains:

"Glorify" means "to make a big deal of." When someone makes a big deal of you, it fills up your heart with joy. God didn't create us so he could get joy—he already had it. He created us so he could share it. He knows it's the thing your heart most needs to be happy. When God says, "Glorify me!", he's really saying, "Be filled with Joy!" He's inviting us into his Forever Happiness.[5]

"Forever Happiness" describes our inner longing, and it's God's desire for us, too. We can share his joy by glorifying him in everything we do. As we make a big deal of God, others can see who he is. Our joy bubbles over and touches them. Especially when we're faithfully doing what God has called us to do.

Jesus told a parable about three servants who received varying amounts of "seed" money from their master before he left on a journey. When the master returned, two servants had doubled the master's money. The master replied, "Well done, good and faithful servant! You have been faithful with a few things; I will put you in charge of many things. Come and *share your master's happiness*!" (Matthew 25:21, emphasis added). The third servant buried his money, and the master rebuked him for not at least putting it in the bank to earn interest.

God is not a hard taskmaster. Because he wants you to share in his joy, he's prepared in advance good works for you to do (see Ephesians 2:10). He designed your life's blueprints, remember? Because of this, you can be confident "that he who began a good work in you will carry it on to completion until the day of Christ Jesus" (Philippians 1:6). This promise alone gives us reason enough "to make a big deal of" God.

Yada Time

Take a moment to glorify God. Praise him for his good plan for you. Thank him for loving you as you are. Seek his FACE. Spend a few minutes in his presence and receive his joy.

How well do you trust God? Do your experiences keep you from trusting him completely? If so, ask God to heal any pain associated with those memories. Tell him you desire to trust him more, and ask for his help. Though God doesn't have to earn our trust, he will prove his trustworthiness.

Day 2: Just Do It

Because I grew up on a farm, I heard many conversations that revolved around the crops and weather. I still ask my dad how the crops look each season. As an avid gardener, I now take a personal interest in the weather. Concerns about adequate rainfall, ample sunshine, or storm threats hold my attention.

The weather may have also consumed Little Red Hen's thoughts while she waited for her wheat to mature. At harvest time, she again asked her friends to help, and once more they declined.

"Then I'll do it myself," she said. And like Nike's motto—she just did it.

Picture her as their spokes-hen, sporting Nike tennies while swinging a sickle in a golden wheat field. As long as you're imagining, pretend she's a Christian and think back to when she first found the seed. How might she have reacted differently? She may have given it to feed the poor. Now ponder what you might have done.

As Christians, we should desire to do God's will and therefore ask him what he wants us to do. His answers will vary because he has a specific, individual plan for each person. We're not all called to plant. Maybe you're wired to water or hooked on harvesting. Our job is to obey God and do our part.

Paul used a similar example referring to winning souls for Christ. He said:

I planted the seed, Apollos watered it, but God made it grow. So neither he who plants nor he who waters is anything, but only God, who makes things grow. The man who plants and the man who waters have one purpose, and each will be rewarded according to his own labor. (1 Corinthians 3:6–8)

Sometimes God will give the same person a different answer to the same situation at a different time because he wants to teach them something new. Staying with the seed scenario, he might first answer, "Eat the seeds, enjoy them. I am your provider." The next time he might say, "Give them away. Trust me. I will provide more." Another time, "Plant them. I will give you increase." Can you see why it's important to ask God every time?

God made each person unique, so he teaches us different things at different times in different ways—and *he* causes our growth. It's no wonder he tells us not to compare, judge, or be concerned about someone else's life (see Matthew 7:5). God has a different timetable for each of us.

As children, my boys frequently bickered over what the other one had or was doing and complained to me about it. For example, they'd say, "Why does he always get to sleep at a friend's house and I don't?" If you didn't read the question with a whiny tone, reread it. I often answered, "John 21:21," and they knew what I meant. In this verse, Peter was referencing John when he asked Jesus, "Lord, what about him?" Even a grown man wanted to compare his situation to his friend's. Jesus had just told Peter "the kind of death by which Peter would glorify God" (John 21:19). Now Peter wanted to know what would happen to John. Jesus told Peter it wasn't his concern and said, "You must follow me" (John 21:22).

God speaks these same words to us today too.

Following Jesus becomes easier as you know and grow into the purposes God has for your life. You'll also become less preoccupied with someone else's life when you're concentrating on yours. Yet fulfilling your God-given calling takes time because everything, including your destiny, starts in seed form.

Genesis 8:22 says, "As long as the earth endures, seedtime and harvest, cold and heat, summer and winter, day and night will never cease." This verse describes seasons and cycles established by God to govern life. Even though these cycles show continuous change, we can find comfort knowing the change is consistent. We can trust the sun to rise the next morning, the trees to bud after a long winter, and the seeds we plant to produce a harvest when mature. God created reliable patterns and principles to guide us.

Sowing and repeating is one such principle: we reap what we sow. Actions have consequences, both good and bad. That which is sown also produces of its kind. Wheat kernels produce wheat. First Peter 1:23 says, "For you have been born again, not of perishable seed, but of imperishable, through the living and enduring word of God." The imperishable seed sown in us is Christ, and at maturity, we'll be like him. Not just resemble him as some weed might that only looks like the real plant, but we will be like him when we see him (see 1 John 3:2). His seed in us will produce nothing less than perfection. Until then, we undergo a gradual, progressive maturation process, conforming us into his image.

God also plants in us his plans and purposes in seed form. That means we must do our part of nurturing those seeds. If we know what God has called us to do, we shouldn't sit back and wait for something magical to happen. We need to *work out* the plans Christ planted in us just as we work out our salvation. We participate with God, pursue learning opportunities, and practice doing what he's called us to do.

In the fifth grade, I wanted to be a writer when I grew up. I enjoyed creative writing classes in high school, but I no longer felt drawn toward a writing career. The writing seed lay dormant in me until I had children. Once it sprouted, I asked God to confirm his calling, and he did, repeatedly, because I kept asking him *when* it would happen. During this time, I wrote when I could and read books on how to write. Eventually, I took writing classes and attended a few writing conferences. I did my part, leaving the outcome in God's hands.

Two decades later, I'm writing full-time, but I don't know how or when God will use my writing. I do know God establishes our callings and gives spiritual gifts for the benefit of others, so I expect that to happen. We don't have to know all the answers to obey God, "for we walk by faith, not by sight" (2 Corinthians 5:7, NASB).

Your journey with its many learning curves is as important to God as your destination. Think about all the lessons Little Red Hen might have learned while farming. A long day digging in the dirt probably increased her ability to persevere. Weather-related perils may have taught her to trust God with the outcome. Watching her tiny seeds sprout, poke their heads through the soil, and grow to become life-giving sustenance surely pointed her to our magnificent Creator.

David's life provides valuable lessons, including what can happen while waiting to fulfill God's calling or purpose. When the prophet Samuel anointed David to be the next king, David was a teenage shepherd boy. The ruling king, Saul, had no intention of giving David his throne. It took approximately fifteen years before David became king of Judah (his tribe) and another seven and a half years before he reigned over all of Israel.

During those in-between years, David fulfilled several other God-appointed purposes, such as killing the giant Goliath. Who could imagine a shepherd boy accomplishing such a feat? His calling as a shepherd prepared him for the battle, so David could imagine success. King Saul was skeptical, however. From all outward appearances, the combatants looked extremely unmatched. But David convinced Saul to let him fight by telling him how he'd protected his sheep from predators. David concluded, "Your servant has killed both the lion and the bear; this uncircumcised Philistine will be like one of them, because he has defied the armies of the living God" (1 Samuel 17:36).

David fought many other battles before obtaining his destiny. He didn't sit back and wait to become King. Nor did he make it happen before God's timing. When given the opportunity to kill King Saul, who'd been trying to kill him, David refused to harm the Lord's anointed (see 1 Samuel 24). Besides being king, David was also a son, brother, husband, and father. God gave David multiple purposes, including the legacy of being included in Jesus' ancestral line.

God has planted multiple purposes in you, too. Giants come in all shapes and sizes, and God may be preparing you right now to face and take one down. If you don't know God's plan or purpose for your life, ask him to reveal it to you. He probably won't provide all the details because then you'd have no opportunity to walk by faith. Therefore, just do what's in front of you. If you're a wife, then do your best to be a loving wife—or be a loving mother, daughter, sister, friend, employee, or boss. Be faithful in the things you already know God has called you to do, and God will give you more. He'll upgrade you with influence, favor, and more responsibilities.

Did you notice that Little Red Hen didn't complain when no one would help her? She didn't whine it wasn't her job. She didn't wait for someone else to do it for her. She just did it. We can stall God's plans by being unwilling to do the menial, everyday tasks. They may not seem pertinent, but they are. Would David have volunteered to kill Goliath had he not first killed lions and bears?

God mercifully doesn't tell us what giants we'll encounter because ill-equipped people run from and not toward their battles. But in God's timing, he prepares us in advance to conquer whatever threatens our destinies. Our part is to do faithfully whatever God sets before us each day. So, let's just do it.

Yada Time

What has God called you to do or be? God created you for many purposes. Make a mental list, including daughter, friend, etc. Which area could you be more intentional in seeking God for help? Talk to him about that now.

Is there anything you've put off doing that you sense God wants you to do? Maybe it's to spend more time with him, read a specific book, take a class, or understand a specific calling better. What's holding you back? Ask God to help you overcome any obstacles to taking your next step.

Day 3: Submission

With a big stick tucked under one wing, Little Red Hen invited Cat, Pig, and Duck to help her beat the wheat kernels off their stems. They declined—despite her big stick. Evidently, they viewed work as a four-letter word. Who could blame them? It wasn't their idea to grow wheat, and they didn't owe some crazy red hen anything! Besides, they received everything they needed from a *real* farmer.

Do you like manual labor? I like the end results that cooking, cleaning, washing clothes, dishes, and other repetitive tasks produce, so I do them. But I'd rather spend my time doing something else. More than once as a child I told my mom I thought she'd had us five kids so we could do all her work! What nerve—and ignorance. As a mother, I know how much work children create, not accomplish.

When I complained about household chores as a child, my mom would say, "There are things in life you won't like doing, but you're going to have to do them anyhow." Maybe not in those exact words, but she was right. I'm thankful she instilled in me a strong work ethic, but I still dislike doing many things.

How can we live happily ever after when we face so many dislikable tasks daily? What do you do to cope? Sometimes I bribe myself. Or I break a task into smaller pieces and spread it out. If faced with thrashing wheat like Little Red Hen, I would listen to praise music on my iPod and keep the beat while beating the wheat. For indoor duties, I watch a favorite pastor on TV and combine a task I dislike with something I enjoy. I'm competitive, so other times I compete with myself by timing myself and trying to break my record. Knowing how long it takes to do a task, such as unload the dishwasher, helps me gain a proper perspective. I tell myself, "What's five minutes out of a 1,440-minute day?" Or I remind myself I could be doing something worse, such as sitting in a dentist's chair or getting chemotherapy. With an upgrade to my attitude, I thank God I'm healthy enough to work. In the next chapter, *The Princess and the Pea*, we'll explore attitude, perspective, and what to do when the worst things do happen.

The Bible tells us the mindset we should adopt toward work. Colossians 3:17 says, "And whatever you do, whether in word or deed, do it all in the name of the Lord Jesus, giving thanks to God the Father through him." Verse 23 adds, "Whatever you do, work at it with all your heart, as working for the Lord, not for men." We serve at our King's pleasure.

The Hebrew word for work is *avad*. "The word avad means 'to serve,' but it also means 'to work' and even 'to worship!'"[6] Viewing work and everything we do as worship puts a positive spin on work. Rick Warren wrote in *The Purpose Driven Life*, "Every activity can be transformed into an act of worship when we do it for the praise, glory and pleasure of God."[7] Romans 12:1 tells us how: "Therefore, I urge you, brothers, in view of God's mercy, to offer your bodies as living sacrifices, holy and pleasing to God—this is your spiritual act of worship."

Our whole existence can be one continual act of worship when we offer ourselves as living sacrifices and submit to God's will. The word submit in Greek is *hupotasso* (hoop-ot-as'-so). It means to subordinate, to be under, or reflexively to obey.[8] Several Bible verses tell us to submit to leaders, spouses, authorities, and to one another out of reverence to Christ. Submitting to someone who lets you have your way is easy. However, our need to have our way is a burden, says Richard Foster. He writes in *Celebration of Discipline*: "The obsession to demand that things go the way we want them to go is one of the greatest bondages in human society today."[9]

Think about that statement for a moment. Have you ever considered having your way as bondage? I hadn't until I considered all the striving, complaining, or manipulating that often accompanies getting my way. It's freeing to allow others to have their way and to submit to them as Scripture tells us to. In doing so, we demonstrate sacrificial living.

Demanding our way or refusing to submit to God and those in authority is rebellion. At least that's what God called it when my employer reprimanded me. In 2000, mortgage lending had slowed to a near halt, and upper management cross-trained me and the other mortgage originators as financial advisors. For six months, I traveled two hours every Wednesday to receive investment training for a job I didn't want. Also, I had to study and pass a test to get licensed to sell life insurance.

There's an old joke about a little girl standing on a chair whose mother repeatedly asks her to sit down. After threats of punishment, the little girl finally obeys but says, "I may be sitting down on the outside, but I'm standing up on the inside." That describes my behavior during this time.

After completing our training, we held weekly meetings via web cameras, which now included upper management. At one early morning meeting, I laid my head on our conference table for all to see. I may have been tired, but I was definitely bored and making the statement I still wasn't "on board" with their plans. For this, I later received a verbal and written reprimand.

I was hurt, embarrassed, and angry. How could management make me do a job I didn't want? "This isn't fair," I cried to God. In his gentle, loving way, he said I had a rebellious spirit and should submit to authority. He also said my rebellion stemmed from not trusting him; I didn't believe that he was in control. I asked God's forgiveness and submitted to my authorities.

Richard Foster wrote, "In submission we are at last free to value other people. Their dreams and plans become important to us. We have entered into a new, wonderful, glorious freedom—the freedom to give up our own rights for the good of others."[10] He also wrote, "Self-denial is simply a way of coming to understand that we do not have to have our own way. Our happiness is not dependent upon getting what we want."[11] If only I had read Foster's book before this happened. Though I obeyed God and changed my attitude, I didn't embrace my employer's dream.

My main objection had been the cyclical nature of home buying. As anticipated, housing sales picked up shortly after we completed training, and I became too busy originating mortgage loans to do financial planning besides. It had all been for nothing—except for the valuable lesson learned in submission.

Submitting to God and others shows God that we trust him. It also gives him a reason to bless us. Shortly after my scolding, an idea popped into my head to take one day off a week to write. I had been away from the office every Wednesday for six months. Why couldn't I continue that schedule? I asked God to confirm if this was his idea. Over the next week, three women, two of whom I barely knew, told me in separate conversations they were working four days a week, and I hadn't even brought up the subject. I took this as confirmation.

Next, I needed approval from the two women who had reprimanded me. It seemed like a long shot, but if God had prompted me, they would grant my request. The following week I was scheduled to meet with one of the women, so I asked God to show me the right time to ask.

When God called Gideon to lead Israel in battle, Gideon asked God for a sign that God would save Israel by his hands. Gideon said, "I will place a wool fleece on the threshing floor. If there is dew only on the fleece and all the ground is dry, then I will know that you will save Israel by my hand, as you said" (Judges 6:37). In the morning, only the fleece was wet. Needing further assurance, Gideon requested another sign, asking God to do the reverse of what had previously happened. The next morning the fleece remained dry and the ground wet.

This concept, called "laying out a fleece," is what I did when I asked God to help me know when to ask the women about working four days a week. I said, "Lord, have this woman ask how my 32-hour work schedule is going. That will be my sign to ask." At our scheduled meeting, the woman didn't ask, so I didn't ask. We shouldn't lay out a fleece lightly as it requires patience, commitment, and faith.

A week later, the other woman scheduled a lunch meeting with me. To my surprise, the first woman joined us, giving me the opportunity to ask them together. But I needed one of them to ask how my 32-hour work week was going—and the first woman did! I answered her question by asking to work four days a week while keeping my shorter work days. They said management would have to approve my request, and not surprisingly, they did.

When we trust God and believe he has a good plan for our lives, then submitting to him and others becomes easier. We'll want what God wants and trust him to cause it to happen. It's a burden to demand we get our way. Freedom awaits us when we willingly submit to God and others—and it can come without someone waving a big stick.

Yada Time

Offer yourself to God as a living sacrifice. Submit to him all areas in which you still want your way. Ask God to enable you to see other's dreams and desires as important. Watch for opportunities to allow someone else to have their way and practice submitting to others. Plan an occasion to submit to someone you love. Make it an easy one at first. Maybe allow your spouse or child to choose where or what you eat, or what you watch on television together. Submission takes practice.

Day 4: To Be or Not to Be

With each new task, Little Red Hen asked Cat, Pig, and Duck for help, and they refused repeatedly. Before hauling the wheat to the mill, she asked. Then she dragged it there herself and lugged the heavy flour sacks home again. She asked one last time before making the flour into dough. Then she kneaded and baked the bread herself.

I imagine Little Red Hen continued to ask because work is often easier and more fun when done with someone else. Ecclesiastes 4:10 says, "Two are better than one, because they have a good return for their work: If one falls down, his friend can help him up."

Yet sometimes it's easier to adopt Little Red Hen's attitude and just do it ourselves. If you're a mom, you know what I'm talking about. We know how we want things done, and we like to control when they get done. Working with others can complicate matters. My husband and I almost always come up with two different ways to do a task, and we both want it done our way and to be in charge—when we're not practicing submission.

My four siblings and I work surprisingly well together as adults, and I think they'd be disappointed if I stopped taking charge. Being the oldest, I fit the typical firstborn stereotype. I organized a surprise party for our parents' fortieth wedding anniversary. Before our guests arrived, I gathered the troops and gave a pep talk my siblings will never let me forget. I told them we were all servants and should pitch in wherever needed. As the evening progressed, I must have thought our guests *needed* my company as I flittered around the room visiting with everyone until cleanup. Social butterfly and slacker rarely describe me, but I was guilty of both. My siblings teasingly complained—and still occasionally recite my "Be a Servant" speech.

Martha from the Bible is well known for serving (and complaining). We don't know how many people gathered at Mary and Martha's home when Jesus visited, but Martha got stuck preparing the meal by herself. She complained to Jesus about her sister, Mary, who was sitting at his feet, listening to him. "'Martha, Martha,' the Lord answered, 'you are worried and upset about many things, but only **one thing** is needed. Mary has chosen what is better, and it will not be taken away from her'" (Luke 10:41–42, emphasis added).

For years, I thought Martha received a bum rap. Who else would have cooked dinner? Martha had to be the dependable, take-charge older sister and Mary the younger, whimsical one. It's hard not to let personal experience color our perspective and bleed into a story.

Sympathetic to Martha, I interpreted Jesus' words as an unfair reprimand for working. I determined that Jesus loved Mary-types more than Martha-types. Though I spent time with the Lord daily, I wasn't one to sit silently doing nothing. I read my Bible and prayed. I tried to be still and listen, but that wasn't how I best heard God's voice.

I imagined Mary-types could sit endlessly in his presence. I couldn't. I was a doer. Give me a Sunday school lesson to prepare and teach, or a committee to organize and lead, but don't ask me to spend endless hours sitting silently at Jesus' feet. Then one day while reading the Bible, the Holy Spirit highlighted the verse: "Jesus loved Martha and her sister and Lazarus" (John 11:5). It was as if the Lord himself had spoken those words and replaced my name with Martha's. I felt incredibly loved and accepted by God even as a Martha.

The Holy Spirit then supplied a new tone for Jesus' voice as I reread the story. I had previously imagined Jesus shaking his head or finger at Martha, and in a scolding manner, saying, "Martha, Martha." Now his voice sounded kind and loving. Jesus had addressed Martha's heart issue—"You are worried and upset about many things"—*because* he loved her. He didn't condemn her work ethic. He stated she wasn't making the right choice. He said, "But only one thing is needed. Mary has chosen what is better, and it will not be taken away from her."

Mary knew the one thing that satisfies is Jesus—being in his presence, hearing his voice, and learning from him. Addressing Satan, Jesus said, "It is written: 'Man does not live on bread alone, but on every word that comes from the mouth of God'" (Matthew 4:4). Mary knew true nourishment comes from hearing God's voice. His words provide life, and his truth sets us free. A continual experience that nourishes our soul should be our goal, too. Why would we want anything less?

But if we're honest, too often we become busy, distracted, self-absorbed, or anxious like Martha. We even become a bit like Little Red Hen when we declare, "I'll do it [life] myself." We're doers. We haven't learned to pursue the "one thing."

The first Wednesday I had off from work, I gathered my Bible, paper, and pen, and waited expectantly at our dining room table for inspiration. Which book idea would I write? Staring at the blank paper, I sensed the Lord calling me to spend time with him. "Won't I be doing that?" I argued. His nudge persisted, and I protested, "I want to write. You called me to write. I'll be doing something for you."

Instead of spending time with the Lord, I journaled my frustration. If sitting at his feet was something I should do, why didn't I feel like it? Why did I still feel more like Martha than Mary? I addressed my questions to God, and I sensed him say, "You have a *do* mentality and not a *be* mentality. Even spending time with me is a *do*, rather than a *be*."

Then the following words flowed onto my paper:

- *Be* in my presence.
- *Be* still and know that I am God.
- *Be*come like me.
- *Be*lieve what I tell you.
- *Be*come what I have planned for you.
- *Be* given direction *be*fore you move.
- *Be*gin to understand my ways.
- *Be*gin and end your day with me and all that's in *be*tween.
- *Be*cause—I love you.

Although I wasn't positive the words were God's and not my thoughts, they seemed biblically sound. With this new insight, I followed God's previous prompting to spend time with him and went to *be* on the living room floor. Shortly after, I fell asleep. As I woke, thoughts raced through my mind that I should do something and not sleep through my writing day. Semiconscious, I prayed, "Lord, wake me up."

Immediately, I heard Doris Day singing, "*Que, sera, sera*, whatever will *be*, will *be*. The future's not ours to see. *Que, sera, sera*. What will *be* will *be*." Now the Lord had my full attention.

Be isn't a complicated truth, but sometimes living it out seems difficult *to do*. We aren't to do, but to be. We'll always find things to do, but God doesn't call us to do everything. He calls us to do what he's already prepared in advance for us (see Ephesians 2:10), and we're to do it yoked with Jesus.

The goal is to *be* even while doing. It's like Sabbath rest. While *being*, we rely on God's direction and strength to accomplish our work. We release all cares and control to him. I love that the word *be* is a linking verb. God created us to be linked with him—attached to Jesus, the Vine. Without him we can do nothing (see John 15:5).

One of my favorite names of God is "I AM." God first revealed himself as I AM in answer to Moses' question of who he should say sent him. "God said to Moses, 'I am who I am. This is what you are to say to the Israelites: 'I am has sent me to you'" (Exodus 3:14). My Bible's footnotes say I AM is "related to the name of God, YHWH, rendered LORD, which is derived from the verb HAYAH, to be."[12] God told Moses, "I will be who I will be."

The eternal Lord, with no beginning or end, created us in his image. If God will be, then how much more shouldn't we? If we focus on the one thing and embrace *being* in God's presence, then our load will be lighter and we won't feel as overworked as Little Red Hen did.

Yada Time

Do you better relate to Mary or Martha? Why? God doesn't love one type more than the other, but he calls every person to *be*. How are *be*, one thing, Sabbath rest, and remaining in the Vine similar? Meditate on these concepts. How will you integrate them into your life? Spend time with Jesus daily. Let him teach you how to be.

Day 5: Golden Receivers

Little Red Hen stepped outside, oven mitts on her wings, and proudly displayed the steaming hot bread. The delicious aroma wafted through the barnyard and gathered Cat, Pig, and Duck to her side. "Who will help me eat this bread?" she asked.

For the first time, her friends sang a different tune. They'd refused to help with the planting, harvesting, threshing, milling, and baking, but now they erupted in a chorus of "I will!" as drool dripped from their watering mouths.

"Oh no you won't," said Little Red Hen, "I'm eating it all myself!"

Who could blame her? She'd done all the work herself. Her friends didn't deserve the tiniest breadcrumb. She allowed them to smell and see the warm, delicious bread so they'd know what they'd be missing.

Day Two introduced the principle of sowing and reaping, and this story's conclusion demonstrates it well. Cat, Pig, and Duck sowed nothing and therefore received nothing. Little Red Hen sowed seeds, worked diligently, and delayed gratification until she eventually received a greater reward for her labor. Although the sowing-and-reaping principle still exists, God offers us a superior system called grace.

Grace, unmerited favor, means God gives us blessings we didn't earn and don't deserve. Instead, we reap the benefits from what Jesus sowed. All he accomplished by his death on the cross becomes ours when we believe and receive. An example of grace would be if Little Red Hen shared the bread with her friends even though they hadn't worked for it.

In John 6:48–51, Jesus said:

I am the bread of life. Your forefathers ate the manna in the desert, yet they died. But here is the bread that comes down from heaven, which a man may eat and not die. I am the living bread that came down from heaven. If anyone eats of this bread, he will live forever. This bread is my flesh, which I will give for the life of the world.

No one deserves to partake of Jesus, the Bread of Life, but he did for us what we couldn't do even if we wanted to. We reap his rewards. He only stipulates that we *receive* by faith what he freely offers. We've touched on several of those gifts already: forgiveness, eternal life, unconditional love, peace, rest, etc. We've also looked at the crucial role faith plays. But we haven't discussed the importance of receiving.

Grace is amazing, but if we're unable to receive God's unmerited favor, it does us no good. In part, our ability to receive determines what we get. Some people receive more easily than others. I'm not a great receiver, but I'm getting better at it.

In college, my boyfriend offered to buy me a new pair of tennis shoes. I'd worn my faded blue Adidas for years, and they finally felt as comfortable as slippers. Putting laces in them may have improved their appearance, but I wasn't concerned—until wearing the shoes embarrassed my boyfriend. As poor as I was, I wouldn't allow him to buy me new shoes. Maybe I was too proud or self-sufficient to receive from him. I felt self-conscious and somewhat humiliated.

Many people have issues keeping them from fully receiving from God. Some issues may stem from negative experiences. We may guard our hearts because gifts came with manipulative strings attached. Or what we received never met our expectations, so now we avoid receiving to keep from being disappointed. For some, receiving stirs up feelings of obligation or a need to reciprocate. Although these scenarios aren't applicable when receiving from God, our fears and unhealed wounds can hinder our ability to receive from him.

Another obstacle could be the mindset, "It is more blessed to give than to receive" (Acts 20:35). We may feel more spiritual when giving. The word blessed can be exchanged for the word happy. When we give, we experience happiness; but we don't have to choose one over the other. We need both because we can't give what we haven't received. If "every good and perfect gift is from above" (James 1:17), we need to receive God's good gifts so we'll have them to give to others.

God created us with the ability to receive. We entered this world as helpless, dependent babies. Initially, we did nothing for ourselves. We received everything we needed from a parent or caregiver. As we grew, we gradually became more self-sufficient. We probably said, "Me do it!" more times than anyone could count. Impatience and independence caused us to strive for what we wanted—when we wanted it.

The food, clothing, and shelter we received as children eventually became our responsibility. We learned to provide for ourselves and may have mistakenly believed we were independent and self-sufficient. As women, God gifted us with the ability to nurture and give tirelessly to others. If we became parents, our giving rose to new levels. By the age of thirty, almost everyone could use a refresher course on receiving, and it would begin with a lesson in asking.

My sister is a great receiver because she dares to ask. In high school during a blizzard one Saturday, she asked our dad to drive her to Rochester (an hour away in good weather) so she could buy a rabbit fur coat—and he drove her! Dad knew her bulldog tenacity would eventually wear him down. And my sister knew our dad loved her so much he would do anything for her.

Jesus told a parable about a woman who obtained justice from a judge because she persistently asked him for it (see Luke 18:1–8). He told another parable about a man whose friend came to him at midnight asking for bread. Jesus said, "I tell you, though he will not get up and give him the bread because he is his friend, yet because of the man's boldness he will get up and give him as much as he needs" (Luke 11:8).

Those who ask boldly and persistently receive.

If we don't have something we want, James 4:2 tells us it's because we haven't asked God for it. By asking, we humble ourselves and declare our dependence on God. We aren't bothering him when we ask; we're obeying him. Jesus said, "Ask and it will be given to you" (Matthew 7:7).

When God taught me about receiving, he stressed the importance of asking and not just for help or material things. He encouraged me to ask him questions throughout the day. He desired a continuous conversation with me, and he still does. He wants one with you, too. While driving to work one day, God confirmed what he'd been teaching me through a billboard for an insurance agent. It said "Ask me" in huge bold letters. God has so much to say and give to us, but he wants us to ask him first.

In John 16:24, Jesus said, "Until now you have not asked for anything in my name. Ask and you will receive, and your joy will be complete." God wants to share his joy with us. He answers our requests because he loves us and loves seeing us happy. What parent doesn't? He also hopes gratitude will prompt us to share our gifts with others. He's not offended when we re-gift what he's given us; he expects it. We can give love because God first gave us love. We can for*give* because he first for*gave* us. God wants us doubly blessed (happy), first by receiving and then by giving away what we received.

God intends we use his gifts to help others. When Jesus sent his disciples out in Matthew 10:8, he told them to "Heal the sick, raise the dead, cleanse those who have leprosy, drive out demons. Freely you have received, freely give." Just as Jesus equipped his disciples, he'll equip us. He said, "I tell you the truth, anyone who has faith in me will do what I have been doing. He will do even greater things than these, because I am going to the Father" (John 14:12). Maybe you don't aspire to raise the dead, but God planted seeds for "greater things" within you. To accomplish them, you must *receive* the faith, power, wisdom, etc. from God that nurtures and matures those seeds.

One way we can increase our ability to receive is to become more childlike. Jesus said unless we become like little children, we won't enter God's kingdom (see Matthew 18:3). We enter his kingdom as children because children are golden receivers. Children are humble, totally dependent on their parents' provision, and ask many questions. They also ask for many things because they have great faith. They don't know money doesn't grow on trees, so they imagine receiving everything they desire. At Christmas, they circle pictures in toy catalogs and compile two-page wish lists, believing they'll receive. Becoming childlike sounds like fun, but it's not a free pass to act childish or selfish. It's to awaken expectancy in your heart that causes you to dream bigger and ask for more.

God created us to accomplish greater things, and when we faithfully use what he gives us we'll receive more. We should long to hear Jesus say, "Well done, good and faithful servant! You have been faithful with a few things; I will put you in charge of many things. Come and share your master's happiness!" (Matthew 25:21). As we continue receiving, God's grace empowers us to respond according to his heart. Our joy is complete as we do work for his kingdom, and in this way, we can worship through work!

Yada Time

How well do you receive? What keeps you from asking God for things? Position your heart as a child and ask God if there is anything blocking your ability to receive. Ask to become more childlike. Talk to God throughout your day, asking him questions and for all your needs. Dream with God about the greater works he has for you. Ask and receive what you need to fulfill your destiny.

Chapter 5
Little Red Hen—Work and Worship
Questions for Reflection or Discussion

Day 1: Sowing Greater Rewards

1. Describe delayed gratification and how it applies to our walk with God. (p. 78)

2. What factor increased a child's ability to delay gratification? (p. 78)

3. What events in your life conditioned you to trust or not to trust?

4. On what basis does God reward us? (p. 79)

5. How can we obtain greater rewards in heaven? (p. 79)

Day 2: Just Do It

1. Why is it important to continually ask God for guidance? (p. 81)

2. Explain the principle of sowing and reaping. Give examples. (p. 82)

3. Why can we be sure we'll eventually be like Jesus? (1 Peter 1:23, p. 82)

4. What are your responsibilities toward accomplishing God's plan for your life? (p. 83)

5. Share an example of how God prepared you for a specific purpose.

6. How do we obtain an upgrade in God's kingdom? (p. 84)

Day 3: Submission

1. What do you do to cope when faced with a dislikable task?

2. How can we put a positive spin on work? (p. 85)

3. How is demanding that we always get our way a burden? (p. 85)

4. How can we learn to submit to others and not demand our way? (p. 86)

5. Describe how submission and being a living sacrifice relate to each other.

Day 4: To Be or Not to Be

1. Do you better relate to Mary or Martha?

2. Jesus said, "Man does not live on bread alone," but on what? (Matthew 4:4, p. 88)

3. How can we apply this to ourselves today?

4. What can keep us from pursuing the *one thing*? (p. 89)

5. What must we do to *be*? (p. 89)

6. How will you integrate *being* and *one thing* into your life?

Day 5: Golden Receivers

1. How does sowing and reaping differ from grace? (p. 90)

2. Discuss the things that can hinder our receiving from God. (p. 91)

3. Had you been Little Red Hen, would you have kept asking for help?

4. Why is it hard for us to ask for things? Do you have the same struggles when asking God?

5. What unselfish motive could prompt us to become better receivers? (p. 92)

6. How can we increase our ability to receive? (p. 92)

Share prayer requests and pray for each other. Let's boldly ask God for what we need as we position our hearts to receive from him.

Chapter 6
The Princess and the Pea—
Perspective, Expectation, and Attitude

Memory Verse:

So we fix our eyes not on what is seen, but on what is unseen,
since what is seen is temporary, but what is unseen is eternal.
2 Corinthians 4:18

Day 1: Princess Problems

As a young girl, the slightest wrinkle set me wiggling. I cried whenever I had to wear a T-shirt under my shirt because it never felt smooth enough. Wearing socks bothered me too, their thick seams pressing angrily against my toes. I still smooth my sheets before getting into bed, unable to sleep amid wrinkles. I sympathize with the princess in this fairy tale who couldn't sleep because a pea lay hidden under her mattresses.

If you aren't familiar with the fairy tale, the instigator behind this princess' problem was her soon-to-be mother-in-law. The protective Queen insisted her son marry a true princess. (As a mother of two sons, I understand.) The Prince's search for his perfect bride was unsuccessful until one evening when a beautiful princess knocked on his family's door to find refuge from a storm. Luckily for him, the maiden knew nothing about the tempest brewing inside his mother.

The Queen believed that a true princess would possess a delicate disposition; her sensitivity would determine her authenticity. The Queen ordered the servants to prepare a place for the Princess to sleep, instructing them to stack mattresses so high that the Princess would need a ladder to get into bed. While no one was looking, the Queen placed a pea under the bottom mattress to test her guest's claim to royalty. If she was indeed a true princess, she would be unable to sleep from the uncomfortable pea.

In God's kingdom, a princess' authenticity is based solely on becoming the King's daughter when she accepts his Son, Jesus, as her Lord and Savior. But even God's princesses encounter tests and problems. To live happily ever after, we must learn to address both. To discuss the topic, I created the acronym PEA—**P**roblem **E**voking **A**nxiety—to represent our problems. Unlike the Princess who couldn't sleep because of the painful pea, God's princesses *will* find rest no matter what causes them discomfort. The only thing that should keep them awake late at night is talking with their daddy, the King!

PEAs come in various shapes and sizes. Unfortunately, some princesses experience bumper crops. But with God's help, we can learn to live happily despite our problems. The Bible says, "For everything that was written in the past was written to teach us, so that through the endurance taught in the Scriptures and the encouragement they provide we might have hope" (Romans 15:4). Hope keeps us afloat on a sea of PEAs, and we gain hope through "the encouragement of the Scriptures."

There's no better place to find answers to life's problems than studying God's Word. The stories about God's chosen people, the Israelites, offer us hope because God will provide the same awe-inspiring miracles and unconditional love for us, too. Being his favorite didn't exclude the Israelites from having problems. They labored in Egypt for over four hundred years as slaves. Then when they were finally freed, they wandered in the wilderness an additional forty years because of unbelief.

As a young girl, I thought it wouldn't take much to surpass the Israelites' faith. God had parted the Red Sea so they could escape on dry land, yet days later they grumbled against him, wishing he'd never rescued them. "The Israelites said to [Moses and Aaron], 'If only we had died by the Lord's hand in Egypt! There we sat around pots of meat and ate all the food we wanted, but you have brought us out into this desert to starve this entire assembly to death'" (Exodus 16:3).

How could anyone so quickly forget their safe passage between walls of water? Previously, God had dispensed ten menacing plagues on the Egyptians so Pharaoh would free the Israelites. God had demonstrated his power and willingness to help, yet they thought he'd allow them to starve or thirst to death. As a naive teenager, I couldn't understand their unbelief. Lack of experience and empathy caused me to judge them harshly. Forty years later, I now understand how easily I forget past miracles and answered prayers when facing a trial. The tiniest PEA (problem evoking anxiety) crops up, and I cry, "Lord, what am I going to do?"

Encountering PEAs is inevitable. We have God-given needs, an enemy who's out to destroy us, and we live in a fallen world with imperfect people. PEAs are all around us, but we should never blame God for our problems. God is good, and the devil is bad. Understanding why God allows problems to exist can help us cope when PEAs threaten to derail our happiness or, worse yet, our faith.

We find the answer in the Israelites' story when they were poised to enter the Promised Land. Forty years prior they had been too frightened to fight the giant inhabitants. Fear and unbelief sentenced them to wandering in the wilderness. Now they faced the giants again. Why hadn't God gotten rid of their enemy? Judges 3:1–2 explains, "These are the nations the Lord left to test all those Israelites who had not experienced any of the wars in Canaan (he did this only to teach warfare to the descendants of the Israelites who had not had previous battle experience)."

God allows PEAs to teach us warfare because our enemy *will* wage war against us. Battles aren't optional. Jesus said we *will* have trials (see John 16:33). When embraced, problems provide opportunities to draw closer to God and become spiritually equipped. God also uses them to test our obedience. The good news is God's tests are open-book (Bible), and he encourages us to ask our teacher, the Holy Spirit, for help. Plus, if we don't pass the first time, we get to retake the test until we do. Could God be any more patient with us?

We need patience, too, because our transformation takes time. PEAs promote the painful process of change, and they give us a reason to enlist God's help. Through warfare, we experience God in new ways, which strengthens our faith and trust in him. Without problems, we'd have no need for solutions. God wants to be our solution to everything.

A true princess understands this, so she faces the PEAs sent to disturb, distract, or even destroy her. She doesn't ignore or pretend they don't exist. She doesn't stack more mattresses on top, hoping to numb her pain. A mattress can be anything we do to avoid a problem: shop, eat, gossip, drink, do drugs, sleep, yell, get angry, withdraw, gamble, hurt loved ones, or any other destructive coping mechanism. A King's daughter draws near to him and implores his help to fight the giants inhabiting her Promised Land.

Even in the heat of a battle, a true princess doesn't allow PEAs to keep her up at night. She's learned to roll PEAs off her plate and onto God's, or she squishes them under her feet by using her authority in Christ. If she's ever awake at night, it's to spend time with her Daddy, not to worry or add another mattress.

Ineffective coping patterns (mattresses) only prolong the real problem and create additional ones. Unfortunately, many of us don't acknowledge our mattress preference. If we do, it's because we see no harm in using it. The enemy knows our mattress choice. He's helped establish it to keep us from addressing our problems.

God also knows when and why we began using mattresses. Maybe we struggled with low self-esteem so we put others down to build ourselves up. Or maybe we were lonely and found companionship in drinking. Feeling left out, we might have gossiped to connect with others. If we grew up feeling unloved, we may have given ourselves too freely in relationships. Instead of learning to deal with our emotions, we swallowed them along with excessive food for comfort. Or when overwhelmed, we used retail therapy to find joy.

Mattresses come in all forms, but they only mask the PEA (problem evoking anxiety). Desiring to conquer her problems, a true princess turns to God when she discovers the PEA and asks for his help, surrendering her mattresses to him. She believes happily ever after is possible and trusts God to work all things for her good. She knows he allows PEAs to teach her warfare, transform her, and bring her one step closer to her Promised Land.

Yada Time

How do you deal with problems? Did a mattress preference come to mind? Acknowledging your mattress use is the first step to freedom. Ask God to show you what or who you turn to other than him first. Talk to him about your use of mattresses. Is there a hurt that needs healing or a lie you need to replace with God's truth? Confess all sinful patterns you've used to deal with your problems ineffectively. Ask God to help you burn old mattresses. Commit to seeking God first when the next PEA rolls into your life. Thank God for being the answer to all your problems.

Day 2: Learning to PIP

The Princess probably had no warning about the bad weather she encountered. Like problems, storms can appear suddenly, as if from nowhere. In Minnesota, travel often becomes questionable during the winter months, so we take blizzard warnings seriously. But it wasn't the weather that threatened to capsize our Christmas celebration with extended family in 1991. It was a cold—the "runny nose, low-grade fever, hacking cough" sort. The kind children trade back and forth all winter. Our one-year-old son, Jordan, acquired his days before Christmas, but we went ahead with our plans.

My husband and I packed our vehicle to the brim with baby gizmos and set off for his parents' home. We arrived early Friday evening in Beardsley, MN, population three hundred. Despite Jordan's sniffles, he demonstrated his talents of "so big" and "patty-cake," his toothy grin capturing everyone's hearts.

That night, Jordan slept in a playpen next to us in an upstairs bedroom. I layered him with blankets; the creaky house was as frigid as an icebox. During the night, he woke crying and burning with fever. I popped a chewable Tylenol into his mouth and crawled back into bed. He continued to cry. On my way to the bathroom, I scooped him out of his playpen and carried him with me. In the hallway, he went limp in my arms. His eyes rolled back in his head, then he stiffened and convulsed.

"Dial 9-1-1!" I screamed, waking everyone up, then my mother-in-law called for an ambulance.

We arrived at the nearest hospital an hour later. Between prayers, I imagined what might have caused his seizure. Guilt fabricated many scenarios. Maybe he had choked on the Tylenol. Had I given him only one tablet? I couldn't be sure because I'd been half asleep. Had his cold been worse than I thought? Maybe I should have taken him to the doctor before we left home. As his mother—it must be my fault.

I'm not sure when Jordan's seizures stopped, but by sunrise, he seemed almost back to normal. His eyes were puffy and red, but his weak smile delivered hope. Unable to find the cause, the doctor referred us to a hospital in Fargo, ND, where Jordan endured more tests, including a spinal tap. Seeing the long needle inserted into his spine hurt me as well.

By late afternoon Saturday, all test results proved negative, and a doctor discharged him. We were free to leave, yet I felt far from free. It would take much longer to recover from almost losing a child. We later learned that the extreme change in temperature from having a fever and being brought out from under warm blankets into the cold had probably caused his seizures.

We celebrated Christmas the next day, thankful in new ways. Jordan shuffled when he walked, his body stiff and sore, and he didn't object when we helped him open his presents. Our gift was the prognosis of his full recovery.

The next week, my New Year's resolution was to PIP—put my Problems In Perspective. No longer would I give significance to life's little irritants. In light of what we'd gone through, what else would ever compare? It's a lesson every princess should learn, but you don't have to lose or almost lose a loved one to master it. I'm confident you can imagine what such a loss might feel like and would agree that little else matters in comparison.

Assessing a problem's severity allows us to shuck all those PEAs (problems evoking anxiety) and gain perspective. It's the first word in another PEA acronym that will help us effectively deal with our problems. That's right, squash a PEA with a different PEA: Perspective, Expectation, and Attitude.

One definition of perspective is "to view things in their true relation or relative importance."[1] Most things in life are relative by comparison. By comparing our problem with a worse situation, we put our problem in perspective. We PIP! For example, a child spilling her milk will seem trivial when compared to her getting seriously hurt or sick. Remembering how much we love a person will help us more accurately assess situations.

Putting our problems in perspective isn't a ploy to sweep them under the rug (or mattress). Princesses should address their problems, but some shouldn't be seen as significant. Life may not be a bowl of cherries, but neither should it be a bowl of spilled PEAs we're constantly dancing around. Sometimes we have to step on a few!

When I dropped a full cardboard container of oatmeal one morning, it splattered into places I knew I'd be discovering for months to come. My husband unknowingly helped me PIP by offering to buy more oatmeal. I had complained about having just opened a new container, so he assumed I was upset over the loss and cost of wasted food. However, my grumbling and anxiety continued.

When I pursued my true feelings, I realized the additional cost wasn't the real problem; it was the time needed to clean the mess. I needed to put time in perspective. So, I timed myself as I swept the oatmeal and discovered my *big* problem stole two minutes from my nine-hundred-and-sixty waking minutes. How upset should I have been?

If I constantly spilled things, I might fear something was wrong with me. Putting time or money into perspective wouldn't help. We must discover our anxiety's underlying cause, and who better to ask than the Holy Spirit? God wants to speak truth into our lives so problems lose their power over us.

Not all problems can be solved by simply putting them in perspective. We may face devastating situations where the outcome could be impossible to imagine. These PEAs (problems) are monumental. We use these events to put all other problems in perspective: loss of life, divorce, cancer, etc. These PEAs bring us to our knees—in prayer.

The Apostle Paul was no stranger to prayer-inducing problems. His adversaries imprisoned, flogged, and repeatedly threatened his life. Five times he received thirty-nine lashes when forty was the highest number given before causing death. Three times he was beaten with rods, once stoned, three times shipwrecked, and many times went without water, food, and clothing (see 2 Corinthians 11:23–28).

Compared to Paul's problems, most of our problems seem ridiculously insignificant. Yet Paul labeled them as "light and momentary troubles" which serve a higher purpose of "achieving for us an eternal glory that far outweighs them all" (see 2 Corinthians 4:17). Besides viewing his problems in relation to their true importance, Paul viewed them from an eternal perspective.

Perspective is also defined as "the aspect in which a subject or its parts are mentally viewed."[2] A heavenly perspective changes how we see things. It's what we use to help us delay gratification to obtain greater rewards. By using it, we see God's bigger picture. Paul told us how to obtain a heavenly perspective. He said, "So we fix our eyes not on what is seen, but on what is unseen, since what is seen is temporary, but what is unseen is eternal" (2 Corinthians 4:18).

We fix our eyes on the unseen in the same way we fix our eyes on Jesus. We choose to focus on God's kingdom and believe this unseen dimension exists. As we position our hearts and minds on the spirit realm, it will become as real to us as the natural. As spiritual beings, we are filled with the Holy Spirit and seated in heavenly places in Christ. We should expect to experience God's supernatural ways. If we aren't, we can pray as Paul did for the Ephesians that the eyes of their hearts would be enlightened (see Ephesians 1:18).

The prophet Elisha prayed a similar prayer for his servant when their enemy surrounded them. For several months, God had been giving Elisha the Arameans' battle plans, which he then passed along to Israel's army. Tired of losing in battle, the king of Aram dispatched an army to kill Elisha. Here's what happened next:

> When the servant of the man of God got up and went out early the next morning, an army with horses and chariots had surrounded the city. "Oh no, my lord! What shall we do?" the servant asked. "Don't be afraid," the prophet answered. "Those who are with us are more than those who are with them." And Elisha prayed, "Open his eyes, Lord, so that he may see." Then the Lord opened the servant's eyes, and he looked and saw the hills full of horses and chariots of fire all around Elisha. (2 Kings 6:15–17)

Many people believe in God and that heaven is real, but how many believe the unseen spirit realm interfaces with their lives daily? It takes a heavenly perspective to recognize many battles are spiritual and hold eternal consequences. Ephesians 6:12 says, "For our struggle is not against flesh and blood, but against the rulers, against the authorities, against the powers of this dark world and against the spiritual forces of evil in the heavenly realms."

We achieve victory over problems by gaining God's perspective from reading the Bible and listening to his voice. We can't effectively wage war until we know how God sees things. Plus, we fight from a place of victory, Christ's victory, because on the cross he declared everything "finished!" As co-heirs with Christ (see Romans 8:17), we battle to obtain what is rightfully ours.

Like the pea under the princess' mattress, our PEAs (problems evoking anxiety) provide opportunities to prove our authenticity as God's children. They test us, teach us warfare, and show the enemy what we're made of. But they won't cause us to lose sleep when we learn to apply Philippians 4:6, which states, "Do not be anxious about anything, but in everything, by prayer and petition, with thanksgiving, present your requests to God." When you do, "the peace of God, which transcends all understanding, will guard your hearts and your minds in Christ Jesus" (verse 7).

A storm forced the Princess to seek shelter, and our storms should cause us to seek refuge in God. He will bring something good from our situation just like when the Princess met the Prince.

Yada Time

Did a specific PEA come to mind while reading this? If so, tell God about it. Ask him to open your spiritual eyes, to help you see your situation from his perspective. Listen to what he would have you know about it. Can you remember a time when putting your problem in perspective would have helped? Think of a situation when you will try to PIP. With what event will you compare your minor problems? I often tell myself, "The world isn't ending" or "No one has died."

Day 3: God's Perspective

From the Queen's perspective, any future daughter-in-law would need a prestigious pedigree to be welcomed into the family. Even today, social and economic factors create barriers between people. Whether you live in a country that operates as a monarchy, democracy, or other socio-economic structure, hierarchies exist. They range from a rigid caste system in India to a more fluid class system in the United States.

From God's perspective, we're all as valuable as the next person. He sees and loves us equally, and he wants us to love, accept, and value others as he does. We'll live happier lives when we view people as seen through God's eyes. Though my next story demonstrates this, it is an area I continually work on.

One blustery morning, like the day the Princess arrived at the Prince's castle, I woke to a howling wind. Remembering it was garbage day, I cringed at the thought of hunting down our garbage container after work again. Who could guess in which neighbor's yard it would end up, or in which block—if it remained in our development? Wanting to avoid the hassle, I suggested to my husband that the garbage bags be put on the curb without the container. He wasn't concerned, so I drove away eyeing the container from my rear-view window convinced I'd seen it for the last time.

When I arrived home, my suspicion was confirmed. In the past, I would have been the first to draw my husband's attention to the missing garbage can, but God was teaching me to see and value others from his perspective. Wrestling with the situation, I sensed God ask, "Isn't Chuck more valuable than a garbage container?"

God often asks rhetorical questions when we've missed the obvious answers. "Okay," I told God, "if we have to buy a new garbage container, so be it. You're right. Chuck is worth more than an old garbage can."

When Chuck came home, I prayed hard that I wouldn't mention the missing container, and two things happened. First, a miracle occurred and I kept my mouth shut, and second, Chuck drove around and found our garbage can. More important, I hadn't said something hurtful to the man I love. I still find it hard to keep my mouth shut, but I try—especially if nothing I say will change the situation. I remind myself that people are more valuable than whatever is upsetting me.

Obviously, people are more important than inanimate objects, so why do we struggle to value people as we should? Jesus said, "A new command I give you: Love one another. As I have loved you, so you must love one another" (John 13:34). Jesus loves us so much he died for us. That's his perspective—we're worth dying for. He commands us to love others as he does. This seems more difficult than "do unto others" and "love our neighbors as ourselves." More than nice sayings, these mantras are words to live—and die by.

Our transformation requires that we die to ourselves so we can love and serve others, which isn't easy considering PEA-ple, including us, can be selfish, self-centered, self-righteous, and easily offended. God took our disagreeable temperaments into account and determined interaction with each other would create opportunities to put our flesh to death, figuratively speaking. Proverbs 27:17 says, "As iron sharpens iron, so one man sharpens another." Unsharpened iron remains dull, jagged, and useless. We become better suited for God's kingdom work when we've been sharpened, but God doesn't wait until then before using us. His plan includes our bumping into each other to knock off our rough edges while serving him.

Like the Princess' pea, we irritate one another well enough to test and prove our authenticity as God's children. But unlike the Princess, we pass our test by loving even those who persecute us. We view problematic people as opportunities for *our* transformation, trusting God is working in them too. If we don't embrace this perspective, we may purposely avoid the people God puts in our lives to sharpen us. We may dream about working alone or living in a quiet cabin in the woods far away from people, but that's not God's plan. He wants us to interact with others to make the world a better place and bring his kingdom to earth.

Too often my gaze wanders from God's big picture and gets stuck on little old me. It's hard to focus on anything else when I'm looking too closely at myself. I become nearsighted. Like looking at my nose without using a mirror, I go cross-eyed. If only that would literally happen so I knew when to refocus. To fix my crossed eyes, I must transfer my gaze from myself onto *the cross* where I see God's extravagant love for mankind.

Like other PEAs (problems evoking anxiety), God orchestrates interaction with people to test us, to teach us warfare, and to draw us closer to him. People aren't our enemy. The only flesh and blood God wants us wrestling against is our self-centered tendency that keeps us from loving others well. Because God commands us to love as Jesus does, we can trust God to give us the grace to love even the most difficult people. Second Corinthians 9:8 says, "And God is able to make all grace abound to you, so that always having all sufficiency in everything, you may have an abundance for every good deed" (NASB). Loving others well falls into the good-works category. When we see others through God's eyes and sense his heart toward them, our perspective toward others will miraculously change.

Yet it's difficult to gain God's perspective if we have an inaccurate view of God. Pause a moment to reflect on your perspective of God.

- Who is God to you?
- What is he like?
- How do you feel about him?
- How do you think he feels about you?

If you struggle to love yourself or others as he does, maybe you don't believe wholeheartedly that God is love. Logically, you may know that God is loving, faithful, merciful, etc., but until you're faced with a new PEA, you may be unaware of any inconsistency between your head and your heart.

Think about a stressful situation or problem you recently faced. When that PEA kept you up in the night, did you believe that God knew about it? Was your first thought to bring it to him? If not, why? Do you believe that he cares about you and your problems? Or do you feel insignificant to him?

Our perspective of God is at best incomplete and at worst inaccurate. From inferior earthly relationships, we've developed misconceptions about God's true nature and character. If a parent was absent, angry, or indifferent, we might subconsciously perceive God as distant, harsh, or uncaring. Other authority figures and relationships also contribute to our perception of God. We build perspective from experience.

God knows everything that has happened to us, and he wants to remove the lies and pain inflicted through fallen relationships. Emotional or inner healing frees us to know God in truth. Renewing our minds by reading Scripture will highlight any wrong views we have of God. With the Holy Spirit's help, you can recognize and displace wrong beliefs. This is an ongoing process, but it can be as simple as paying attention to God's promptings and dealing with negative thoughts and emotions.

Paul prayed that God would give the church in Ephesus "the Spirit of wisdom and revelation" so that they would know God better (see Ephesians 1:17). This can be our prayer too. God wants us to know him truly; therefore, he allows PEAs to roll into our lives so we will seek him. He promises to be found, and when he is, he reveals new aspects of himself to us. This has been his mode of operation throughout history.

In the Old Testament, when a person experienced God in a new way, they would often call him by a new name. When God provided a ram for Abraham to sacrifice in place of Isaac, Abraham called God Jehovah-Jireh, meaning the Lord will provide (see Genesis 22:14). When God defeated the Amalekites, the Israelites called God Jehovah-Nissi, meaning the Lord is my banner (see Exodus 17:15). Jehovah-Shalom means the Lord is peace (see Judges 6:24). Experiencing God in new ways through problems can be a part of your life's journey too.

While putting myself through college, I worked part-time and received financial aid, but it was seldom enough. I needed extra for the basics. With God's help, I always had enough. Several times I received scholarships; some I didn't remember having applied for. The money came from surprising sources. Through my financial trials, I came to know God as my provider, which enables me to trust him in this area today.

Hindsight provides the clearest perspective of God. But to get there, we have to overcome some PEAs. Afterward, we can look back and remember how we came to know God better. Because God never changes, we can expect him to help us again. Eventually, we'll have experienced God in so many ways we'll affectionately call him our All in All.

Yada Time

Which past relationships most influenced your perspective of God? Explore both negative and positive examples. Thank God for the people who positively displayed his character and forgive those whose actions contributed to distorting your perspective of God. Ask the Holy Spirit to heal any hurts hindering you from seeing God as he truly is.

Meditate on the characteristics of God that you've experienced. What new name would you like to know him by?

Day 4: Expectations

When the Princess went to bed that evening, I imagine she expected to sleep well after her traumatic tussle with a storm. She might have perceived the stacked-high mattresses as her royal welcome, not expecting them to be harboring a pea—to test her authenticity, no less. By morning, the painful pea had left her black and blue. Showing her bruises to the Queen at breakfast, the Princess complained she hadn't slept all night. The Queen, not expecting the maiden to be a true princess, changed her perspective of her.

As perspective relates to sight, expectation—the second letter in our acronym—relates to our belief system. Expectations can cause problems when they are unmet, unspoken, or unrealistic. We all have them because everyone believes something, and some things we believe more emphatically than others. We expect people (family, friends, strangers) to act a certain way, places (home, church, work) to remain a certain way, and things (cars, houses, computers) to operate a certain way. With so many everyday expectations, we rarely acknowledge them. Yet, we notice when one goes unmet.

When Jordan was six, I took him to the movie *Harriet the Spy*. Jesse, only three at the time, went with Chuck for ice cream. When Jordan heard that Jesse got ice cream, he was upset I hadn't given him that option. The next day while Jordan played with friends, Chuck took Jesse with him to a tire store. On their way home they stopped for ice cream. A few days later, when Jordan learned that Jesse was with Chuck again, he broke into tears. "It's not right," he sobbed. "The Bible says the oldest should get everything, and Jesse's getting all the ice cream." He'd been learning in school about the biblical brothers Jacob and Esau. Because Jordan was the oldest, he expected to receive birthright privileges.

Although Jordan's expectation was unrealistic, it went unmet because he hadn't expressed it. When he did, we made sure that he got ice cream too. Many expectations go unmet because we never speak them. We assume that others know and share similar expectations. We label these as common sense, common knowledge, or common courtesy, inferring everyone should think and behave as we do. Because we believe this, we seldom state our expectations. Why bother, when everyone already knows them?

When we realize someone doesn't believe or behave as expected, a PEA (problem) pops up. If the annoyances are small, such as a person smacking her gum, shuffling her feet, or driving more slowly than the speed limit while in the fast lane, we call them pet peeves. But who needs peeves as pets? I like to think of small unmet expectations as *pest peas*. These annoyances may seem insignificant, but, over time, several pest peas in a relationship can create a kettle of split pea soup. We must treat them like real problems and address them, not always with others, but at least with God.

Our spouses, children, and friends can't read our minds nor can we read theirs. In healthy relationships, people express their expectations in loving ways. This doesn't mean we point out each other's flaws. We must allow others to be themselves, idiosyncrasies and all, but we can't *expect* another person's behavior to change if we don't say something. Communication and compromise are crucial to living happily with others.

There's an adage that when a man and a woman marry, the husband expects his wife never to change, and the wife expects to change her husband. I hadn't heard that saying before I married the first time, but I had expected to change him. Going into my second marriage, I knew better, at least regarding my ability to change anyone. The only person we can change is ourselves, but our change can often be the catalyst that helps another person change.

In the eleven weeks that Chuck and I dated before marrying, we never had a fight. I later heard that couples shouldn't marry before having a fight, and I learned why. Though knowing this wouldn't have stopped me from marrying him, the first year was extremely difficult. Chuck wouldn't fight, he'd withdraw. Little got resolved when we couldn't discuss our problems.

My first husband and I argued too much. Going into my second marriage, I expected that Chuck and I would argue a little. When he wouldn't, I pressed him harder, causing him to withdraw for entire weekends. From his perspective, fighting would cause a marriage to fail. It was like chopping down a tree, each disagreement taking an irretrievable chunk out of the relationship until it toppled.

Because I couldn't change him and I disliked the consequences of his withdrawing, I changed. I learned to bring my hurt, complaints, and frustrations to God. Instead of pushing Chuck away by prodding him to talk, I went to my bedroom and poured my heart out to God. It wasn't until I consistently did something different that our destructive cycle broke, which enabled Chuck to change. Twenty-five years later, with much inner healing received by both, he no longer fears that arguments will topple our marriage.

Expecting never to argue with your spouse is unrealistic. It is also unrealistic to ask your five-year-old child to fold towels while she's watching television. It's not only unrealistic but unfair. Her brain isn't developed enough to do two tasks at the same time. It's somewhat like asking your husband to listen to you while he's watching sports. You expect him to focus on you, and he expects you not to talk to him until there's a commercial.

Having unrealistic expectations causes problems, but assessing if they are realistic can be difficult to do yourself. Expectations are what you believe, so why would you think any differently? You wouldn't without objectivity, which a friend can offer, or better yet the Holy Spirit. Seek God's truth regarding your situation. Expectations are neither right nor wrong; they are realistic or unrealistic based on the people and circumstances involved.

Begin by stating your expectation in specific terms. For example, if you expect your parents to be involved in your children's lives, identify in what ways and how often. Be specific: you expect them to attend your child's sporting events four times each season. You communicate this to your parents, but they rarely show up. Is this too much to ask? You'll probably defend your stance, telling God or a friend that other grandparents attend their grandchildren's events. Remember, your expectations are neither right nor wrong. Your objective is to determine whether they are realistic.

Also, don't choose a friend who you know will agree with you; she will likely fuel your frustration. You want someone who can be objective, offer godly counsel, and help you gain God's perspective. If possible, ask the Holy Spirit yourself. Staying with the previous example, God may show you all the other ways your parents interact with your child, giving you a fresh perspective. Or God may remind you of how it hurt as a child when your parents didn't attend *your* sporting events. Healing past wounds can release the unrealistic expectations we have of others.

Expectations, like PEAs, must be dealt with. First, by assessing whether they are realistic, and second, by communicating those that are. Despite our diligence, some people may be incapable of meeting our expectations. We all have issues. Our goal then becomes to find peace amid an unmet expectation. To accomplish this, we must rely on God to see from someone else's perspective and gain understanding.

We don't know what others have gone through or what they deal with daily. Even if we try to walk in someone else's shoes, our feet aren't the same. When I went to college, my parents had four children still living at home. My teenage sister was struggling in school, my only brother had come home a different person after a summer at Army boot camp, and my two youngest sisters were nine and six. At nineteen, I hadn't experienced parental demands and responsibilities yet. Expecting frequent visits from my parents while I lived three hundred miles away was unrealistic.

The many variables involved can make it seem burdensome to address our expectations. But if we learn to bring our expectations to the Lord, we'll gain insight, direction, healing, and peace even if they remain unmet. In Psalm 5:3, David wrote, "In the morning, Lord, you hear my voice; in the morning I lay my requests before you and wait expectantly."

The Bible tells us what we can expect from God. We can expect peace that surpasses all understanding, forgiveness from sin, unconditional love and favor, power to do greater works, the fullness of joy, a way of escape when tempted, and much more.

God expects us to expect great things from him. He calls us to live by faith, meaning that he expects us to believe and trust him to fulfill his word and make good on his promises. When our perspective of him (the ways he reveals himself to us) becomes clearer, then we'll expect (believe) more from him.

Yada Time

Think about a current unmet expectation you have. Is it realistic? Have you told the person your expectation? Discuss the situation with God and ask his insight in how to proceed so you can gain understanding and peace.

In what area would you like to increase your expectations of God?

Day 5: I'd Rather be Queen

Wedding bells chimed by the story's end, but we don't know if any turbulence occurred between the Princess and Queen while planning the royal affair. It would be surprising if the wedding went off without a hitch. Even happy events produce stress and complications, making them memorable in unique ways.

Many years ago, some friends invited my husband and me to attend the dedication ceremony of their five-year-old daughter, Mia. Instead of baptizing infants, their church dedicated children to God at various ages. On this joyful occasion, several parents stood beside their young children on the stage, struggling to keep them reigned in while awaiting their turn. Mia swayed in her frilly pink dress next to her parents.

After her dedication, the pastor declared that she was now a princess, the daughter of the King of kings. As they walked back to their pew, her mother affectionately called her princess. Mia placed both hands on her hips and, with the sass of a teenager, announced, "I'd rather be a queen." This young girl had a big attitude, and her confidence serves her well as she pursues her dream of becoming a singer/songwriter.

Chuck Swindoll gave proper perspective to attitude when he said, "Life is ten percent what happens to us and ninety percent how we react to it. Our attitude is everything."[3]

Like how perspective is linked to how we see things and expectation is connected to our belief system, attitude is allied with our emotions and influenced by perspective and expectation. It's the last word in our PEA acronym, and it often seems the most powerful and hardest to manage. We may not always *feel* like acting, believing, or seeing life the way we should, making our attitude problematic at times.

We label unfavorable attitudes as negative, wrong, or bad. We easily recognize them in others but frequently fail to see them in ourselves. Conversely, we expect others to display a proper, positive, or good attitude. Life would be so much more enjoyable if everyone possessed an attitude like the one displayed by this woman:

Noticing that she had only three hairs left on her head one morning, she declared, "What a perfect day to wear my hair braided." And her day was perfect. The next morning, seeing only two strands of hair when looking into the mirror, she said, "Won't my hair look lovely parted down the middle." And she enjoyed a lovely day. The third day, when only one strand of hair remained, she exclaimed, "I've always wanted to wear my hair in a ponytail." And her day was filled with childlike wonder. On the fourth day, all her hair was gone. "Yay!" she squealed. "No more decisions about how to fix my hair!"[4]

Sometimes it doesn't feel like we have a choice regarding our attitude, but we do. God gave us free will. When we ask for help, God will provide the strength and insight needed to choose a biblical attitude. The Apostle Paul described that attitude:

Have this attitude in yourselves which was also in Christ Jesus, who, although He existed in the form of God, did not regard equality with God a thing to be grasped, but emptied Himself, taking the form of a bond-servant, and being made in the likeness of men. Being found in appearance as a man, He humbled Himself by becoming obedient to the point of death, even death on a cross. (Philippians 2:5–8, NASB)

Whether you're genuinely seeking to become more like Jesus or desiring to live happily ever after, both require embracing a humble attitude. We discussed becoming a servant in Cinderella's chapter and submitting to others in Little Red Hen's. Humility plays a role in our ability to serve and submit. When we won't do either, our attitude becomes a problem, such as my rebellious attitude toward becoming a financial planner.

Jonah displayed a similar attitude when God told him to go to Nineveh. He was so against obeying God he boarded a ship and set off in the opposite direction. When a storm came, Jonah told his fellow sailors to throw him overboard because he had caused the storm. After they had tossed him overboard, a gigantic fish swallowed him. At least I only received a written reprimand for my rebellion.

Finding myself in the belly of a whale, tangled in seaweed and my nostrils burning from the stench of decaying fish, would quickly change my attitude. Or would it? I'm not convinced that Jonah's attitude improved. After three days, the fish spit Jonah onto dry ground—possibly from the sour taste in his mouth.

Jonah eventually delivered God's message. But it doesn't seem like his big-fish experience fixed his poor attitude. While witnessing God's mercy, Jonah's stinky attitude resurfaced, and he became angry.

> He prayed to the Lord, "Isn't this what I said, Lord, when I was still at home? That is what I tried to forestall by fleeing to Tarshish. I knew that you are a gracious and compassionate God, slow to anger and abounding in love, a God who relents from sending calamity. Now, Lord, take away my life, for it is better for me to die than to live." (Jonah 4:2–3)

Seriously, Jonah? You'd rather be dead than fulfill your God-given purpose? I'm learning not to judge lest God provide a similar situation to help me see from someone else's perspective. I prefer to eat fish rather than be swallowed by one. In Jonah's defense, being a prophet may have seemed like a pointless job. Why should he proclaim God's wrath when he knew the people would repent and God wouldn't have to make good on his threat?

Our multitasking God didn't send Jonah to Nineveh solely for Nineveh's benefit. God sent Jonah for Jonah's benefit also because he needed an attitude adjustment. After Jonah's rant, God asked him, "Is it right for you to be angry?" (Jonah 4:4).

Jonah didn't answer, but he stuck around. Maybe he hoped God would change his mind and destroy the Ninevites after all. He hadn't yet learned what God wanted him to learn. The story continues:

> Then the Lord God provided a leafy plant and made it grow up over Jonah to give shade for his head to ease his discomfort, and Jonah was very happy about the plant. But at dawn the next day God provided a worm, which chewed the plant so that it withered. When the sun rose, God provided a scorching east wind, and the sun blazed on Jonah's head so that he grew faint. He wanted to die, and said, "It would be better for me to die than to live." (Jonah 4:6–8)

Again, Jonah declared he'd rather be dead than alive. When God asked if he had a right to be angry about the withered vine, Jonah said he did, repeating that he was "angry enough to die" (verse 9). Jonah was having a bad week, possibly a bad life. God wanted to bring truth to Jonah and help him gain a better attitude, a humbler attitude.

"But the Lord said, 'You have been concerned about this plant, though you did not ... make it grow. .... And should I not have concern for the great city of Nineveh, in which there are more than a hundred and twenty thousand people ...?'" (Jonah 4:10-11).

The story ends there. We don't know if Jonah ever understood God's heart, his loving and forgiving nature toward all people. God loves everyone, and so should we. Instead of viewing another person as the problem, we should ask God if the problem lies within us. Like Jonah, God may try to help us better understand how much he loves people. Or he may point out an area in which we need to change.

An attitude reveals what's going on in us at our core level. Some might call it our disposition. It is how we feel and act toward someone or something. Because external circumstances can disrupt our inner equilibrium, having an occasional poor attitude is likely. Thankfully, we can learn to displace the attitude we don't want with one that's humble, happy, hopeful, grateful, confident, etc.

Because our perspective and expectations influence our attitude, we should first assess how well we're doing in those areas. If we want an optimistic attitude, we should focus on God's promises, expecting to receive them. Comparing ourselves to the creator of the universe should put us in proper perspective and produce humility in us. We can become grateful by reflecting on our blessings. Choosing the right focus will influence our attitude.

Yet, at times, we may struggle to see straight. When something devastating happens, our focus can blur and our expectations deplete. God doesn't expect us to act as if everything is sunshine and rainbows when it's not. He expects us to mourn a loss. Prolonged sorrow or hopelessness often disables our ability to choose a positive attitude. Sometimes we need someone to lead us to God's perspective and help us become expectant again.

After my divorce, I had to surrender my dream of a perfect family. Life seemed unfair. I sought Christian counseling for depression, needing someone with a compassionate ear to listen and impart God's truth and healing. It didn't take many visits with my counselor before God got through to me. Surprisingly, God agreed with my assessment of life being unfair. Then he pointed out that I had done nothing to deserve the grace, forgiveness, love, and salvation he'd given. With this change in perspective, my attitude shifted. I could then focus on my blessings and expect that things would soon change.

Every day we choose our attitude, but we don't have to choose it by ourselves. We can ask God to help, and we can seek help from others when needing objectivity, a fresh perspective, or refocusing. By learning to PIP and assessing your perspective and expectations, you'll acquire an attitude acceptable to you and to God.

Yada Time

How would you describe your attitude most days? If you could receive an attitude upgrade, in what area would you want it adjusted? What steps might you take to achieve this?

Many of us struggle with humility. What things contribute to pride sneaking into your attitude? What helps you recognize it when it does?

Chapter 6
The Princess and the Pea—
Perspective, Expectation, and Attitude
Questions for Reflection or Discussion

Day 1: Princess Problems

1. How do the Scriptures provide hope? (see Romans 15:4, p. 97)

2. List at least three reasons God allows problems to exist. (p. 97)

3. Do you have a mattress preference? Share if you want to.

4. Why is using a mattress not helpful? (p. 98)

5. What should a true princess do when facing a problem? (p. 98)

Day 2: Learning to PIP

1. What does it mean to PIP? (p. 99) Share an example.

2. What causes problems to lose their power over us? (p. 100)

3. From what perspective did Paul view his problems? (p. 100–101)

4. How can we obtain the same perspective? (p. 101)

5. Explain what it means to battle from a place of victory. (p. 101)

Day 3: God's Perspective

1. Why do we struggle to value people as much as God says we should? (p. 103)

2. How can we love others as Jesus does? (p. 103)

3. Without naming the person, tell about a time God used someone to knock off some of your rough edges.

4. Discuss in what ways you have a healthy perspective of God.

5. In what area would you like to improve your perspective of him?

6. What new name would you like to know God by more personally?

Day 4: Expectations

1. When can expectations cause problems? (p. 105)

2. Why don't we always express our expectations? (p. 106)

3. Why is it difficult to assess whether an expectation is realistic? (p. 107)

4. Share if you've ever changed your behavior and it helped someone else change.

5. Tell about assessing or expressing an expectation this week and how it worked out.

6. How do we find peace with unmet expectations? (p. 107)

Day 5: I'd Rather be Queen

1. Which is the most difficult for you: perspective, expectation, or attitude?

2. What does a biblical attitude look like according to Philippians 2:5–8? (p. 109)

3. Why might God have specifically chosen Jonah to prophesy to Nineveh? (p. 110)

4. Instead of viewing another person as the problem, what should we ask God? (p. 110)

5. If you could receive an attitude upgrade, in what way would you want it adjusted?

Share prayer requests and pray for each other. Let's gain God's perspective of our problems.

Chapter 7
Chicken Little—Discernment and Maturity

Memory Verse:

But solid food is for the mature, who by constant use
have trained themselves to distinguish good from evil.
Hebrews 5:14

Day 1: The Sky is Falling

If a person drops a penny from the top of the Empire State Building and it hits someone standing below, will it kill the person it hits? Can a penny accelerate to a lethal velocity? Some people mistakenly believe it can, but a penny isn't heavy enough to kill anyone at any speed. A clunk on the head from an assumed object, however, can be deadly if you're Chicken Little. That's what happened while she was out for a walk one day. It wasn't the hit on her head that caused her demise; it was a wrong assumption and her lack of discernment. Looking upward and seeing only blue sky overhead, she shouted, "The sky is falling! The sky is falling!"

Chicken Little reasoned that something this ominous needed the king's immediate attention, so she raced off to tell him. Here's where I imagine the author named the main character Chicken Little versus a masculine name such as Big Rooster. To make the story believable, the author needed a female lead—because everyone knows that males rarely stop to ask directions. Not knowing the way to the king's palace, Chicken Little stopped the first animal she met, Henny Penny, and asked, "Could you please show me the way to the king's palace?"

Henny Penny didn't know where the king lived either, but after hearing Chicken Little describe the imminent danger, she joined the urgent expedition to warn the king. The next three animals they encountered, Ducky Lucky, Goosey Loosey, and Turkey Lurkey, also had no idea where the king lived. Yet without questioning Chicken Little's story, they naively joined her crusade.

The group then crossed paths with Foxy Loxy, and he assured them he knew the way to the king's palace. If only one of the fearful five had used discernment upon meeting Foxy Loxy their outcome might have been different. Trusting their self-appointed leader, the animals followed Foxy Loxy straight into his den. There they learned the new meaning of having guests for dinner.

Before addressing discernment's importance, let's discuss a more urgent matter: knowing the way to the King's palace. By this, I mean heaven or eternal life. "Jesus answered, 'I am the way and the truth and the life. No one comes to the Father except through me'" (John 14:6). Jesus is the only way to our Father, the King. As tempting as it may be to believe that God provides other options to gain entrance to heaven, the Bible states otherwise. There is but one way: Jesus. The world wants us to believe that many paths (religions) lead to God. This deceptive belief provides false hope with dire consequences. As Christians, we discount Jesus' sacrifice if we believe any way other than through him leads to salvation.

Years ago, I visited an elderly friend who held different spiritual beliefs than I did. I soon realized that she was as equally ambitious to convert me to her faith as I was to convert her to mine. After she told me that only 144,000 would be saved when Jesus returned and everyone else would come back to the earth for a second chance, I asked, "Then why did Jesus have to die? Doesn't it seem cruel that God sacrificed his only Son if so few would be saved or if we could eventually gain salvation by receiving another chance?" She admitted that she had wondered the same thing for years. Our time together was too brief before she died, but I was grateful to know that she believed Jesus is God's Son and that he died for her sins. This gave me hope I'll see her in heaven one day.

If you believe that Jesus is the only way, can you lead others to him? It's as simple as teaching someone the ABCs: **A**dmit you're a sinner and in need of a Savior; **B**elieve Jesus is God's Son and that he paid the penalty for your sins; **C**onfess Jesus as your Lord and Savior and **C**ommit your life to him. It's helpful to share with them the supporting Bible references found in Appendix A.

We should tell others about Jesus so they too can experience his love, joy, peace, etc. John 17:3 says, "Now this is eternal life: that they know you, the only true God, and Jesus Christ, whom you have sent." We find true happiness through a personal relationship with Jesus. Not only do we know the way to the King's palace, we also know the King intimately. So when we don't introduce others to him, we're withholding their greatest need.

The Apostle Paul boldly preached the good news of salvation through Jesus Christ wherever he went. Besides being an Old Testament scholar, Paul encountered Jesus and received revelations about salvation from the Holy Spirit. He could answer any skeptic's question, showing through Scripture as far back as Genesis that Jesus was the promised Messiah. Jesus' life, death, and resurrection fulfilled over three hundred Old Testament prophecies about him.[1]

Paul encountered persecution because he preached a message contrary to the religious leaders' beliefs. During his travels, he escaped those trying to kill him in Thessalonica and landed in Berea. "Now the Berean Jews were of more noble character than those in Thessalonica, for they received the message with great eagerness and examined the Scriptures every day to see if what Paul said was true. As a result, many of them believed, as did also a number of prominent Greek women and many Greek men" (Acts 17:11–12).

Christians refer to the Bible as God's love letter because it discloses God's extravagant love toward humanity through Jesus. The Bible provides valuable information and life lessons, so we also call it our instruction manual. With a Bereans' diligence and eagerness to examine Scripture, we can use the Bible as a resource to live happily ever after. Second Timothy 3:16–17 says, "All Scripture is God-breathed and is useful for teaching, rebuking, correcting and training in righteousness, so that the servant of God may be thoroughly equipped for every good work." To glean the instructions and treasures found in Scripture, we need the Holy Spirit's help, the Spirit of truth, who will guide us into all truth (see John 16:13).

The greatest deception of this age may be the distortion of the truth. We've been duped into believing that truth is subjective or relative and that absolute truth doesn't exist. By championing tolerance, our culture resembles the biblical era of the Judges: "In those days there was no king in Israel; every man did what was right in his own eyes" (Judges 17:6, NASB). This mindset has lulled the world into perversion, complacency, and ignorance. Political and social correctness dictate that we must accept others' behaviors, ideas, and values with no regard to truth. Are we acting lovingly if we don't share God's truth with those deceived?

The attack on truth shouldn't shock anyone because absolute truth is Jesus (see John 14:6). Is it surprising that many Christians lack discernment?

John MacArthur, senior pastor of Grace Community Church, defines discernment:

> In its simplest definition, discernment is nothing more than the ability to decide between truth and error, right and wrong. Discernment is the process of making careful distinctions in our thinking about truth. In other words, the ability to think with discernment is synonymous with an ability to think biblically.[2]

Discernment aids our efforts to live happier lives. Without it, we make wrong decisions with harmful consequences and possibly fall prey to the devil's schemes, such as Chicken Little and her friends did with Foxy Loxy.

In the letter to the Hebrews, the author scolded them for being immature and lacking discernment. They were "slow to learn" and needed a refresher on "the elementary truths of God's word." The author compared them to infants living on milk. "But solid food is for the mature, who by constant use have trained themselves to distinguish good from evil" (see Hebrews 5:11–14).

This last verse teaches us how to become more discerning. It is by constant use and training, which means we must practice to gain discernment. Rarely does anyone do anything well without first investing time and effort. We may find practice dull, draining, or difficult before we become proficient at something. Discernment requires commitment and persistence, which explains why many lack this skill. Add in the risk of making a mistake and fewer become motivated to practice. We will make mistakes—that's how we learn.

First Thessalonians 5:21 tells us to "Test them all; hold on to what is good." The words test, examine, prove, try, and judge are derived from the same Greek root word *dokimazo* and are used interchangeably in the New Testament.[3] We learn discernment by examining and testing what we see, hear, read, sense, and encounter.

When we examine something, we must check to see if it's congruent with God's truth. Therefore, we must first know the truth, as found in Scripture and interpreted by the Holy Spirit. Without knowing the truth, we have nothing by which to compare and recognize the false. A person learns to identify counterfeit dollar bills by studying and becoming familiar with the real ones.

Because Jesus is the truth, the more intimately we know him, the easier it will be to distinguish between good and evil, right and wrong, or the best choice among several good options.

The Apostle Paul wrote, "And this is my prayer: that your love may abound more and more in knowledge and depth of insight, so that you may be able to discern what is best and may be pure and blameless for the day of Christ" (Philippians 1:9–10). As our love for God grows through our knowledge (yada) of him, so will our ability to discern correctly, but we must still practice. By practicing discernment, we can then distinguish false fears and not run frantically like Chicken Little.

Yada Time

Pray Paul's prayer: Lord, I ask that my love "may abound more and more in knowledge and depth of insight, so that [I] may be able to discern what is best and may be pure and blameless for the day of Christ" (Philippians 1:9–10).

Practice discernment by testing if something aligns with Scripture. When making decisions, ask, "What would Jesus do?" Find the answer in the Bible, or better yet, ask Jesus.

Day 2: Cause and Effect

Like Chicken Little, I've made a wrong assumption before—several, actually. I often assume a cause-and-effect relationship exists when one doesn't. For example, I once thought a wall-mounted air freshener dispenser in the ladies' room at work was rigged to the toilet seat. I first noticed the new dispenser when it sprayed a fragrant mist into the air and startled me as I lifted my derriere off the seat. The second day, having forgotten about it, I jumped again as a burst of perfume shot into the air as I stood. If toilets could flush via motion detectors, why couldn't an air freshener operate similarly?

Determined not to be surprised again, the third day I rose ever so slowly—and nothing happened. No cause-and-effect relationship existed, to my chagrin. Thankfully, I hadn't discussed my theory with coworkers. The Lord used this to begin teaching me about faulty cause-and-effect thinking. We need to understand true cause-and-effect relationships, both in the natural and spiritual realms, when we are learning discernment.

Life experiences provide a mental database of cause-and-effect relationships from which we draw, such as sticking a bobby pin into a light socket will hurt. I only did that once. If we pay attention, we can also learn from others' experiences and avoid unpleasant situations.

When my boys were young, they took baths together. Jordan usually finished first and would jump out of the tub and run. He had only one speed, and he'd invariably slip on the water they'd splashed on the floor and hit his head. When Jesse wanted to get out, he stood in the tub as if the water had frozen him in place and cry until I rescued him. He learned many cause-and-effect relationships from watching his brother.

We draw from experience when making decisions or assessing new situations, but we don't always make accurate causations, such as when I assumed that a relationship existed between a fragrance dispenser and a toilet seat. We can also misapply information or make wrong associations regarding our spiritual lives. Experience alone can be an unreliable teacher. Therefore, God gave us a reliable teacher, the Holy Spirit, and a reliable database, the Bible.

In God's Word, we can read of numerous cause-and-effect relationships, many of which include if-then statements. For example, "If my people, who are called by my name, will humble themselves and pray and seek my face and turn from their wicked ways, then will I hear from heaven and will forgive their sin and will heal their land" (2 Chronicles 7:14). We refer to these biblical cause-and-effect verses as conditional promises. Acts 16:31 provides a New Testament example: "Believe in the Lord Jesus, and you will be saved." Salvation is free, but it won't take *effect* until a person believes.

When we understand biblical cause-and-effects, we can apply their principles or foundational truths and learn to live happier lives. We discussed the example of sowing and reaping in Little Red Hen's story. Matthew 6:33 is another: "But seek first his kingdom and his righteousness, and all these things will be given to you as well." Ignoring or living in opposition to God's principles contributes to an unhappy life. We find examples of sin's effect throughout Scripture.

Consider the story of the Israelites who escaped captivity and fled to Egypt. There they offered sacrifices to the Queen of Heaven. After the prophet Jeremiah told them it was wrong to do that, they said, "But ever since we stopped burning incense to the Queen of Heaven and pouring out drink offerings to her, we have had nothing and have been perishing by sword and famine" (Jeremiah 44:18).

One could almost laugh at their faulty cause-and-effect thinking. The Israelites weren't perishing because they had stopped worshiping the Queen of Heaven. Their troubles began when they worshiped her. They had disobeyed the first commandment: "You shall have no other gods before me" (Exodus 20:3). Jeremiah set them straight. "Because you have burned incense and have sinned against the Lord and have not obeyed him or followed his law or his decrees or his stipulations, this disaster has come upon you, as you now see" (Jeremiah 44:23).

Living under the New Covenant, we might assume the Old Testament cause-and-effects no longer apply to us. Jesus paid the penalty for our sins when we accepted him as our Lord, so we need not fear God's judgment. However, we will one day stand before God's throne and give an account for our words and actions (see Romans 14:10–12). The Bible also says, "For he who does wrong will receive the consequences of the wrong which he has done, and that without partiality" (Colossians 3:25, NASB). God tells us not to sin because sin has an irrefutable effect: it hurts us and others.

Both the New and Old Testaments provide many cause-and-effect relationships that teach us how to live godly lives. And a godly life is a happy life. This next verse is a cause-and-effect principle we've looked at before. "So I say, live by the Spirit, and you will not gratify the desires of the flesh" (Galatians 5:16). Living by the Spirit enables (causes) us *not* to gratify sinful desires (effect) and assists us in discerning right from wrong.

In Chapter 3, we learned how crucial a renewed mind is to effective spiritual warfare. A renewed mind is also necessary for discernment. Romans 12:2 says, "Do not conform to the pattern of this world, but be transformed by the renewing of your mind. Then you will be able to test and approve what God's will is—his good, pleasing and perfect will." To be transformed (effect), we must not conform to worldly patterns, and we must renew our minds. A renewed mind enables us to discern God's will.

There is no better place to be than in God's will. Knowing his will requires that we "test and approve" (discern) what his will is. This is discernment's ultimate purpose. If we want to live happily ever after, we must know and obey God's will. This requires that we renew our minds and practice using discernment.

Learning God's truths, promises, and principles found in the Bible will renew our minds, but it is only part of the equation. We also need the Holy Spirit to help us understand and apply them. God doesn't limit our learning mode to studying the Bible. He also teaches us through everyday experiences and interaction with him. He wants more than rule followers; he wants committed lovers who will give their lives to him. Jesus chastised the Pharisees, saying, "You study the Scriptures diligently because you think that in them you have eternal life. These are the very Scriptures that testify about me, yet you refuse to come to me to have life" (John 5:39–40).

Whether the Holy Spirit teaches us through Scripture or personal experience, he provides opportunities to practice what we're learning. His tests increase our ability to retain the truth. The tests themselves can be memorable, such as the one I received while attending a Christian conference years ago.

At one session, a speaker taught that God doesn't always get his way, which sounded blasphemous. He illustrated his point by telling a story about when God had tried to get his attention, but the speaker hadn't responded and something bad happened. God works through people, so when we aren't listening and making ourselves available to be his hands and feet, God doesn't get his way. The enemy gets his way when bad things happen. I hadn't accepted this as true yet, so God provided an opportunity to apply this teaching and confirm its validity.

The pop quiz came at lunch. While waiting to order a bratwurst from a street vendor, the thought came that the bratwurst would give me food poisoning. Thinking I was being paranoid, I dismissed the thought. Job 33:14 says, "For God does speak—now one way, now another—though no one perceives it." Sure enough, I got food poisoning. God had spoken, and I had ignored his warning, similar to the speaker's experience. When I flew home the next morning, I was still sick, which left a lasting impression on my friends too.

If only I had paused to discern if the thought originated from me, God, or the devil. Because I hadn't tested what I'd heard, I made a wrong assumption and believed the thought originated with me. We must test our thoughts to renew our minds and become proficient at discerning. As this story illustrates, we can't find all our answers in the Bible. Therefore, we need the Spirit's continual guidance.

Don't mistake intuition and conscience for the Holy Spirit. They can be useful, but they aren't the Holy Spirit. People say things such as "Follow your heart," or "Let your conscience be your guide." Although said with good intention, these phrases offer poor advice. Our hearts get wounded, and we can make unwise decisions based on hurt feelings. Hearts can also lead us astray, having carnal desires. Only when God speaks to your heart by giving you peace and assurance is following your heart good advice. When that happens, you've heard from God, so why not say "follow God" and give credit where it belongs.

God gave us a conscience to act as our moral compass. But when sin entered the world, our conscience also fell. Like us, our conscience needs to be renewed, which happens when we upgrade its database with God's standards as found in Scripture and from the Holy Spirit. As we become more discerning, our conscience becomes more reliable. The Holy Spirit uses our conscience to convict us of sin, causing us to feel guilty. Our enemy can also cause us to feel false guilt and condemnation. The Holy Spirit never condemns. Therefore, we must rely on the Holy Spirit and not our conscience to discern the truth.

The same goes for intuition. Some use the word interchangeably with guidance from the Holy Spirit, but it is not. One dictionary defines intuition as "a natural ability or power that makes it possible to know something without any proof or evidence: a feeling that guides a person to act a certain way without fully understanding why."[4] The problem is the word natural. God is *super*natural. We should confess he's the source of our knowing, when he is. If he isn't, we may have other spirits leading us that won't have our best interest in mind.

Our ability to discern correctly and judge good from evil isn't gained through using reasoning, intuition, or conscience but through a personal relationship with the Holy Spirit. He guides us into all truth, so learning to recognize his voice is crucial to everything, especially discernment. We must take the time to enlist God's help when making decisions or judgments. Learning true cause-and-effects and practicing discernment will help us live godly lives.

Yada Time

Continue to renew your mind by discerning where your thoughts originate. While reading the Bible, watch for true cause-and-effect relationships and implement their truths and teachings. Ask the Holy Spirit to show you an area in your life you need to align with God's Word or his will. Submit that area to God and turn to him for the power needed to change.

Day 3: Maturity

Without a map or GPS navigation system, Chicken Little and her friends wandered aimlessly while searching for the king's palace. We don't know how much time passed between her chance encounters, but traveling a long distance can become boring. Possibly they played games to entertain themselves. Instead of counting semi-trucks, they may have counted scarecrows. Or maybe they played Slug Bug, but instead of punching someone when they saw a Volkswagen, the bugs were literally slugs, and they ate them.

Children love to play games, especially at birthday parties. Few childhood pleasures compare to being the birthday girl or boy at a party with friends. Better yet was a slumber party. There, friends found refuge discussing the uncomfortable questions about puberty and other taboo topics. The game Truth or Dare created a forum to share personal and embarrassing moments. We used games to learn about life and each other. Unfortunately, the information we gleaned wasn't always reliable, as with Chicken Little's message.

If the "Little" in the chicken's name refers to her being young, we might find her silly assumption about the sky falling cute. Children say the funniest things. My son Jesse once asked my mom why her legs had cracks in them. He'd never seen varicose veins before. Children lack knowledge, experience, and rational thought processes. The rational part of a human's brain doesn't fully develop until we're twenty-five.[5] It's no wonder that children are naïve and believe whatever anyone tells them.

Though lacking discernment, children have other admirable attributes, such as being creative, resilient, forgiving, and eager to learn. They don't pretend to have all the answers, not until their teenage years anyhow. Jesus said we must become like little children, believing and trusting him, to enter his kingdom. "Truly I tell you, unless you change and become like little children, you will never enter the kingdom of heaven" (Matthew 18:3).

Children also display less than commendable behaviors, such as temper tantrums, irrational fears, and an inability to be reasoned with. It's far from adorable when adults emulate these childish behaviors, including when they believe everything they hear or read—especially from the internet—or when they take everything literally like children often do and forego using discernment.

When my nephew was young and shopping with his mom one day, the legs of his sweatpants hiked up to just below his knees. He looked goofy, so my sister told him to pull down his pants—and he did. He dropped them in the convenience store for all to see, exposing his Superman undies.

That may be an extreme example, but I don't think that God wants us to interpret every word in the Bible literally. I'm not saying how much of the Bible shouldn't be taken literally, but Jesus spoke in parables. He frequently used figures of speech or exaggerated statements (hyperbole) while teaching and never intended his audience to take his examples literally. Unless you think that a man *should* chop off his hand if it causes him to sin or gouge out his eye if he lusts after a woman (see Matthew 5:29–30). Many Scripture passages use symbolism, and it takes a diligent student to interpret the intent and meaning accurately.

Those who follow Jesus are his disciples. The word disciple in Greek means learner or pupil.[6] Although we're lifelong students, Hebrews 5:12 states we're to become teachers one day. This doesn't mean that we stop learning; it means that we understand and incorporate a truth into our lives well enough to pass it along. God's discipleship program includes mentoring relationships. We need people more mature than we are to speak God's truth into our lives. At some point, we're to do the same for others. This is how the body of Christ matures.

When you were a child, you probably gave little thought to your growing body's needs. Your parents may have taught you the importance of rest, exercise, and healthy food choices. They possibly gave you age-appropriate responsibilities and increased them as you matured. More than once they probably let you know when you weren't acting your age. You learned from them. You imitated their behavior and adopted their beliefs. God intends for us to mature in loving, mentoring relationships.

When a parent doesn't nurture a child as God intended, the emotional and spiritual maturation process gets stalled. Children become stunted as adults and suffer various problems. They might struggle to trust others and thereby try to control them. They might feel disconnected, depressed, and unable to express their needs. They might be self-centered or obsessed with finding pleasure, fulfillment, or purpose. Many problems occur when a child's emotional maturity process gets short-circuited.[7]

Immaturity can often cause problematic behaviors in adults, but it's never too late to grow up. As God intended, maturity happens through honest, loving relationships. If you lacked them as a child, God can provide loving relationships with others now. This is his intent for the body of Christ—to help one another mature. To learn about maturity indicators, I recommend the book *Living from the Heart Jesus Gave You* by James Wilder.

The Bible explains another route to spiritual maturity:

And He gave some as apostles, and some as prophets, and some as evangelists, and some as pastors and teachers, for the equipping of the saints for the work of service, to the building up of the body of Christ; until we all attain to the unity of the faith, and of the knowledge of the Son of God, to a mature man, to the measure of the stature which belongs to the fullness of Christ. (Ephesians 4:11–13, NASB)

God calls us to service, unity, maturity, and the fullness of Christ. To accomplish this, he's gifted his body with apostles, prophets, evangelists, pastors, and teachers. We refer to these five titles together as the fivefold ministry. Their role is to "prepare God's people for works of service." That doesn't make them more important than anyone else; they're merely the equipping team. It takes everyone doing their part to obtain unity and maturity in Christ's body.

The Greek word used here for "building up" is *oikodome*. It's derived from two root words: *doma*, meaning to build, and *oikos*, referring to "a dwelling (more or less extensive, literal or figurative); by implication a family."[8] God created us to be a family *and* his dwelling place. It is within this secure, loving structure that we attain unity, maturity, and the fullness of Christ. Amen! We become like him, resembling our Savior in character and in service.

> As a result, we are no longer to be children, tossed here and there by waves and carried about by every wind of doctrine, by the trickery of men, by craftiness in deceitful scheming; but *speaking the truth in love*, we are to grow up in all aspects into Him who is the head, even Christ, from whom the whole body, being fitted and held together by what every joint supplies, according to the proper working of each individual part, causes the growth of the body for the building up of itself in love. (Ephesians 4:14–16, NASB, emphasis added)

Truth in love is like Miracle-Gro for the body of Christ. It is the elixir that encourages growth. Without truth spoken in love, we remain immature. We are childish, jealous, easily offended, and seek to have our way. Truth spoken without love is difficult to receive. Immature people tend to state the truth in a condemning rather than loving way.

God doesn't call us to set everyone straight. He calls us to love. When I first learned about "speaking the truth in love," I thought it meant God wanted us to correct people compassionately. I imagined I'd make sure God wanted me to say something before correcting anyone. As usual, God provided a test to correct my misunderstanding when someone did something wrong to me, and I was hurt. I wrestled with God, but not as I'd thought I would. I wanted to correct the person who had offended me, but God wouldn't let me. He knew my motivation wasn't to be helpful or loving. If I couldn't speak the truth in love, I wasn't to speak at all.

This verse isn't as much about bringing correction as it is about bringing loving truth. Jesus said, "Do not judge, or you too will be judged. For in the same way you judge others, you will be judged, and with the measure you use, it will be measured to you" (Matthew 7:1–2). He followed these words with the example of someone having a plank in their eye yet wanting to take a speck of sawdust out of someone else's eye.

Many people quote Jesus' words about not judging to dismiss practicing discernment. In the previous verse, Jesus used the word *krino* for judge, meaning "to try, condemn, punish."[8] It is different from the word dokimazo, the judgment needed to discern.

We must judge to determine right from wrong, good from evil, but we must not *condemn* those who are not walking in truth. Judging others intending to condemn is not the same as discernment. Anyone can do that. Too frequently our minds make snap judgments about people. Discernment without love is judgment. It takes maturity to distinguish between the two.

God places people before us to help us grow or for us to help them grow. We nourish each other when we speak and hear the truth in love. As we mature in our faith, we will be less child-like and more Christ-like, demonstrating God's love and truth to the world.

Yada Time

In what ways has someone mentored you in the past? Are you mentoring anyone now? You don't have to establish mentoring relationships formally; they can happen as God places people in your life. We also mentor each other through friendships. If you want a specific mentor, ask God to provide someone to fill that role for you. Allow him to bring someone to mind and ask that person. They will likely consider it an honor. Pray about mentoring someone yourself, too.

Day 4: Ponderings and Prophecies

When something goes wrong, I try to learn from my mistakes. I question whether I could have done something differently, but I don't always find answers to my questions. Sometimes pondering possibilities is as far as I can get. Life holds many mysteries, and God rarely fills in all the blanks. When bad things happen, answers seem scarce. What do you do when a situation doesn't make sense?

Job's story reminds us that good people experience bad things through no fault of their own. "Then the Lord said to Satan, 'Have you considered my servant Job?" (Job 1:8). God gave Satan permission to wreak havoc in Job's life. He lost his children, his health, and all his wealth. His wife said, "Curse God and die!" (Job 2:9). Covered with painful boils, Job's friends arrived to console him. Eventually, they discussed what he had done to deserve such calamity.

Most people search for cause-and-effect relationships when things go wrong. Job's friends were no different. After empathizing with him for seven days, they broke their silence to speculate on the cause of his suffering. Obviously, Job had sinned and God was punishing him, they rationalized. But no one knew the real reason. I heard a preacher once say it was because Job had opened the door to the enemy by allowing fear into his life. They quoted Job saying, "What I feared has come upon me; what I dreaded has happened to me" (Job 3:25).

Fear is from the enemy, and I don't discount the negative effects fear produces. But Job lost ten children! Most parents fear a child's death at one time or another. If having fear causes what we fear to happen, most parents would lose their children. Not just one child, but all of them like Job. But how often do our fears come to pass? Statistically, it's seldom.

In Job 1:8, God described Job to Satan as "blameless and upright, a man who fears God and shuns evil." I'm not convinced Job's fears caused his calamities. We may never know why God allowed Satan to destroy all that Job had. Some circumstances are difficult to comprehend. It's tempting to make assumptions or fabricate answers when trying to understand. When we offer opinions or theories when no answer exists, we often hurt others.

Imagine if Chicken Little had crossed paths with Job's friends—or others offering advice. Would they have suggested the hit on her head was her fault? Maybe they'd insinuate she had sinned and God was punishing her. We may not blatantly say this to someone, but our minds can drag us in that direction.

At the end of an enjoyable Bible study with friends, one friend asked for continued prayers for her grandson. He had been born with a heart defect and had undergone another surgery, this time to fix his pacemaker. She had once seen him healed in a vision and questioned why God hadn't done that yet.

Well-meaning friends attempted to explain the unexplainable. They suggested it wasn't God's timing yet, our perspective differs from God's, and heaven is a better place anyhow. Words meant to console weren't helpful. After they had left, it felt as though we had behaved like Job's friends, offering reasons without basis. Though no one had blamed her grandson for his condition, we discussed how sin could block healing. No one truly knew why God hadn't healed this child yet.

Most often when we ask someone an unanswerable question, we don't want them to answer it. We want them to love, comfort, sympathize, and agree that our situation is unfair. The Bible tells us to "weep with them that weep" (Romans 12:15, NASB). We shouldn't try to explain suffering to those hurting.

Not knowing what to say can keep us from reaching out to those in need. Job's friends did something right. They mourned with him for seven days. We don't have to provide answers. If we remember to listen and be slow to speak, our presence will show those hurting we care.

Second Corinthian 1:4 says, "[God] comforts us in all our troubles, so that we can comfort those in any trouble with the comfort we ourselves receive from God." We're called to reach out to those experiencing what we've gone through. God will connect us with those who need the comfort we can provide.

After my divorce, several Christian women confided in me about their troubled marriages. Many were looking for a way out, and I sensed they hoped I'd persuade them to do what Jesus said is wrong. God led them to me so I could speak the truth in love and pray for their marriages. I shared divorce's many downsides and told them they'd be trading their current problems for new ones, especially if children were involved. There are situations that warrant a divorce, such as abuse, and I believe God forgives those who divorce. But consequences still exist.

During the difficult first year of my current marriage, it would have been easy to give up. Instead, I sought counsel from an older Christian woman whom I barely knew. She had spoken at a women's group I attended, and God prompted me to call her. She invited me to pray with her and her friends weekly, and these women never strayed from offering godly advice and praying according to God's Word.

We don't get to choose the words of comfort, encouragement, or advice that people offer. People eagerly share their opinions. They may be well-intentioned friends, like Job's, who recite bad theology, or they might be new acquaintances like Chicken Little's followers who were just as lost. Discernment enables us to recognize bad advice and thoughtless comments as not true so we can discard them.

We do, however, get to choose whom we allow to speak truth into our lives. Therefore, it's important that we seek counsel from mature Christians who will be honest and not mince words. Unlike a biased friend, they won't tell you what you want to hear; they'll tell you what you *need* to hear—truth, spoken in love. Even a trusted friend may give advice contrary to Scripture if you persuade her to see things your way. Therefore, it is wise not to discuss our lives with just anyone. We must discern truth from the many voices hoping to influence us.

Rehoboam, King Solomon's son, had to discern whose advice to take after becoming Israel's king. The people came to him and said, "Your father put a heavy yoke on us, but now lighten the harsh labor and the heavy yoke he put on us, and we will serve you" (1 Kings 12:4). Before he answered, Rehoboam consulted the elders who had served his father. They advised him to become a servant to the people and agree with their request. Rehoboam also sought his friends' advice. They replied, "Tell them, 'My little finger is thicker than my father's waist. My father laid on you a heavy yoke; I will make it even heavier. My father scourged you with whips; I will scourge you with scorpions'" (1 Kings 12:10–11).

Solomon is remembered for having wisdom; his son is not. Rehoboam couldn't discern godly advice from his friends' foolishness. Therefore, he and many others suffered the consequences. The people rebelled, and the twelve tribes split into the northern kingdom, Israel, and the southern kingdom, Judah. One bad decision affected multitudes of people for centuries.

Jeroboam then became king over the northern kingdom, and God sent a young prophet to prophesy against him. To prove he had spoken God's words, the prophet prophesied that the temple altar would split in two—and it did. The king invited the prophet to dine with him, but he declined, saying, "For I was commanded by the word of the Lord: 'You must not eat bread or drink water or return by the way you came'" (1 Kings 13:9).

When an old prophet heard what had happened, he searched for this young prophet and found him resting under an oak tree. He too invited him home for supper, but the man declined, reciting his instructions from the Lord. The old prophet wouldn't take no for an answer. He said, "I too am a prophet, as you are. And an angel said to me by the word of the Lord: 'Bring him back with you to your house so that he may eat bread and drink water.' (But he was lying to him.)" (1 Kings 13:18).

This story saddens me. The young prophet didn't use discernment. He didn't test the old prophet's words, and he went home with him. While they were eating, a word from the Lord came to the old prophet, for the young prophet: "You have defied the word of the Lord and have not kept the command the Lord your God gave you … Therefore your body will not be buried in the tomb of your fathers" (1 Kings 13:21–22). On his way home, a lion killed the young prophet, and the old prophet buried him in his tomb.

If you've received a prophetic word before, you know how exciting it is to hear God's message to you through someone else. Prophetic words edify, encourage, and empower a person, many times confirming what God has already said. Prophecy is a valuable gift, but we must test the words spoken. We can't blindly believe what others say. Our lives may depend on our discernment. The Bible says, "Dear friends, do not believe every spirit, but test the spirits to see whether they are from God, because many false prophets have gone out into the world" (1 John 4:1).

Although receiving a prophetic word involves risk, the Bible says, "Do not treat prophecies with contempt, but test them all; hold on to what is good" (1 Thessalonians 5:20–21). We test a prophecy by seeing if it aligns with Scripture, and we study the character and fruit evident in the prophet's life. No major life decision should be made based on one prophetic word alone. God encourages us to ask him to confirm his word.

Besides prophets who speak into our lives, friends, teachers, pastors, the media, and even strangers try to influence us. Discernment enables us to know if we should receive or reject others' words and ideas. If we don't test them, we could follow ungodly counsel and experience devastating consequences. While we may ponder life's mysteries, discerning God's will is available to all who search for it.

Yada Time

Which mysteries do you ponder the most? What experiences have equipped you to comfort others with the comfort you received from God? Did God bring someone to mind who could use a friend right now? Stay alert to God's promptings to reach out with compassion to someone. Don't worry about what you'll say; your presence alone will comfort them.

Day 5: Signs of the Times

Did you ever play the children's game What time is it, Mr. Fox? The person chosen as the fox stands facing a wall with his back to the other players who repeatedly shout, "What time is it, Mr. Fox?" The fox replies with random times between one and eleven o'clock while the players sneak up behind him. The game's objective is to touch the wall before the fox touches you, but when the fox senses you're near, he answers the question with "Twelve o'clock MIDNIGHT!" and turns to chase everyone.

Timing is important: in a game, a good joke, knowing when to discuss a sensitive subject with a boss, friend, or husband—and knowing where we are on God's timetable.

Each January, members of the Science and Security Board of the Bulletin of the Atomic Scientists set a symbolic clock, indicating how close they believe the world is to a global catastrophe, such as nuclear annihilation. In 2015, the Doomsday Clock moved to 11:57 p.m., one minute closer to midnight than the previous year.[9] The clock's hands advanced thirty seconds closer in 2017. Not since 1953 when the United States and the Soviet Union both tested thermonuclear devices has it been closer than now at two minutes from midnight.[10]

Without a doubt, the sand in Time's hourglass is running out. Ever since Jesus promised to return, some have believed that he will return in their lifetimes, and one generation will someday be correct. In the 70s, many Christians anticipated Jesus' return at any moment. The song "I Wish We'd All Been Ready" by Larry Norman told about the rapture of Christians to heaven. The movie *A Thief in the Night* depicted the beheading of Christians who refused to take the mark of the beast written about in the book of Revelation. Preachers foretold planes crashing and cars colliding when their pilots and drivers mysteriously vanished at the rapture. Stories about end-time events brought fear to my young heart. Jesus could return at any moment. Was I ready?

Immaturity caused my fear. When I became assured of my salvation, I knew I wouldn't miss the rapture. As my knowledge of heaven increased, so did my eagerness to live there someday. Whether I'm raptured alive or die before Jesus returns, I joyfully anticipate my home in heaven. Until then, it's important that we faithfully do what God has called us to do—and not be deceived or distracted by doomsday fanatics.

Jesus said this about his return: "But about that day or hour no one knows, not even the angels in heaven, nor the Son, but only the Father" (Matthew 24:36). Despite this verse, people continue to predict the day the world will end. Do you remember the Y2K frenzy, the 2012 Mayan calendar, and the four blood moons in 2015 and 2016? It seems as if end-time predictions are happening more frequently.

Unfortunately, a negative or fearful mindset usually accompanies these predictions. Those who repeatedly warn of impending doom are often said to suffer from Chicken Little Syndrome. They stockpile food and water to prepare for what they believe is imminent danger. Others amass gold and silver and then buy weapons to protect their stash. They believe they're ready—but are they?

Only those who have placed their trust in Jesus will be ready to meet him. As Christians, we need not fear the future or the world's ending. Fear comes from the enemy. The Bible says, "For you have not received a spirit of slavery leading to fear again, but you have received a spirit of adoption as sons by which we cry out, 'Abba! Father!'" (Romans 8:15, NASB). We can trust God to keep calamity from us or provide the strength to endure it. Deuteronomy 31:8 says, "The Lord himself goes before you and will be with you; he will never leave you nor forsake you. Do not be afraid; do not be discouraged." Instead of allowing fear to paralyze us, we should draw near to God and learn to discern the present time.

The religious leaders in Jesus' day didn't recognize the time in which they lived.

[Jesus] said to the crowd: "When you see a cloud rising in the west, immediately you say, 'It's going to rain,' and it does. And when the south wind blows, you say, 'It's going to be hot,' and it is. Hypocrites! You know how to interpret the appearance of the earth and the sky. How is it that you don't know how to interpret this present time?" (Luke 12:54–56)

Through prophecies, God promised the Jews that he would send a Messiah to save them. But they didn't believe that Jesus was the Anointed One because he wasn't doing what they expected him to do, which was to destroy their enemies and set up an earthly kingdom. They didn't recognize the time of God's visitation.

Fortunately, after Jesus' departure, he sent the Holy Spirit to *abide* with us, not just visit. Second Corinthians 6:2 says, "For [God] says, 'In the time of my favor I heard you, and in the day of salvation I helped you.' I tell you, now is the time of God's favor, now is the day of salvation." What an amazing time to be alive!

The Greek language uses at least two different words for time. One is *chronos*, from which we get the word chronology. It refers to ordinary time.[11] The other word is *kairos*, "which designates a fixed or special occasion."[12] It can also mean an "opportune or seasonable time."[13] In the previous verse, the author used the word kairos because we live in an extraordinary time, "a time of God's favor." Jesus proclaimed God's favor when he read Isaiah 61:1–2 in the temple. Speaking about himself, he said:

> The Spirit of the Lord is on me, because he has anointed me to proclaim good news to the poor. He has sent me to proclaim freedom for the prisoners and recovery of sight for the blind, to set the oppressed free, to proclaim the year of the Lord's favor. (Luke 4:18–19)

God's favor hasn't ceased, it's increased because the Lord's Spirit lives in every believer. "As He is, so also are we in this world" (1 John 4:17, NASB). God calls us to be Jesus' hands and feet and to do greater works than he did. Jesus said, "As you go, proclaim this message: 'The kingdom of heaven has come near.' Heal the sick, raise the dead, cleanse those who have leprosy, drive out demons. Freely you have received; freely give" (Matthew 10:7–8). Jesus also said to disciple all nations, baptizing and teaching them to obey God (see Matthew 28:19–20).

To accomplish all God has commissioned us to do, he provides favorable times (kairos) individually and corporately when his Spirit is notably present to do amazing things. Some kairos moments are so obvious we can't miss them, such as when miracles happen without anyone asking for them. God removed a painful ganglion cyst from my wrist one evening when I was simply seeking him. Unexpected kairos moments often happen when we're in his presence.

Other times, we must discern the Spirit's presence and what he wants to do. These kairos moments require our participation before something miraculous happens. We might sense God wants us to share a prophetic word with someone. Or maybe he wants us to pray for a person's healing. These kairos moments depend on us recognizing God's presence, discerning the time, and obediently doing what God asks us, which often requires boldness and courage. If you've ever led anyone to the Lord, you've seized a kairos moment.

Other kairos moments can be as simple as being in the right place at the right time and doing the right thing, such as when someone needs your help. When we make ourselves available to God, we can expect him to involve us in many kairos moments. We live in God's favor. We can pray for and expect kairos moments when we pursue God. Like storm chasers, we can chase after God and be alert to shifts in the spiritual atmosphere. When we discern the times, opportunities to join God in his work will abound. We can learn to become more aware of the glorious, grace-filled time we live in and the kairos moments God orchestrates for our participation.

Romans 13:11 says, "And do this, understanding the present time: The hour has already come for you to wake up from your slumber, because our salvation is nearer now than when we first believed."

Every day we are one day closer to Jesus' return, so we should use our time wisely and be alert to favorable kairos moments and the glorious time we live in. There is no need to fear a Doomsday Clock or the sky falling when we have Jesus in our lives. His Spirit will guide us toward maturity and increased discernment.

Yada Time

Jesus could return soon. Are you ready or does the thought cause fear? Talk to God about any anxiety you have about end-time events. What do you believe about them? Listen for God's truth. Draw near to your loving Father and receive his peace.

Ask the Lord if you are faithfully doing what he's called you to do. It's never too late to make each day count. Ask for and expect kairos moments, being willing to join God in what he's doing.

Chapter 7
Chicken Little—Discernment and Maturity
Questions for Reflection or Discussion

Day 1: The Sky is Falling

1. Why do we at times hesitate to lead others to Jesus?

2. If someone called you a Berean, would you be complimented? Why or why not? (p. 115)

3. How can reading the Bible help us live happier lives? Give examples. (2 Timothy 3:16–17, p. 115)

4. What dangers do people face when they believe absolute truth doesn't exist? (p. 116)

5. Define discernment. How does knowing Jesus help us with discernment? (p. 116)

6. Tell about a time you used discernment and the outcome.

Day 2: Cause and Effect

1. When can life experience be an unreliable teacher? (p. 117)

2. What or who are reliable teachers? (p. 117)

3. What is discernment's ultimate purpose? (p. 119)

4. What role does renewing our minds play in discernment? (p. 119)

5. Share a time you failed to discern a situation and what happened.

6. Why shouldn't we trust our intuition or conscience? (p. 120)

Day 3: Maturity

1. In what types of relationships does maturity happen best? (p. 122)

2. What can cause our maturity process to get stalled? (p. 122)

3. What might that look like in an adult? (p. 122)

4. Share an example of speaking the truth in love.

5. How do judgment and discernment differ? (p. 123)

Day 4: Ponderings and Prophecies

1. What do you do when a situation makes little sense?

2. What can keep us from reaching out to those hurting? (p. 125)

3. Why is it important to seek counsel from a mature Christian? (p. 126)

4. How do we test a prophetic word we receive? (p. 127)

5. Who or what else tries to speak into our lives? (p. 127)

6. How can we keep others from influencing us?

Day 5: Signs of the Times

1. Why don't we need to fear the future? (p. 128)

2. Why is it an amazing time to be alive? (1 Corinthians 6:2, p. 129)

3. Define a kairos moment. Give an example. (p. 129)

4. How can we experience more kairos moments? (p. 129)

5. Are you ready for the Lord's return? Share why or why not.

Share prayer requests and pray for each other. Let's boldly ask God for more kairos moments.

Chapter 8
Rapunzel—Rescued and Free

Memory Verse:

The name of the Lord is a fortified tower; the righteous run to it and are safe.
Proverbs 18:10

Day 1: Bringing Down the Vows

Rapunzel's parents named her after a lettuce that her mother craved while pregnant. Rapunzel's father stole this luscious lettuce from a witch's garden, and one day he got caught. As retribution for his crime, the witch demanded that the couple give her their firstborn child. Rapunzel's parents tried to keep their daughter's birth a secret, but when lilting lullabies drifted through the air from the couple's cottage, the witch came to investigate. Discovering the beautiful child, the witch snatched Rapunzel from her mother's arms and carried her away.

Lettuce for a child's life seems like an unfair trade, but it wasn't a trade—it was payback for stealing. Rapunzel was an innocent victim, such as many children are when a parent makes a wrong choice. The witch locked Rapunzel in a tower deep in the forest, removing her from all human contact.

Parents often isolate their children from others as a discipline tactic. They place them in a timeout, send them to their rooms, or ground them from leaving the house to restrict their interaction with others. For those found guilty of committing a crime, our correctional system separates them from society by sending them to prison. Wardens relegate prisoners who require further discipline to solitary confinement. Extended isolation can be more than punishment—it can be torture.

If the devil had his way, he'd place us all in solitary confinement. Because he can't, he tempts us to withdraw when someone hurts us. He encourages us to build walls for our protection, which keep others at a distance. "The higher the wall, the better," he whispers. "If only you lived alone in the woods. People! Who needs them?"

We all need people, and on some level, we instinctively know this. The devil knows this too, so he entices us to isolate ourselves. He's crafty, but his schemes aren't complicated. At an opportune time, he feeds us a lie, such as when I believed my mom didn't love me. He tells us, "You don't belong," or "You're not good enough." He whispers, "So-and-so is mad at you," or "No one likes you." We believe these lies and feel unwanted or unloved. To stop the pain, we avoid certain people or social situations altogether.

Several years ago, I befriended a woman who had expressed her loneliness through our church's prayer chain. As our friendship grew, so did the list of people who had hurt her. Every few months a new name appeared on her list. I never heard anyone else's side of the story, but I doubted they were all guilty, as she claimed. A year or so later, my name appeared on her list, and nothing I said or did changed her mind. Although I'd seen the handwriting on the wall, her rejection still hurt. More so, I hurt for her. Driving people away doesn't keep us from getting hurt, it keeps us in pain. We add one more brick of self-protection to our tower of isolation.

We lay many foundational walls in childhood. This is true of my wounded friend who experienced abuse as a child. Satan desires to destroy relationships—especially within families.

Rapunzel's story isn't about a witch who desperately wanted a child. She took Rapunzel to punish her parents, similar to how the devil wants to get back at God by hurting us. Satan doesn't want us for a relationship either because he's incapable of having one. He wants to separate us from our Father, to cause us both pain. But as God's children, nothing "will be able to separate us from the love of God that is in Christ Jesus our Lord" (Romans 8:39).

Though Satan can't separate us from God, he strives to get us to believe we're separated. He may tell us we've done something so terrible God won't forgive us, or we've committed the same sin one too many times for God to forgive us. If the devil tells us we don't deserve God's love and forgiveness, we can agree with him because it's true. We don't. That's what grace is about. We receive what we don't deserve (forgiveness) because Jesus paid our debt.

God loves us and promised, "Never will I leave you; never will I forsake you" (Hebrews 13:5). As Christians, we will never be separated from God. We need to take God at his word and believe he is with us even when we don't sense his presence or our circumstances make it appear otherwise. He is our refuge and strong tower (see Psalm 61:3), which we will address on day five.

Although Satan can't separate us from God, he can try to separate us from our spouses, friends, and families. Besides wishing to cause us harm, he does this because we're a greater threat to him when we walk in love and unity. Jesus said the world would recognize his followers by their love (see John 13:35), and unity commands a blessing (see Psalm 133). Jesus prayed, "I in them and you in me—so that they may be brought to complete unity. Then the world will know that you sent me and have loved them even as you have loved me" (John 17:23).

Love and unity should be our calling card.

Unfortunately, we often fail to love well, which keeps us from being unified and causes us to protect ourselves from pain. Relationships make us vulnerable; we risk getting hurt, embarrassed, rejected, and more. We've all been there. That's why we unconsciously build walls to keep others at a distance. If you don't think you've erected any walls, could it be you've gotten used to your view?

Walls are hard to detect because we make them out of lies that seem true and from harmful vows that we probably don't remember making. Fear of being hurt binds our bricks together like mortar. Until we uncover our lies and vows, we'll stay in our tower of isolation, right where our enemy wants us. We make these inner vows. "An inner vow is a determination set in the mind and heart to protect us from pain."[1] It's like a promise we make to ourselves that influences how we process life. Most often they occur when we've been hurt, and they usually include the words always or never. For example, we may vow:

- I will never let anyone hurt me again.
- I will always remember …
- I will never be like (a parent or someone else)."
- I will always love …

On the surface, many vows seem like good advice. No one wants to acquire a parent's negative traits, but inner vows often judge others and encapsulate more than we realize. Subconsciously, they dictate our future. Our inner-self enforces our vows in unhealthy ways while attempting to protect us.

As a teenager, I vowed I would never forget what it felt like to be a young person. Even when the Lord reminded me of the vow, I didn't recognize its negative effects. I assumed the feelings from childhood would be useful as a parent, failing to see the impact it was having on my children. I struggled to discipline them because I didn't want them to experience the pain I vividly remembered. That vow kept me from parenting well until I received healing.

Discovering vows and lies isn't difficult when you ask the Holy Spirit to uncover them for you. He may not show them immediately, but at some time you'll encounter a problem and find it difficult to make a needed change even though you want to. When this happens, ask God if there is a lie or vow impacting your situation. Linda Godsey shares an example of this:

One woman struggling to get pregnant discovered she had vowed as a teenager, "I will never have children when I grow up." When she repented and broke her agreement with the words she had spoken, she conceived a baby in a short period of time.[2]

Once when I was praying with a friend, I heard the Lord tell me my friend needed inner healing in a specific area. It seemed unlikely, but I shared this with my friend. When she told me she didn't, I felt as if it was impossible for me to hear the Lord correctly. After she left, I asked God why I didn't trust I could hear his voice. A memory immediately came to me. I was nine years old, sitting at our family's kitchen table writing a poem. The words I had written, but not remembered until then, came readily to mind:

Fiddle de dum, fiddle de dee, life is just a mystery.
No one knows, no one will, know the mystery of God's will.

At that moment, I knew I had believed the lie I'd written. Subconsciously, I had lived my life by this fallacy, unable to trust I could hear the Lord correctly. He wanted to free me from my doubts and convince me that I could hear his voice and know his will. Later, my friend acknowledged needing inner healing in that area. Jesus said, "Then you will know the truth, and the truth will set you free" (John 8:32).

It is amazing how our beliefs impact our lives. That's why we must continually renew our minds. We built our towers one lie or vow at a time, and God wants to replace each with his truth. He also wants us to risk being vulnerable again even before we allow him to demolish our walls. We can do this by taking refuge in him when someone hurts us rather than add another brick to our walls of loneliness and isolation. We must risk being hurt or rejected to live as God intended us to live, in community with others and not alone. God never intended that we live as isolated as Rapunzel.

Yada Time

Ask the Lord to reveal any vows you've made. Sit quietly and listen. Use the following prayer whenever you realize any previously made vows.

> "Lord, I take back from myself and from Satan those words/vows I made by an act of my will. Those words were not from You and I refute them. I renounce the statements I made that I will (never let anyone hurt me again, always be the strongest, smartest, prettiest …, never be like my father or mother, always have a plan B, never have expectations). Release me from the power of those vows and set me free to make the choices that please You and enrich my life."[3]

I forgive (name of the person who hurt you associated with making the vow). I ask you, Lord, to forgive me for trying to protect myself and for not having trusted you. I receive your forgiveness, and I give you permission to destroy all walls and self-protection strategies I use. Reveal your truth and set me free. I ask this in Jesus' name. Thank you! I love you. Amen.

Day 2: Trapped

Twenty years ago, we built our last home a few houses from where we were living, toward the end of a cul-de-sac, and our family enjoyed watching its progress. The boys were five and eight, active and adventurous. One Saturday they ventured off alone to inspect the cement walls and basement floor that had been poured days earlier. The massive concrete hole beckoned their exploration.

Like typical boys, they jumped into the deep pit—probably just to prove they could—and ran around. All was well until they wanted to leave. With no stairs, they had no way up or out. They were trapped, the walls insurmountable. Their pitiful pleas for help caught a neighbor girl's attention, and she ran to get me. As I lowered a ladder into the basement to rescue them, their expressions turned from grateful relief to boisterous joy at the prospect of climbing a ladder.

Rapunzel would have needed a much longer ladder to escape her imprisonment than the one I lowered to my boys. Even a fire truck's extension ladder might not have reached her. But a bigger problem existed; the tower was hidden deep in the woods. Without neighbors, no one would have heard her cry for help.

We may not be physically trapped, but circumstances can cause us to *feel* trapped. We may believe there's no way out of a situation or there's no one who cares enough to help us. We're convinced things will never change, and life seems hopeless. Maybe we feel trapped by an addiction, a health issue, or the debt we owe. Maybe we're in a lifeless marriage, can't shed our excess weight, or work at a dead-end job. Sometimes the same, old, everyday drudgery imprisons us. We feel powerless to change.

I've been there many times, and the Lord has faithfully pulled me out of every pit. Sometimes God gives us the escape strategy we need. Other times he reveals a choice we haven't considered, or he provides the courage to make the choice we know we should. The methods he uses to rescue us vary, but the result always increases our freedom.

Galatians 5:1 says, "It is for freedom that Christ has set us free." God values freedom so much he gave us free will when he created us. Jesus died so that we might experience freedom from sin and the devil's power. In Cinderella's story, we saw how Jesus rescues, saves, heals, and forgives us. Today, we'll explore a principle that ensures our rescue.

Like my boys, we can find ourselves trapped after making one bad decision—one wrong leap. Our motivation may have been innocent enough, but we lacked foresight. Maybe our circumstances changed without our consent, or we've changed. Rapunzel's parents caused her captivity. No matter what precipitated our predicaments, Jesus wants to free us.

In my first marriage, I felt trapped. I didn't consider divorce an option because God hates divorce (see Malachi 2:16), but I was miserable. Without sharing details, our marriage needed a miracle. After years of trying to change my husband, I eventually learned I was the only person I could change, and I couldn't even do that without God's help. Feeling helpless and hopeless, I cried, "Lord, do whatever it takes. Just change things." In heartfelt submission, I unknowingly stumbled on the powerful principle of surrender.

When I was five months pregnant with our second son, I released my marriage to God. I quit trying to control my husband's behavior by bargaining, withholding, or making threats. My methods hadn't worked anyway. I made decisions based on what God wanted me to do instead of manipulating a situation or worrying about the aftermath. I allowed my husband to experience the consequences of his actions even if they affected me negatively. I trusted God more and placed our marriage in his hands.

To arrive at heartfelt surrender, we often have to encounter something so beyond our control that we can see no other option than to release our situation to God. That's a great place to be and how we're supposed to live. Living happily ever after requires that we surrender all areas of our lives to God. He works best in that environment because he won't violate our free will. But like sanctification, total surrender can be a process. God allows problems to help us recognize the areas we haven't submitted to Jesus' lordship yet.

Jesus demonstrated a surrendered life. On the night before his death, he experienced great anguish in the Garden of Gethsemane. "'Abba, Father,' he said, 'everything is possible for you. Take this cup from me. Yet not what I will, but what you will'" (Mark 14:36). Jesus surrendered his will to God's will, knowing he'd die by crucifixion. Sometimes *not* knowing what lies ahead is a blessing, especially when our rescue happens differently than we hope, or it includes dark paths along the way toward freedom.

A few months after asking God to do "whatever it takes," I gave birth to a beautiful baby boy. On the day he and I were supposed to be discharged from the hospital, I learned he had been running a fever, and a pediatric specialist transferred him to the neonatal intensive care unit. Fear crept in and tested my ability to stay surrendered. In my previous prayer, I'd given God permission to do whatever it took to change things. Could I trust God in this crisis and surrender my child to him too?

Abraham faced a worse situation. His son was a teenager when God said, "Take now your son, your only son, whom you love, Isaac, and go to the land of Moriah; and offer him there as a burnt offering on one of the mountains of which I will tell you" (Genesis 22:2, NASB). Losing a child for any reason is difficult enough, but purposely causing your child's death would be inconceivable as a parent.

It's hard to imagine traveling on such a mission, your son carrying the firewood for his incineration. Isaac asked his father, "Behold, the fire and the wood, but where is the lamb for the burnt offering?" (Genesis 22:7, NASB). How would you respond? In the next verse, "Abraham said, 'God will provide for Himself the lamb for the burnt offering, my son.' So the two of them walked on together." Hebrews 11:19 tells us Abraham's perspective: "Abraham reasoned that God could raise the dead, and figuratively speaking, he did receive Isaac back from death."

God never intended for Abraham to kill Isaac. As Abraham raised his knife to slay his son, an angel called to him. "And he said, 'Do not stretch out your hand against the lad, and do nothing to him; for now I know that you fear God, since you have not withheld your son, your only son, from Me'" (Genesis 22:12, NASB). Abraham passed God's test by surrendering what he cherished most to God. Through this encounter, God also revealed an aspect of himself that Abraham didn't yet know.

Back then, people sacrificed their children to appease their gods. God wanted Abraham to know he wasn't like other gods; he would provide the sacrifice himself. A ram appeared, caught in the bushes, for Abraham to sacrifice on the altar. "So Abraham called that place The Lord Will Provide. And to this day it is said, 'On the mountain of the Lord it will be provided'" (Genesis 22:14). This story beautifully describes God's love for us, and it foreshadowed God sacrificing his only son two thousand years later.

Not knowing if our newborn son would live or die tested my faith. After multiple rounds of antibiotics, the doctor finally allowed me to bring Jesse home. When we say things like "God spared my son's life," it infers we thought God had contemplated killing him. We forget it's the devil that kills, steals, and destroys. Jesus came to give abundant life. God wants no one to die prematurely.

As parents, living happily ever after requires that we surrender our children to God, repeatedly if necessary, but we don't sacrifice them for any reason. God gives children as gifts. Surrender means we hold loosely all gifts we receive, not allowing anything to take God's place in our heart. God also expects us to steward his gifts well, which means as parents we're to bring our children up in the Lord, teaching and training them in God's ways while guiding them toward their relationship with him.

God didn't use Jesse's health crisis to change my marital situation, nor did my rescue happen overnight. God was changing my heart as I daily, sometimes hourly, surrendered my marriage to him. Even after our divorce, I continued hoping that things would work out between us. Whenever I asked God about the future, I repeatedly heard, "Be still, and know that I am God" (Psalm 46:10). He reminded me he was in control and I could rest in him. Jesus spoke the same words "Be still" to the waves threatening to capsize his disciples' boat (see Mark 4:39). Through Jesus, we can still the storm stirring inside us by trusting God to rescue us.

Though I didn't get the happy ending I thought I wanted, God gave me more than I had ever asked or imagined—including abundant joy. We escape imprisonment by surrendering to God. We place ourselves on God's altar and declare as Paul did, "I have been crucified with Christ and I no longer live, but Christ lives in me. The life I now live in the body, I live by faith in the Son of God, who loved me and gave himself for me" (Galatians 2:20).

Yada Time

Reflect on the circumstances that once brought you to a place of surrender. How would you describe your relationship with God at that time? Are you as close to him today as you were then? How did he resolve your situation? How were you changed?

Is God prompting you to surrender something, or someone, to him today? It could be as serious as a family problem or as simple as how much time you spend watching TV. Rely on God to give you the strength to surrender what he requests. He only asks because he wants you to live truly free.

Day 3: Singing in His Reign

While driving to pick up my son from a friend's house, I passed through our city's ritziest neighborhood. Frosted evergreens glistened in the moonlight, and decked-out mansions sparkled with bright multicolored lights. Lawn decorations greeted passersby with holiday wishes, and my heart became giddy with anticipation. Christmastime brings out the child in me. A song popped into my mind, but it wasn't a familiar Christmas carol. It was an unexpected Beatles tune, its lyrics about all the lonely people.

Sadness replaced my holiday joy as I contemplated the true condition of many people's lives. On the outside, we might look as cheerful as Christmas lights, but on the inside, we're emotionally bankrupt. We feel alone and disconnected, as if our lives were void of meaningful relationships.

In a world filled with over seven billion people, experiencing loneliness is seldom caused by being alone. I've felt alone in a crowd before, haven't you? That's because "loneliness is a condition of relational disconnection, social awkwardness and prolonged bouts of solitude."[3] Life's transitions can make us more susceptible to loneliness, such as when a spouse dies, a child leaves home, we start a new job, or we move to a different city. In the adjustment period, we may feel alone.

If loneliness extends beyond a transitional period, a person should seek help. Loneliness can lead to or result from depression, and we must take depression seriously. But if you've ever been depressed, you know how difficult it is to seek help for yourself. When feeling alone or depressed, we isolate ourselves even more. Emotional and psychological barriers produce low energy and lack of courage. Like Rapunzel, we're unable to venture out or call for help.

In contrast, some people stay busy to combat their loneliness. Then when they return to their empty homes at night, they find the day's conversations make for haunting company. Things they or others said replay with undertones of judgment, rejection, and self-doubt, causing them to wish they had stayed home. Deep emotional wounds fuel loneliness. We may feel ashamed, unloved, unworthy, inadequate, rejected, etc. Only Jesus can rescue us from our hurts.

When I moved to a new city for my second year of college, I struggled with loneliness and depression. Looking back, I can see how both began years earlier. The details aren't important, but recognizing the signs of depression, which include feeling hopeless and alone, are important. Fortunately, my family recognized the signs and encouraged me to get help. I talked with a counselor, and she suggested I make a few changes. Following her advice, I moved into a dormitory where I was less isolated and developed new friendships by joining a Bible study.

The loneliness I experienced in my first marriage wasn't as easily solved. Though I had felt emotionally distant from my husband for years, when he moved out, my loneliness escalated from not seeing my boys every day. I had agreed they could stay overnight at their dad's two nights a week and every other weekend. I never thought he'd be able to handle their care long term, but he never missed his time with them. Handing my precious little ones over to their father who had rarely taken care of them created another opportunity to surrender them to God.

My heart ached for my boys on the nights I didn't have them, and the only way home after work involved driving past their daycare provider's house. I'd see them playing in her yard and desperately want to stop, but I knew I couldn't. It would be too hard for them and me. So, I drove by, tears streaming down my face.

Loneliness was only a symptom of my real problem: my heart was breaking. Many who struggle with loneliness also suffer from a wounded heart, possibly from a pain-inflicted childhood or a life-altering event later on. Until our hearts receive the care and healing they need, loneliness will persist. We cannot risk being vulnerable, so we stay trapped in our self-made lonely towers.

By God's grace, I continuously surrendered my situation and did three things. I purged, professed, and praised. Through journaling, I purged my pain and negative emotions, conversing with God through writing. I poured out my heart to him and listened for his voice. I surrendered all new circumstances, and any old ones I'd taken back, and cried to God until I received his comforting words or peace. I still use this principle today. I tell God about my situation, purging my feeling until I'm able to turn my problem over to him and leave it there.

During this heart-wrenching time, music ministered to me more than usual. The song "The Anchor Holds," sung by Ray Boltz, *professes* God as our anchor who keeps us upright despite our storm's battering.[5] The lyrics of many Christian songs profess Scripture and God's promises. I professed Ephesians 3:20 in song, which states "[God] is able to do exceeding abundantly beyond all that we ask or think" (NASB), and I claimed this for my future. Besides singing and professing God's Word, I memorized it. I wrote it on notecards to carry with me, and I bought plaques with faith-filled Bible verses and hung them on my walls. I believed and professed God's truth and promises over my situation.

Another song I played repeatedly was "Praise the Lord," sung by Russ Taff. It declares the chain-breaking power invoked when we *praise* God despite our problems.[6] I sang this song often with my arms raised and tears streaming down my face. I purged my pain through praise, and I entered into God's presence. Psalm 22:3 tells us God inhabits the praises of his people, and praise helps us stay surrendered to God's will.

When Paul and Silas were in prison, Acts 16:25 says, "About midnight Paul and Silas were praying and singing hymns to God, and the other prisoners were listening to them." Here's what can happen when we praise God in our trial. "Suddenly there was such a violent earthquake that the foundations of the prison were shaken. At once all the prison doors flew open, and everybody's chains came loose" (Acts 16:26). Wow! Praise loosens chains. It shakes foundations. It topples towers. A simple shout caused the walls of Jericho to fall (see Joshua 6:16–20), and I imagine the Israelites shouted, "Our God is awesome!"

In another story, the Bible describes how God honored the Israelite's praises and defeated their enemies when Jehoshaphat was Judah's king.

> Jehoshaphat appointed men to sing to the Lord and to praise him for the splendor
> of his holiness as they went out at the head of the army, saying: "Give thanks to
> the Lord, for his love endures forever." As they began to sing and praise, the
> Lord set ambushes against the men of Ammon and Moab and Mount Seir who
> were invading Judah, and they were defeated. (2 Chronicles 20:21–22)

In their first battle after Joshua's death, the Israelites asked the Lord which tribe should lead the charge against the Canaanites. "The Lord answered, 'Judah shall go up; I have given the land into their hands'" (Judges 1:2). Judah, the tribe from which our Lord descended, means praise. We fight from a position of victory because Jesus has already won every battle. He conquered sin, death, and the devil. Therefore, praise should be our weapon of choice as we fight to apply all Jesus has accomplished on our behalf.

Hebrews 13:15 says, "Through Jesus, therefore, let us continually offer to God a sacrifice of praise—the fruit of lips that openly profess his name." We won't always feel like praising God, but we can *choose* to praise him regardless of our circumstances by reflecting on his sacrifice. Our praises will catch God's attention as Rapunzel's singing caught the Prince's.

In her loneliness, Rapunzel sang lullabies to pass the long, lonely days. The wind must have been blowing in the right direction as it carried her melodies to the Prince's ears. As he followed the enchanted tunes, he discovered a tower deep in the woods and the beautiful woman singing them.

Rapunzel didn't blow a trumpet. She didn't shout. She sang the songs buried deep in her heart and hastened her rescue. Our praises will do the same for us. Psalm 34:17 says, "The Lord hears his people when they call to him for help. He rescues them from all their troubles" (NLT).

Yada Time

If you suffer from a broken heart or other pain, express your sorrow to God through journaling. Tell him how you feel, and *purge* all negative emotions by releasing them to God. Search God's Word for verses that bring hope to your situation, then memorize and *profess* them. Listen to a favorite praise chorus and *praise* God despite your sadness.

If you struggle with severe loneliness or depression, please consider getting help from a professional. If you aren't lonely, call someone who you suspect is lonely or depressed and let them know you're thinking about them. Share an encouraging word or a Bible verse with them. Ask if you may pray for them and do it with them. Don't worry about what you'll say; allow the Sprit to lead you as you deliver God's love. Encourage them to seek professional help if you sense they should.

Day 4: Leap of Faith

The Prince hid behind a tree as the witch approached the tall tower. She cupped her hands to her mouth and hollered, "Rapunzel, Rapunzel, let down your long hair." Moments later, golden locks cascaded out a window and down the tower's side. The witch climbed the hair and disappeared into the tower. After a while, she descended using the same rope of hair.

Having your hair used as a ladder gives new meaning to a bad hair day. At least Rapunzel never suffered from getting a bad haircut. Nor did she experience peer pressure or sibling rivalry. She didn't worry about fitting in or keeping up appearances either. No one hurt her feelings or offended her, excluding the witch, who I imagine was plagued by bad hair days herself. Yes, isolation has its benefits.

All kidding aside, no one truly wants to live alone in the woods. Not even the witch, who stole a baby for company. Though Rapunzel may not have known that other people existed, she must have sensed that something was missing. Eventually, she discovered what.

After the witch had departed, the Prince called, "Rapunzel, Rapunzel, let down your long hair." She flung her hair out the window, and soon the handsome prince came into view. Imagine her shock. "Do not be afraid," he said. "I heard your beautiful singing and followed it. I wanted to meet you." The two fell in love at first sight and made plans to run away together. The Prince climbed down her hair and called to Rapunzel, "Jump into my arms. I'll catch you!"

To gain her freedom, Rapunzel needed to take a leap of faith.

We studied faith's importance in chapter one. "Without faith it is impossible to please God" (Hebrews 11:6). Because faith is vital to living happily ever after, let's explore faith in another context to understand it better. Recall that believing and trusting God defines faith, which makes faith foundational to receiving what we cannot yet see. It supports us while we wait to receive everything God has promised us.

People often misunderstand what taking a leap of faith means. They equate it with blind faith, which it isn't. One dictionary defines blind faith as "belief without true understanding, perception, or discrimination."[7] God doesn't require blind faith from anyone. Though we may never understand God completely, blindness doesn't describe a Christian's faith. God invites us to know him personally, so he's the basis of our faith.

When we take a leap of faith, unlike blind faith, we understand what God wants us to do, and we do it despite our unanswered questions. It's like when God told Abram, "Leave your native country, your relatives, and your father's family, and go to the land that I will show you" (Genesis 12:1, NLT). Abram's departure was a leap of faith because he didn't know where God would lead him. Because he understood what God wanted him to do, he wasn't walking blindly. He trusted God and watched for further direction along the way. Randomly deciding to go on a journey in hopes it pleases God is blind faith. Such a decision lacks "understanding, perception, or discrimination" and doesn't please God.

Rapunzel's leap of faith shows the faith God desires us to exhibit. The Prince said, "I will catch you," and she took him at his word. She believed and trusted the Prince would do what he said he would. If he hadn't instructed her to jump, it would have been foolish for her to do so. What if he hadn't been near enough or paying close enough attention to catch her? Jumping without someone to catch you is blind faith—and unwise.

God doesn't want us moving through life blindly. He wants us to know him personally, to know his ways, nature, character, and promises. We learn what pleases him by reading Scripture and daily interacting with him. He expects our faith (belief and trust) to be grounded in truth and not in guesswork or our imagination.

Years ago, I surveyed my friends by asking them the following question: If someone relayed a request for you to do something but they didn't give all the details, which missing piece would you most want to know—who, what, where, when, or why?

Take a moment and ask yourself that question.

I'm a curious *why* person, and I wanted to learn if others needed to know why as much as I did. After stating their choices, almost everyone wanted to know the correct answer. Several became irritated when they learned there wasn't a right or wrong response and that I had only asked out of curiosity. Their attitudes afterward soon became my survey's most intriguing part. Though the variety of answers surprised me, I learned a valuable lesson from one friend's response. He said, "I would have to know *who* is asking me to do this. If it is God, then none of the other questions matter."

What a great answer—and an example of great faith. I hadn't considered the question as spiritual until then. Habakkuk 2:4 says, "The righteous person will live by his faithfulness." Romans, Galatians, and Hebrews quote this verse along with many other books that emphasize our need to live by faith. If we understand faith as believing and trusting God, living by faith means we make decisions based on what God has said, striving to do his will. Therefore, it would benefit us to increase our faith.

Romans 10:17 says, "So faith comes from hearing, and hearing by the word of Christ" (NASB). In context, the author is referring to saving faith, the message of salvation. He said we must tell others about Jesus because if they never hear about him, they can't believe in him. This principle applies to increasing daily faith as well. If we don't hear from God on a subject through the Bible or the many other ways he speaks, our faith doesn't increase in that area. We need to know what God says so we can believe it. But we won't find all our personal questions answered in the Bible.

God's Word doesn't spell out whether we should buy a certain house, start a new business, or marry a particular person. God may provide answers to our questions through the Bible, as he did when directing me to change jobs, but my faith didn't increase until I heard from God. Because God wants us to live by faith, and faith comes from hearing, we must study the Bible, listen for his voice, and become familiar with how he speaks.

After fasting forty days in the wilderness, Jesus was hungry. Satan seized the opportunity and tempted Jesus to turn stones into bread. Jesus replied, "Man shall not live on bread alone, but on every word that comes from the mouth of God" (Matthew 4:4). Hearing from God sustains us better than food nourishes our bodies. But hearing alone is not enough. Once we know what God wants us to do, we must do it. James 1:22 says, "Do not merely listen to the word, and so deceive yourselves. Do what it says."

Not doing what we're supposed to do is a sin, and sin produces consequences. Ignorance is no excuse. If we unknowingly drink poison, we will still suffer the consequence. It's better to know God's will and obey it than not know it and take our chances. Besides, obedience brings blessings.

Obeying God and exercising faith don't always require that we take a leap. Both get easier the more we know, love, and trust God. When we struggle to obey God, it may indicate that the enemy has erected a stronghold in our lives. Like the tower that held Rapunzel captive, a wrong belief or desire can trap us in sin and disobedience. As a military term, a stronghold is a place of safety. In our context, the enemy has found a safe place in us to wreak havoc. He has a strong *hold* over an area of our lives from which he influences our attitudes, mindsets, behaviors, etc. Obedience seems impossible when a stronghold exists. Only Jesus can break the enemy's hold on us.

Jesus came to give us abundant life (see John 10:10). This doesn't mean we won't encounter problems and persecutions, but even during our trials, we can access God's love, joy, peace, etc. by faith. God wants us to live happy, fulfilled, and abundant lives. Jesus' encouraging words in Matthew 11:28–30 bear repeating. He said:

> Come to me, all you who are weary and burdened, and I will give you rest. Take my yoke upon you and learn from me, for I am gentle and humble in heart, and you will find rest for your souls. For my yoke is easy and my burden is light.

Jesus invites us to leap into his arms. We won't be jumping blindly because he's called us to come. He's waiting, watching, and ready to catch us no matter how big or small the enemy's stronghold. God wants us to depend on him. Go ahead, jump!

Yada Time

What new insight did you gain about faith? Is the Lord encouraging you to take a leap? If you need more faith, spend time listening to the Lord. Get to know him and understand his request better. Hearing from him will increase your faith. If you're caught in the enemy's stronghold, call out to Jesus and jump into his loving arms. Trust God to rescue you and rely on his strength to make any needed changes.

Day 5: Our Strong Tower

Rapunzel heeded the Prince's command and leaped into his waiting arms. She escaped the witch and the tower that had held her captive, and she enjoyed endless fellowship with the Prince. Jesus wants this for us too, and he speaks to us to increase our faith, destroy our walls, and draw us closer to him.

We've looked at the metaphoric walls we build to protect ourselves, and how the enemy constructs strongholds in our lives through fear, lies, and pain to influence or control our attitudes and behaviors. Today, we will explore what it means to know the Lord as our stronghold or strong tower. David wrote in Psalm 61:3, "For you [God] have been my refuge, a strong tower against the foe."

In biblical times, towers were a big deal, literally. Massive walls encased most cities to protect them from invaders. A city's entrance often included secured gates and immensely high towers as lookout posts. People in agricultural areas also erected watchtowers, as the watchman's role was crucial to everyone. A tower's elevated height enabled watchmen to see for miles and keep watch over the crops and the city. At the first sign of approaching danger, watchmen blew their horns to alert the people. The city's gates closed and a call to arms sounded.

Within a city's walls, an additional tower existed. This fortified, impenetrable tower provided protection, food, water, and weaponry—like the bomb shelters in the 50s. If an enemy breached the city's walls or gates, the people ran to this tower for refuge.

Judges 9:50–53 depicts such a situation.

Next Abimelech went to Thebez and besieged it and captured it. Inside the city, however, was a strong tower, to which all the men and women—all the people of the city—had fled. They had locked themselves in and climbed up on the tower roof. Abimelech went to the tower and attacked it. But as he approached the entrance to the tower to set it on fire, a woman dropped an upper millstone on his head and cracked his skull.

It's a morbid story, but its happy ending illustrates my point. The people found protection and provision in a strong tower. The Bible provides many references to God as our stronghold or strong tower. Proverbs 18:10 says, "The name of the Lord is a fortified tower; the righteous run to it and are safe." And Psalm 27:1 says, "The Lord is my light and my salvation—whom shall I fear? The Lord is the stronghold of my life—of whom shall I be afraid?"

King David, a mighty warrior familiar with battle, wrote most of the Book of Psalms. During the four years before becoming king, the ruling King Saul hunted David like a wild animal. David credited God for his many escapes from Saul. He wrote, "I will say of the Lord, 'He is my refuge and my fortress, my God, in whom I trust'" (Psalm 91:2).

We may never face as great a danger as David did, but that doesn't mean we don't need a strong tower ourselves. Our battles at home, work, or in our minds can seem as threatening. Everyone needs a place where the enemy can't reach them. God provides such a place in Jesus. He is our stronghold, the fortress in which we find refuge.

In Old Testament times, God designated certain cities as places of refuge. Because the punishment for killing someone was a life for a life, God instructed Moses to designate cities where those who unintentionally committed manslaughter could find safety (see Numbers 35:15). Though this was good news for the innocent, the guilty had no such hope.

Jesus expanded the law, stating if anyone has anger or hatred in his heart toward anyone, he has committed murder in his heart (see Matthew 5:21). By Jesus' standard, none of us could enter a city of refuge and be safe. Jesus made the law a heart issue. Who then does God allow into his refuge?

On the day of Pentecost, Peter answered this question. He said, "And *everyone* who calls on the name of the Lord will be saved" (Acts 2:21, emphasis added). It doesn't matter how many sins we've committed, anyone who calls on the Lord's name can enter his stronghold. Calling on

Jesus' name is like using a password, such as "Open Sesame," because Jesus is the door—and he is much, much more. He is our strong tower, our city of refuge.

If a person who accidentally killed someone entered a city of refuge, he was safe as long as he stayed in that city. One step outside the boundary lines and his avenger could kill him. The same goes for entering a strong tower. If an enemy surrounded a tower, you were safe as long as you remained inside with the door bolted shut. Both scenarios describe a Christian's life in Christ. As long as we trust in Jesus as our Savior, we're safe inside the city of refuge. Still, an even more secure place exists within the city—a strong tower, where God provides everything we need.

We enter God's stronghold by believing and trusting in Jesus, and we abide in him through love, faith, and obedience. Jesus said, "Anyone who loves me will obey my teaching. My Father will love them, and we will come to them and make our home with them." (John 14:23). In *The Stronghold of God*, the author, Francis Frangipane, writes:

> How shall we find this spiritual place? We simply begin by loving Jesus. He said, "He who loves Me shall be loved by My Father, and I will love him, and will disclose Myself to him" (John 14:21). If we persevere in love and obedience, Jesus has promised to progressively reveal Himself to us.[8]

Frangipane continues: "This unfolding revelation of Jesus Christ to our hearts is the path to the abode of God. It is this shelter of the Most High that is the stronghold of God."[9] Because God reveals himself progressively, it may take a while before we discover every spiritual blessing Christ provides. It would be like learning the provisions stored in a massive strong tower. Some things we'd expect to find there, but others we'd have to search the merchandise list (the Bible) to know if they were there. It is our job to seek for what is ours in Christ. Second Peter 1:3 says, "[God's] divine power has given us everything we need for a godly life through our knowledge of him who called us by his own glory and goodness."

Our Strong Tower provides more than we can imagine. But until we need or want something, we probably won't go looking for it. When we pursue knowing Jesus better, we'll discover many things by accident—or rather, by his purpose as he reveals himself to us. Abiding in our Strong Tower, we'll no longer need to hide behind our self-protective walls. We'll feel safe enough to risk being vulnerable and work with the Lord to remove our walls.

Have you ever watched a building get demolished? Before a demolition specialist decides on the best technique, he considers such factors as the structure's height, the material, and its proximity to other buildings.

A few years ago, I witnessed the demolition of a brick dormitory deemed unsafe to house students. It looked like a tower, its circular shape stretching many stories into the sky. Its height alone made it impossible for any demolition machinery to reach the top. Also, two other buildings sat nearby on both sides. Skillful workers placed dynamite in strategic places within the building's structure. Once the explosive sticks ignited, the brick tower crumbled within seconds. It was a spectacular sight.

Recall that the word dynamite comes from the Greek word dunamis, which means power. Though used to describe the Holy Spirit, dynamite doesn't come close to the Spirit's power that raised Jesus from the dead—and we have the same power working to change us! (See Romans 8:11).

The Holy Spirit's power can breach the enemy's strongholds and destroy our self-protective walls. But God rarely brings our walls down all at once with one majestic BANG! It's not that he couldn't. He prefers to dismantle the lies, vows, and hurtful memories one brick at a time. Through this process, he reveals truth and aspects of himself unknown to us. He values relationship.

While wishing that God would "fix" me all at once, I complained to him about the lengthy process. He brought to mind a painful massage I once suffered. Any movement afterward caused pain for weeks. I sensed that tackling all our issues simultaneously would be too painful. God works gently and patiently with us, calling us to abide in him, our Strong Tower, where he reveals himself and meets all our needs.

Though we may feel trapped like Rapunzel, our towers are not hidden from God. He sees and hears us. He wants to rescue us from feeling trapped or alone. He wants to heal our broken hearts and dismantle our self-protective walls. He loves us and has amazing plans for our lives. When his rescue seems delayed, he's often waiting for us. We may be holding on to something he wants us to surrender, or maybe we haven't taken the leap of faith he's asking us to. Sometimes we forget to call on his name. If you want to gain his attention, sing what's in your heart. Even if your heart is breaking, praise the Lord. Run into your Strong Tower and find safety and healing. Prince Jesus is waiting to rescue you.

Yada Time

We dwell in God's stronghold by abiding in Christ. It's like enjoying his presence and Sabbath rest. Recall how we can enter his presence by seeking his FACE (faith, attributes, creation, or experience), calling on his name, or praising him. Even if you don't sense God's presence, trust that he is with you. He hears and loves you. Talk to God about your needs. Pour out your heart to him and listen to what he says. Commit to dwelling in God's Strong Tower, Jesus. Trust that no matter how hard the enemy attacks you, God will always rescue you.

Chapter 8
Rapunzel—Rescued and Free
Questions for Reflection or Discussion

Day 1: Bringing Down the Vows

1. Discuss reasons people isolate themselves.

2. How does Satan entice us to isolate? (p. 133)

3. What can cause us to build walls around ourselves? (p. 134)

4. What is an inner vow? Share an example. (pp. 134–135)

5. How can an inner vow affect the person making it? (p. 135)

6. What should you do instead of placing another brick on your wall? (p. 136)

Day 2: Trapped

1. Tell about a time you felt trapped.

2. How can not knowing what lies ahead be a blessing? (p. 138)

3. Share about a time you surrendered a situation or person to God and the outcome.

4. What did God reveal about himself after he stopped Abraham from sacrificing Isaac? (p. 138)

5. How do we escape imprisonment? (p. 139)

6. Reflect on or discuss how surrender brings freedom?

Day 3: Singing in His Reign

1. What can fuel loneliness? (p. 140)

2. Has a broken heart ever caused you to be lonely?

3. What 3 things did the author do to navigate negative situations? (p. 141)

4. How can we purge our negative emotions? (p. 141)

5. Share a song that ministered to you during a painful season.

6. What can happen when we praise God during a trial? (p. 141)

Day 4: Leap of Faith

1. How does blind faith differ from a leap of faith? (p. 143)

2. In what should we ground our faith? (p. 143)

3. Describe living by faith. How can we increase our faith? (p. 144)

4. Define a stronghold of the enemy. (pp. 144–145)

Day 5: Our Strong Tower

1. Describe a strong tower in biblical days. (pp. 145–146)

2. Who does God allow into his strong tower? (p. 146)

3. How do we enter God's stronghold/strong tower? (pp. 146–147)

4. How is Jesus like a strong tower? How do we abide in Jesus? (p. 147)

5. Why might Got not bring all our walls down at once? (p.148)

6. Is there anything else in this chapter you want to discuss?

Share prayer request and pray for each other. Let's demolish our walls together!

Chapter 9
Rumpelstiltskin—Redeemed and Righteous

Memory Verse:

That at the name of Jesus every knee should bow, in heaven and on earth
and under the earth, and every tongue acknowledge
that Jesus Christ is Lord, to the glory of God the Father.
Philippians 2:10–11

Day 1: Jeopardy

Pretend you're a contestant on the game show *Jeopardy*, and you've chosen the category Fairy Tales for one hundred dollars. Ready? The answer is: her father bragged she could spin straw into gold. Hurry—buzz in! If you guessed "Who is the unnamed maiden?" you are correct, for our purposes anyhow. This mystery maiden who eventually married the King was never named in "Rumpelstiltskin," and neither was her father. He's referred to as the poor miller who delivered flour to the King's palace.

The miller desperately wanted the King to notice his daughter, so he boasted of her beauty, attributes, and talents hoping to secure a better future for her. In his exuberance, he fabricated her abilities beyond human capabilities. "She can spin straw into gold!" he proclaimed, and with that, he caught the King's attention—and put his daughter's life in jeopardy.

"Take her to my castle," the King ordered his servants. "Lock her in a room and fill it with straw. If she cannot do as her father stated, she shall surely die."

Have you ever found yourself in trouble for pretending to be someone you're not? "Fake it 'til you make it" only works if you can eventually "make it," but this maiden had no possibility of ever making gold from straw.

Our call to perfection is not so different from the desperate situation imposed on this maiden. Jesus said, "Be perfect, therefore, as your heavenly Father is perfect" (Matthew 5:48). Since we were born sinners, this command seems as impossible as turning straw into gold. By determination alone, we can't keep God's law perfectly. We will only be perfect through Jesus. But God commands us to live godly lives.

Like salvation, the call to perfection, maturity, or completion is impossible in our strength. We may know this, but we can easily forget and strive to become righteous through our efforts. We fall into performance-based perfection, striving to do good without relying on God's power to transform us. We will never gain true righteousness by our merits.

The Galatian church faltered in this area too. Paul wrote to them, saying, "I would like to learn just one thing from you: Did you receive the Spirit by the works of the law, or by believing what you heard? Are you so foolish? After beginning by means of the Spirit, are you now trying to finish by means of the flesh?" (Galatians 3:2–3). The Galatians trusted in their Jewish laws, customs, and celebrations to make them righteous instead of relying on the righteousness found in Jesus. They neglected the Spirit's transformation power at work within them.

Living by rules rather than by the Spirit can seem easier. We're accustomed to rules because they're everywhere. But no matter how hard we attempt to live by the Spirit, most of us still measure our acceptance with God based on works, such as how often we pray, attend church, read our Bibles, obey his commands, help the less fortunate, tithe and give offerings. God wants us to do these things, but these spiritual disciplines position us before God to receive from him; they don't earn us a way into his good graces.

Paul warned, "You who are trying to be justified by law have been alienated from Christ; you have fallen away from grace" (Galatians 5:4). When we measure our righteousness by our actions, we are in jeopardy of falling from God's grace. The Bible refers to anyone who believes they've achieved righteousness by their actions as self-righteous. Jesus told the following parable as an example:

> Two men went up to the temple to pray, one a Pharisee and the other a tax collector. The Pharisee stood by himself and prayed: "God, I thank you that I am not like other people—robbers, evildoers, adulterers—or even like this tax collector. I fast twice a week and give a tenth of all I get." But the tax collector stood at a distance. He would not even look up to heaven, but beat his breast and said, "God, have mercy on me, a sinner." I tell you that this man, rather than the other, went home justified before God. For all those who exalt themselves will be humbled, and those who humble themselves will be exalted. (Luke 18:10–14)

A Pharisee in biblical times belonged to a Jewish sect that gave strict interpretation and adherence to the law. Today we might call them legalistic or the religious Goody Two-Shoes. Sadly, I wore those shoes once. Though God desires that we live moral, upright lives, the Pharisees mistakenly believed they were more spiritual than everyone else. Pride was their issue. They could list all the bad things they had never done and all the good things they had. Modern-day Pharisees don't stand on street corners and announce these things, but in their hearts, they keep a running tally.

Pharisee tendencies can be hard to recognize, especially if you've grown up attending church religiously. I've listed some clues to help you determine where you fall on the Pharisee spectrum. You might be a Pharisee if you:

- Get nose bleeds from standing so high on your spiritual ladder.

- Feel condemned if you miss church, Bible study, or other spiritual activities.
- Talk *at* God instead of *with* him—and your favorite topic is you.
- Establish rules and judge others by how well they follow them.
- Believe you are more pleasing to God than others are.

When the Holy Spirit convicted me of my self-righteousness, I felt regret and sorrow. Yet, to repent, I also needed to change my thoughts and attitude, and I didn't know how. I had grown up in the church following spiritual to-do lists. Though I didn't realize it, I needed to understand God's grace better. God used a friend, whom I'll call Joni, to begin this process.

I met Joni at a Bible study we attended, and her love and devotion to the Lord were boldly evident. I assumed she had lived her whole life for God because she radiated his love and displayed the Holy Spirit's fruit and gifts. Her passion for the Lord ignited a desire in me to know him more intimately.

After some time, I asked Joni how she maintained her zeal for the Lord. Paraphrasing Luke 7:47, she replied, "Those who are forgiven much, love much." She told me she'd lived in rebellion for years and had committed horrible sins. I blushed at hearing her stories, but Joni knew she was a new creation in Christ Jesus, and that's all that mattered to her and to God (see 2 Corinthians 5:17).

The verse Joni shared haunted me for weeks. Jesus had spoken those words to a sinful woman like Joni. How could I obtain greater love for God when I had done nothing as scandalous as she? I asked God to help me love him more, and I foolishly thought I might have to hurt someone accidentally, such as by causing a car accident, to experience greater forgiveness.

During this time, another friend and I agreed to meet and confess every sin we'd ever committed. Besides wanting a clean slate, we hoped to comprehend the weight of our sinfulness. The plan sounded good, but such self-reflection and debasement opened the door for the enemy's attack. For the two weeks before our meeting, Satan pointed out all my faults and every sin I'd ever committed, causing me guilt, shame, and condemnation. Then a car accident happened. Had I been driving seconds faster, mine would have been the car they hit. Instead, I only witnessed the accident, and the revelation of God's grace grew a little clearer.

By the time my friend and I met to confess our sins, I knew there was nothing good in me apart from Christ. Comprehending my unworthiness, I experienced the weight of my sin and saw myself as the woman in the Bible, sitting at Jesus' feet and receiving his forgiveness. When the heaviness lifted, I experienced God's grace toward me, a sinner. A deeper love and passion for the Lord ignited in me, and like grace, it too was a gift.

Even with my Pharisee tendencies, I had lived many years feeling as if my efforts to please God were never enough. When we complete spiritual to-do lists out of obligation, we miss the joy of living by his Spirit and the loving interaction that occurs. God values relationships, remember? Besides, even the best rule followers seldom measure up to their standards. Grace frees us to live every moment as God directs, basking in his love and acceptance, "For by one sacrifice he has made perfect forever those who are being made holy" (Hebrews 10:14).

We need not live in jeopardy of falling from God's grace when we embrace all Jesus did on our behalf. Jesus' sacrifice made us perfect in God's sight, and the Holy Spirit works to perfect Jesus' likeness in us. Both are impossible tasks for us—but not for God. Our part is to believe, receive, and yield ourselves to God's process of turning sinners into saints, who are more precious to him than gold.

Yada Time

Where do you fall on the Pharisee spectrum? How well do you know that God loves and accepts you as you are? If you desire a greater passion for the Lord, let him know. Ask God to show you the weight of your sin and the price Jesus paid for your becoming righteous before God.

Is there a behavior or mindset you're trying to change without God's help? Talk to God about your problem. Ask him to help you yield to his Spirit and help you make better decisions. Allow the Spirit to direct your steps by talking to him throughout the day. Listen to what the Spirit reveals to you. Hearing from God will change your mindset and will ultimately change you.

Day 2: Let's Make a Deal

While locked in a room full of straw, the unnamed maiden found herself in quite a pickle. If she didn't turn the straw into gold by morning, the king would have her killed. Often at this point in a fairy tale, a handsome prince gallops in on a white horse and rescues the damsel in distress. But this unnamed maiden only received a surprise visit from a strange little man.

Not only could this magical man appear out of nowhere, but he could also spin straw into gold—for a price. In a bargaining mood, he suggested they play *Let's Make a Deal*. "What will you give me to turn this straw into gold?" he asked the maiden. When she offered her necklace, he greedily accepted and got busy spinning.

Day two, the maiden faced the same dilemma with a new stack of straw, and the peculiar man reappeared to haggle another deal. This time she offered him her ring. He took it, spun the straw into gold, and the maiden lived to see another day.

Although she received more straw on the following day, the maiden had nothing left to offer. "Surely you will become queen," the peculiar man said, "and when you do, you must give me your firstborn child."

When facing death, people will do or say almost anything to survive. Some even bargain with God, promising to serve him if he saves them. Martin Luther made such a deal. While he was traveling one night, a severe thunderstorm erupted, and lightning struck the ground nearby. Luther promised he'd become a monk if God spared his life.[1] Luther fulfilled his promise, and God used him to bring the message of Jesus' saving grace to a legalistic religious system.

Fulfilling a promise is important, especially when we've vowed to do something in exchange for God's help. Several Bible stories tell about deals made with God. One barren woman named Hannah promised God her firstborn child if God would open her womb. After giving birth to a baby boy, "She named him Samuel, saying, 'Because I asked the Lord for him'" (1 Samuel 1:20). After Hannah weaned Samuel, she brought him to the Lord's house and left him with Eli, the priest. Samuel became a mighty prophet that God used to anoint Israel's first king.

The next story has a sober ending. While making a deal with God, a man named Jephthah said, "Whatever comes out of the door of my house to meet me when I return in triumph from the Ammonites will be the Lord's, and I will sacrifice it as a burnt offering" (Judges 11:31). His daughter greeted him outside their door.

Playing *Let's Make a Deal* with God is serious business.

Thankfully, we don't have to concoct deals with God. He's already given us the deal of a lifetime—Jesus. We need only accept his offer. The Bible says, "For no matter how many promises God has made, they are 'Yes' in Christ" (2 Corinthians 1:20). When we trade our life for Christ's, we gain all of God's promises—and none of them are zonks.

A zonk was the booby prize given on the television game show *Let's Make a Deal*. I watched the popular show when I was growing up, imagining what zany costume I would wear if ever on the show. Audience members dressed in costumes to catch the attention of their host, Monty Hall. Uncle Monty, as he called himself, bartered with the audience members he chose. He referred to them as traders, and he gave each an item, such as cash, an appliance, or a box of candy, and offered them the chance to exchange it for an unknown hidden prize. But their first item might also contain a hidden prize. The show revolved around taking risks through trading.

Each show's finale gave two previous traders the option to trade what they had won for a chance at the Big Deal hidden behind one of three doors. The risk wasn't as great for those who'd won lesser-valued prizes. But for those who had already won an expensive prize, such as a car, the risk of losing what they possessed seemed too great to play for the Big Deal. Similarly, Jesus said, "Truly I tell you, it is hard for someone who is rich to enter the kingdom of heaven" (Matthew 19:23). Because following Jesus requires that we risk everything (see Luke 14:33).

Some people take risks more easily than others. I'm a conservative person by nature. In the fourth grade, my classmates and I were given the opportunity to invest fifty cents in a short-term popcorn business. For one week each spring, the fourth graders popped and sold popcorn to students after school to learn business principles and terms, such as capital, investment, and profit. I didn't invest in the popcorn business, but the students who did doubled their money—a lesson I never forgot.

Playing it safe has both pros and cons. As a youth, not being a risk taker kept me from trying unsafe activities, such as smoking or drugs. Unfortunately, it also kept me from going to Bible camp until I was in my thirties. But I didn't consider it risky to build our first home with no experience—or to marry Chuck after dating only eleven weeks. Passion can cause us to take risks we otherwise wouldn't.

In the United States, we rarely consider it risky to become a Christian. But in other parts of the world, becoming a Christian guarantees that you will be persecuted, disowned by family and friends, and often killed because of your faith. A supernatural passion and love for the Lord must empower us to risk our lives for Christ. Jim Elliott, a martyred missionary to the Auca Indians in Ecuador, South America, once said, "He is no fool who gives what he cannot keep to gain what he cannot lose."[2]

In Luke 14:26–30, Jesus addressed the cost of following him. He said:

If anyone comes to me and does not hate father and mother, wife and children, brothers and sisters—yes, even their own life—such a person cannot be my disciple. And whoever does not carry their cross and follow me cannot be my disciple. Suppose one of you wants to build a tower. Won't you first sit down and estimate the cost to see if you have enough money to complete it? For if you lay the foundation and are not able to finish it, everyone who sees it will ridicule you, saying, "This person began to build and was not able to finish."

Though salvation is free, Jesus said it would cost us to follow him. If it doesn't, we may not be following Jesus as we should. After Jesus told his wannabe followers to count the cost, he said, "In the same way, those of you who do not give up everything you have cannot be my disciple" (Luke 14:33). Many turned away at this point.

Following Jesus should cost us everything because it cost God his only Son. In his book *The Cost of Discipleship*, German Theologian Dietrich Bonhoeffer wrote, "What has cost God much cannot be cheap for us."[3] He referred to grace that doesn't cost us as cheap. He explained:

Cheap grace is the grace we bestow on ourselves. Cheap grace is the preaching of forgiveness without requiring repentance, baptism without church discipline, Communion without confession … Cheap grace is grace without discipleship, grace without the cross, grace without Jesus Christ, living and incarnate.[4]

To follow Jesus, we must give him our will, desires, interests, rights, reputation, finances, future, etc. Jesus said we must carry our cross, which means we must put to death anything in us that doesn't align with his will. Someone once said, "Your cross is where your will and the will of God cross." As we surrender to his lordship, the ultimate exchange happens—our life for his.

You may be familiar with the New York Stock Exchange, but how familiar are you with God's exchange system? How much stock (faith) do you have in God? How have you invested in his kingdom?

God's exchange system is free, but the transaction fee is faith. By faith, we release our inferior reality and exchange it with God's superior one. Jesus' death provided everything we will ever need, and the Holy Spirit helps us "understand what God has freely given us" (1 Corinthians 2:12). We needn't wonder if what's behind one of God's doors is good; everything he offers is great! It's whether we will let go of what we already have to take hold of what God has promised. The cost to follow Jesus seems minimal when we consider all we can gain.

Here are exchanges we can make:

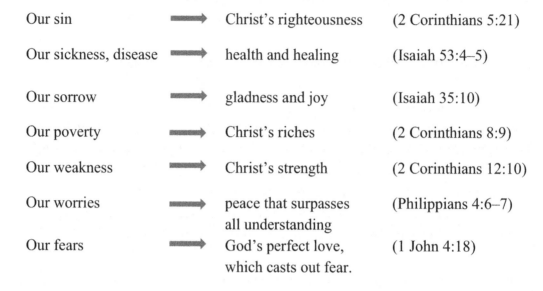

Our sin	→	Christ's righteousness	(2 Corinthians 5:21)
Our sickness, disease	→	health and healing	(Isaiah 53:4–5)
Our sorrow	→	gladness and joy	(Isaiah 35:10)
Our poverty	→	Christ's riches	(2 Corinthians 8:9)
Our weakness	→	Christ's strength	(2 Corinthians 12:10)
Our worries	→	peace that surpasses all understanding	(Philippians 4:6–7)
Our fears	→	God's perfect love, which casts out fear.	(1 John 4:18)

Who wouldn't make those trades? When we don't, it's often because we won't let go of selfishness, greed, lust, anger, bitterness, resentment, jealousy, hatred, etc. The cost can seem too great, for we must release our hurt or hatred to love our enemies as God commands. We must relinquish our right for revenge before we can forgive. It will cost us our self-will to follow Jesus and not lead a lifestyle of our choosing.

However, hanging onto the things we shouldn't is like keeping a zonk prize instead of trading it for the Big Deal—especially when we know which door to choose. Jesus said, "I am the door; if anyone enters through Me, he shall be saved, and shall go in and out, and find pasture" (John 10:9, NASB).

There is no deal you can offer God that will ever exceed what he's already offered you—your life in exchange for Christ's. It's the deal of a lifetime because all of God's promises are "yes and amen" in Christ. Paul said, "What is more, I consider everything a loss because of the surpassing worth of knowing Christ Jesus my Lord, for whose sake I have lost all things. I consider them garbage, that I may gain Christ" (Philippians 3:8). We should do no less than trade everything to gain Christ, the Biggest Deal ever.

God doesn't limit the number of trades you can make either. In fact, he encourages you to trade everything for his kingdom. Jesus compared the kingdom of heaven to a hidden treasure (Big Deal). When a person finds it, their joy is so great they sell everything they own to buy it (see Matthew 13:44). Jesus is worth making a Big Deal over, and the joy you receive will far outweigh any price you pay.

Yada Time

Are you totally invested in God's kingdom? If not, what keeps you from doing so? In what ways might you be holding out on God? What costs have you incurred by following Jesus? What have you received in exchange?

Consider all Jesus paid on your behalf. What zonk do you need to trade for God's promise? Is there something you need to let go of first? Talk to God about the transaction, and by faith make the exchange.

Day 3: The Price is Right

In desperation, the unnamed maiden agreed to the strange little man's price of her firstborn child. If the payment sounds familiar, the Witch required the same from Rapunzel's parents.

The firstborn's worth is a familiar biblical theme. It's first mentioned in the account of Cain and Abel, and it is more than a story about a jealous brother who killed his younger sibling. Their story reveals the importance of approaching God on his terms—through a sacrificial firstborn. Cain worked the land and grew crops while Abel raised livestock. "In the course of time Cain brought some of the fruits of the soil as an offering to the Lord. And Abel also brought an offering—fat portions from some of the firstborn of his flock. The Lord looked with favor on Abel and his offering" (Genesis 4:3–4). The Lord received Abel's offering but not Cain's.

God didn't accept Cain's offering because Cain had labored to produce it from the cursed soil. Our "works" will never fulfill God's requirement. God demanded the death of a spotless *firstborn* male animal, which foreshadowed Jesus' sacrificial death. Also, to create a covenant, God required the shedding of blood (see Hebrews 9:18). By not approaching God on his terms, Cain could not enter a covenant relationship with God.

But God gave Cain another chance. He said, "If you do well, will not your countenance be lifted up? And if you do not do well, sin is crouching at the door; and its desire is for you, but you must master it" (Genesis 4:7, NASB).

The word crouching in Hebrew is *rabats,* and it means to be down on four legs like an animal ready to pounce—because sin desires to have us.[5] The Hebrew word for desire is *teshuwqah.*[6] The Bible uses the same word when God pronounced a curse over Eve. "Your *desire* will be for your husband, and he will rule over you" (Genesis 3:16, emphasis added). Both verses also contain the Hebrew word *mashal*—"to have you" or "rule over."[7] Their similarities show sin's desire to become one with us intimately in order to rule over us. This imagery should encourage us not to answer the door when sin knocks.

Fortunately, a door (decision) stands between us and sin, and we can choose whether we open the door or keep it closed. As Christians, we gain victory over sin by answering Jesus' knock, the true door. Cain, however, didn't heed God's warning. He answered sin's knock and killed his brother.

God made it clear we must approach him on his terms. The Old Testament disclosed God's terms through the Law, rituals, festivals, etc., but God's purpose for them was always to point us to Jesus, "the image of the invisible God, the firstborn over all creation" (Colossians 1:15). God gave significance to the firstborn because of his firstborn, Jesus. No one comes to the Father except through Jesus (see John 14:6).

We find another example of the firstborn's significance in the Passover. It's a familiar story, so I'll give the highlights. When the Israelites were slaves in Egypt, God spoke to Moses in a burning bush and called him to deliver his people from bondage. Pharaoh wouldn't let the Israelites go, so God inflicted the Egyptians with plagues. After the ninth plague, God said to Moses, "Then say to Pharaoh, 'This is what the Lord says: Israel is my *firstborn* son, and I told you, 'Let my son go, so he may worship me.' But you refused to let him go; so I will kill your *firstborn* son'" (Exodus 4:22–23, emphasis added).

The tenth plague killed all firstborn men and animals throughout Egypt, excluding the Israelites who had sacrificed a spotless lamb and sprinkled the lamb's blood on their doorposts as God had directed (see Exodus chapters 5–12). By following God's specific instructions, the Angel of Death *passed over* the Israelites' homes. Had they not believed and obeyed God, their firstborn sons would have died along with the Egyptians' sons. Doing things God's way is the only way to live—literally.

God told the Israelites to celebrate the Passover annually, to remember when he had rescued them from slavery. Jesus celebrated the Passover meal with his disciples the evening before his crucifixion. Paul recounted the event:

> The Lord Jesus, on the night he was betrayed, took bread, and when he had given thanks, he broke it and said, "This is my body, which is for you; do this in remembrance of me." In the same way, after supper he took the cup, saying, "This cup is the new covenant in my blood; do this, whenever you drink it, in remembrance of me." For whenever you eat this bread and drink this cup, you proclaim the Lord's death until he comes. (1 Corinthians 11:23–26)

Jesus embodied the Passover by becoming our spotless lamb. His shed blood covered our sin and enacted a New Covenant with God. Through faith in Jesus, we can approach God as our loving Father. "Because you are sons [or daughters], God sent the Spirit of his Son into our hearts, the Spirit who calls out, 'Abba, Father'" (Galatians 4:6).

As God's children, God promises to take care of us. Jesus said, "If you, then, though you are evil, know how to give good gifts to your children, how much more will your Father in heaven give good gifts to those who ask him!" (Matthew 7:11). God fashioned the natural family system after a spiritual reality. Unfortunately, our sin nature causes us to demonstrate poorly God's intended purpose for the family.

In 1922, my paternal grandmother, Eva, and her five siblings were taken from their home by a government agency because their father was physically abusing their mother. Eva, the oldest, went to live in a state-run school similar to an orphanage at age seven until she turned eleven. If the school had seemed harsh, she experienced unspeakable abuse at her next home. Through an indentured program, the school gave her to a farm couple to help raise their children.

Like Cinderella, a handsome prince eventually rescued my grandma from servitude and abuse. But she kept an orphan's heart because she'd never experienced a parent's love. Grandpa was the first person to love her, and when he died, abandonment issues surfaced and triggered anxiety attacks. My aunt thought finding Grandma's birth family might bring healing, and so the search began.

At age sixty-one, Grandma learned that her father and two oldest brothers were the only immediate family members still alive. When she visited them, the reunion wasn't as she had hoped. Abused as children, her brothers were mentally impaired, and her unrepentant father, age eighty-six, suspected she'd come for his money. Judging by his dilapidated shack and outhouse, he had nothing of value. He withheld, or didn't possess, the love she had hoped to receive.

We don't have to be an orphan to get an orphan's heart. Life's hurts and hardships can also produce this in us. If we felt unloved as a child, we might struggle to receive God's love. If our parents divorced or one of them died, we might feel abandoned by God. If our behavior determined our parents' acceptance, we might doubt God's approval.

Those with an orphan's heart struggle to find their rightful place in any family, including God's. They fear punishment if they do anything wrong. They determine their worth by their achievements and try to earn love through servitude. They haven't embraced the spirit of sonship. "For you have not received a spirit of slavery leading to fear again, but you have received a spirit of adoption as sons by which we cry out, 'Abba! Father!'" (Romans 8:15, NASB).

It grieves God when we treat him as if he's a harsh taskmaster and not a loving Father. He paid an unthinkable price—his firstborn Son—so we could call him Daddy. Ephesians 3:12 says, "In him [Jesus] and through faith in him we may approach God with freedom and confidence." Though we understand that we must approach God through Jesus, we may not comprehend that we can do so with freedom and confidence. Someone with an orphan's heart might be afraid.

God knew we would struggle to approach him as his beloved children. Therefore, he sent his firstborn Son into the world to reveal God to us. Jesus said, "Anyone who has seen me has seen the Father" (John 14:9). When Jesus taught his disciples how to pray, he said to address God as "our Father." Jesus demonstrated the Father's love, and the Father gave us the spirit of sonship to help us believe we're his children. Also, God heals the wounds that cause us to feel like orphans.

God used my firstborn son's birth to heal my orphan's heart. The indescribable love I felt toward my baby overwhelmed me. I had experienced no emotion as deep or as strong. There wasn't anything I wouldn't do for that child, including die for him. I then knew (yada) God felt the same way about me, yet incomprehensibly greater. Whenever I doubt God's love or approval, I recall how much I adore my sons. Nothing could stop me from loving them, not anything they said or did. That's how much God loves us.

Romans 8:38–39 says:

> For I am convinced that neither death nor life, neither angels nor demons, neither the present nor the future, nor any powers, neither height nor depth, nor anything else in all creation, will be able to separate us from the love of God that is in Christ Jesus our Lord.

God didn't offer his Son's life in a moment of desperation as our maiden did. He planned this from the beginning. Jesus' sacrifice allows us to approach God as our Abba, Father, with freedom and confidence. We are God's children—no longer orphans. For us, the price was right.

Yada Time

Could you relate to having an orphan's heart? If so, ask the Holy Spirit to heal the wounds causing you to doubt God's goodness and help you embrace your identity as his child. Talk with God about your hurts as they surface. He may ask you to forgive someone, or he may bring truth to a lie you believe. Trust the Holy Spirit to continue this work within you. It is a process. Spending time with God and experiencing his love will increase our confidence and freedom when we draw near to him.

Day 4: I've Got a Secret

The King married the unnamed maiden, and before long she gave birth to a baby boy. The strange little man appeared soon after to retrieve the pledged child from the Queen, but because of the mother's pleading and the man's addiction to bargaining, he gave her a chance to win the child back. "If in three days you can tell me my name," said the man, "I'll let you keep your child."

We discussed earlier that God offers us the deal of a lifetime through his Son, Jesus. Although God's plan originated before the world's foundation, he set his Big Deal in motion with Abraham when he promised to make his name great, give him more descendants than there are stars, and bless all the nations of the earth through his lineage. Abraham didn't ask for this blessing; it was part of God's plan. Abraham did, however, negotiate a different deal with God later. This happened after God shared another secret with him.

Yes, God has secrets. Once upon a time, Jesus was his biggest secret. Colossians 1:26 refers to Jesus as "the mystery that has been kept hidden for ages and generations, but is now disclosed to the Lord's people." But it's not as if God didn't provide clues. Many biblical prophecies described Jesus' coming. Amos 3:7 says, "Surely the Lord God does nothing unless He reveals His secret counsel to His servants the prophets" (NASB).

The Bible refers to Abraham as both a prophet (see Genesis 20:7) and God's friend (see James 2:23). Abraham enjoyed a close relationship with God, and because of their friendship, God confided in Abraham. He told Abraham his secret plan to destroy the wicked cities of Sodom and Gomorrah. Since Abraham's nephew, Lot, and his family lived in Sodom, Abraham found the courage to negotiate with God. He said, "What if there are fifty righteous people in the city? Will you really sweep it away and not spare the place for the sake of the fifty righteous people in it?" (Genesis 18:24).

God agreed not to destroy the city if he found fifty righteous people living there. But Abraham didn't know how many righteous people God would find, so he continued bargaining. He asked if there were only forty-five, then forty, then thirty-five, etc. until God agreed not to destroy the city if he found only ten righteous people. God didn't find even ten righteous people. But because Abraham was his close friend—and God is just—God sent angels to bring Lot and his family to safety before he destroyed Sodom (see Genesis 18:17–19:29).

The prophet Moses was another close friend of God's (see Exodus 33:11). Most prophets are, since they speak on God's behalf. After Moses had led the Israelites to freedom, his brother and sister questioned his authority. God responded:

When there is a prophet among you, I, the Lord, reveal myself to him in visions,
I speak to them in dreams. But this is not true of my servant Moses; he is faithful
in all my house. With him I speak face to face, clearly and not in riddles; he sees
the form of the Lord. (Numbers 12:6–8)

Who wouldn't want God to speak to them face to face and more clearly? How do we develop that friendship with God? Moses obeyed God and spent hours in his presence. He hung out with God so much that it showed—his face literally glowed. He took on God's likeness. Friends look and act like each other the more time they spend together. They finish each other's sentences. They anticipate each other's next move. Best friends' hearts beat as one, and God longs to be that close to us.

After Jesus had spent over three years with his disciples, he said to them, "I no longer call you servants, because a servant does not know his master's business. Instead, I have called you friends, for everything that I learned from my Father I have made known to you" (John 15:15). Like God did with Abraham and Moses, Jesus let his disciples in on his secrets. He spoke to them clearly, but to everyone else he spoke in parables. When Jesus' disciples asked him why he spoke in parables, he answered:

This is why I speak to them in parables: "Though seeing, they do not see; though hearing, they do not hear or understand. In them is fulfilled the prophecy of Isaiah: 'You will be ever hearing but never understanding; you will be ever seeing but never perceiving. For this people's heart has become calloused; they hardly hear with their ears, and they have closed their eyes. Otherwise they might see with their eyes, hear with their ears, understand with their hearts and turn, and I would heal them.'" (Matthew 13:13–15)

Jesus' disciples didn't understand the parables' meanings any more than the crowd did, but their hearts weren't calloused. They believed in Jesus and spent endless hours with him. They hungered to understand his teachings, so they asked him to explain each parable's meaning.

In his book *Dreaming with God*, Bill Johnson writes:

It is the mercy of God to withhold revelation from those who have no hunger for truth, because if they don't hunger for it, the chances are they won't obey it when they hear it. Revelation always brings responsibility, and hunger is the thing that prepares our hearts to carry the weight of that responsibility. By keeping revelation from those without hunger, God actually protects them from certain failure to carry the responsibility it would lay on them.[8]

Besides protecting those who aren't ready to receive more, God also hides things to create an opportunity to reward those who are hungry. We must seek God to gain understanding or new revelation, and Hebrews 11:6 says, God "rewards those who earnestly seek him." Those who draw near to God distinguish themselves as God's closest friends. Not everyone pursues knowing God intimately.

After Moses received the Ten Commandments, he descended the mountain and recited the Law to the Israelites. This was their response:

When the people saw the thunder and lightning and heard the trumpet and saw the mountain in smoke, they trembled with fear. They stayed at a distance and said to Moses, "Speak to us yourself and we will listen. But do not have God speak to us or we will die." Moses said to the people, "Do not be afraid. God has come to test you, so that the fear of God will be with you to keep you from sinning." The people remained at a distance, while Moses approached the thick darkness where God was. (Exodus 20:18–21)

God, who is light, possibly cloaked himself in darkness to give the people an opportunity to walk by faith. Or maybe he did so to learn who would or wouldn't follow him when life got scary. Only a true friend will follow another friend with no concern for her own life. God wants us to be that kind of friend, one who walks with him despite our fears and follows him no matter what it costs.

God never intended to speak solely through the prophets, but the Israelites chose this method of hearing. God wants to speak to everyone personally. Through Jesus, God extends this offer to us today. Not all will listen and nurture an intimate friendship with him. Those who do will be privy to God's secrets.

Another reason God tells his friends secrets is so that they, like Abraham, will negotiate with him. The Bible refers to this as intercession. God wants us to cry out to him on behalf of others. Moses interceded for the Israelites after they had fashioned a golden calf to worship. God wanted to destroy the Israelites, but Moses convinced him not to (see Exodus 32:11–14). Several prophets interceded for Israel throughout history. God knew no *human* could provide a permanent solution to sin through intercession.

Isaiah 59:16 says, "And [God] saw that there was no man, and was astonished that there was no one to intercede; Then His own arm brought salvation to Him; And His righteousness upheld Him" (NASB). Today Jesus sits at the Father's right hand, interceding for us (see Romans 8:34). And when we don't know how or what to pray, "The Spirit himself intercedes for us through wordless groans" (Romans 8:26).

God's secrets fall into many categories. Like the strange little man's unknown name, God has aspects of himself he keeps hidden, such as a quality or characteristic we haven't yet experienced. Other secrets may be solutions to problems or answers to questions. Some could be discoveries waiting to happen—think inventions or cures for diseases. The Bible contains secret wisdom, revelation, and prophecies yet to be fulfilled. In Jesus, God hid "all the treasures of wisdom and knowledge" (Colossians 2:3). God will share these secrets with those who hunger to know him more.

We determine how intimate a friendship we enjoy with God. He shares his heart and his secrets with those who hunger to know him. He wants friends who will love as he loves, and who will intercede for others as Jesus does for us.

Yada Time

What one thing could you do to improve your friendship with God? If nothing comes to mind, ask God what he thinks. He might say you're his best friend—no improvement needed. Keep in mind that God never condemns. If he offers a suggestion, you may feel remorse, but this godly sorrow will lead you to make a change. The enemy, however, condemns. He will tell you that you don't measure up. God's loving corrections will draw you closer. Thank God for his friendship.

Has God brought to mind anyone for whom you could intercede? Pray what comes to mind and trust the Holy Spirit to relay to the Father exactly what the person needs. Thank God for what he's about to do in that person's life.

Day 5: Name that Tune

The strange little man's propensity to bargain bought the Queen some time, but her firstborn's fate rested on her ability to guess the man's name. What an impossible task she faced. Since a mother's love is fierce, she sent her servants far and wide to discover this man's name. While searching the forest, one servant came upon the strange little man dancing a pre-victory jig and singing:

> Merrily the feast I'll make. Today I'll brew, tomorrow bake.
> Merrily I'll dance and sing, for next day will a stranger bring.
> Little does my lady dream, Rumpelstiltskin is my name!

The servant rushed back and told the Queen, and when the strange little man appeared the next day, the Queen recited Rumpelstiltskin's name to his dismay and displeasure.

The authors Brothers Grimm no doubt chose the name Rumpelstiltskin because of its inherent meaning: a goblin that rattles posts to make noise.[9] Their German readers would have made this connection and characterized the strange little man as ghoulish. Names have a meaning, and whether we like or dislike our names, they represent us.

In biblical times, the Israelites believed a name signified a person's nature or personality. Parents often named a child after a characteristic or circumstance surrounding their birth. Abraham and Sarah named their son Isaac, which means laughter, because Sarah laughed when God told her she'd have a child at age ninety.[10] During childbirth, when Jacob's wife Rachel realized she was dying, she named their newborn son Ben-Oni, meaning "son of my pain."[11] Jacob changed the child's name to Benjamin, "son of my right hand."[12]

God changed several people's names to more accurately portray them. He changed Abram's name, which means "exalted father," to Abraham, "father of a multitude," because God had promised Abraham he'd father many nations.[13] God changed Jacob's name to Israel after Jacob had wrestled with God. Israel means "because you have struggled with God and with humans and have overcome" (Genesis 32:28).

We discussed earlier that the Israelites gave descriptive names to God after they experienced him in new ways, such as Jehovah-Jireh, which means God will provide (see Genesis 22:14). "The oldest Semitic word meaning 'God' is El. Linguists believe its base meaning is strength or power. 'El' is the Strong One, or the Deity (God)."[14] The Jews added attributes to El to create new names, such as El Roi, the God who sees me.[15] Yahweh (YHWH) is the most personal of God's names.[16] God used the root meaning of this name when Moses asked what he should call him. "God said to Moses, 'I AM WHO I AM. This is what you are to say to the Israelites: 'I AM has sent me to you'" (Exodus 3:14).

It was no accident Jesus used seven I Am titles when referring to himself. He declared himself God by saying:

- "I am the bread of life." (John 6:35)
- "I am the light of the world." (John 8:12)
- "I am the door." (John 10:9, NASB)
- "I am the good shepherd." (John 10:11)
- "I am the resurrection and the life." (John 11:25)
- "I am the way and the truth and the life." (John 14:6)
- "I am the true vine." (John 15:1)

If the people hadn't made the connection, they did when Jesus said, "Before Abraham was born, I am!" (John 8:58). At this, they picked up stones to kill him. They understood his message and considered it blasphemous to infer he was God, but Jesus *is* God—the great I AM.

Jesus told his disciples, "Remember what I told you: 'A servant is not greater than his master.' If they persecuted me, they will persecute you also. If they obeyed my teaching, they will obey yours also. They will treat you this way because of *my name*, for they do not know the one who sent me" (John 15:20–21, emphasis added).

Even today, Jesus' name is the most controversial of all God's names. Many people mistakenly believe that we all worship the same God, reasoning that non-Christian religions simply call him by different names. That would be like saying that all people with the name Kim Larson are me. Sure, some people call me by other names, such as Kimmi, Kimberly Clark, or Kimosabe. But if someone wanted to find *me* among several Kim Larsons, they would ask personal questions about me, such as "Does she have two sons named Jordan and Jesse?" and "Is she married to Chuck Larson?" The answers would distinguish me from all other Kim Larsons.

Though there is but one God, we do not all worship him because our definitions of who he is are not the same. Not every faith believes that Jesus is God's son. Nor do they believe that Jesus is God. Jesus came to reveal the Father, and he said those who persecute him do not know the Father. God is Father, Son, and Holy Spirit—three persons in one. Those who don't believe in the triune Godhead don't worship the one true God. But God loves those who do not yet know him, and because he does, he asks us to lead others to him.

Although Jesus is God, he became a man and humbly obeyed the Father, becoming the perfect Passover sacrifice. Philippians 2:9–11 says:

Therefore God exalted him to the highest place and gave him the name that is above every name, that at the name of Jesus every knee should bow, in heaven and on earth and under the earth, and every tongue acknowledge that Jesus Christ is Lord, to the glory of God the Father.

There is no higher name than Jesus. It means God saves or Jehovah is salvation (see Matthew 1:21). Jesus saves (sozo) us from our sins and eternal damnation, and he also heals, delivers, rescues, and makes us whole. Romans 10:13 says, "Everyone who calls on the name of the Lord will be saved." Jesus' name represents him, so by calling on his name we're petitioning him for help.

When we use a famous person's name to impress others or get preferential treatment, we call that name-dropping. We often feel special because of who we know. God's not impressed by name-dropping—unless it's his Son's name we're using. Jesus told his disciples, "Truly, truly, I say to you, if you shall ask the Father for anything, He will give it to you in My name. Until now you have asked for nothing in My name; ask, and you will receive, that your joy may be made full" (John 16:23–24, NASB).

Asking in someone's name wasn't something new to Jesus' disciples. They would have understood this concept and what it implied. Masters gave their trusted servants the authority to do business transactions on their behalf. Businesses today authorize only certain people to make decisions and to sign checks. Jesus authorized his trusted friends to do business in his name and to withdraw from his account whatever they needed. He knew they would represent him and his interests well.

Unfortunately, some people drop God's names without calling on him. They dishonor him by flippantly saying his name when surprised, excited, angry, or disappointed. Some even use it to curse others. When a society no longer honors God, using his name as the latest slang isn't surprising. But Christians should know better. The third commandment says, "You shall not misuse the name of the Lord your God, for the Lord will not hold anyone guiltless who misuses his name" (Exodus 20:7).

We may not utter God's name as profanity, but we misuse it when our lives don't reflect his nature and character. As Christ's followers, we bear his name, but not always do we bear it well, such as when we lie, cheat, steal, backbite, gossip, divorce, and act selfishly. If we disrespect his name by our actions, we give the world little reason to revere his name—or even believe in him. We need to live up to Jesus' name and model his nature, character, attributes, and his love for others.

Jesus commanded his disciples to "heal the sick, raise the dead, cleanse those who have leprosy, drive out demons" (Matthew 10:8). Wouldn't his name receive the honor it deserves if we who bear his name worked miracles as he did?

In John 14:12–14, Jesus said:

Very truly I tell you, whoever believes in me will do the works I have been doing, and they will do even greater things than these, because I am going to the Father. And I will do whatever you ask in my name, so that the Father may be glorified in the Son. You may ask me for anything in my name, and I will do it.

Asking in Jesus' name is more than dropping Jesus' name to the Father. It means we come in his authority, desiring to do what Jesus did or would do. We re-present him to the world, reflecting his character and attributes, loving others as he loves. We ask in Jesus' name because his name is above all other names, and we bear that name.

When we come before the Father in Jesus' name, we approach God on his terms—through the sacrifice of his firstborn Son. Wearing Jesus' righteousness, we can come freely and confidently before our holy God, no longer as orphans but as beloved children. When we hunger to develop a deeper friendship with God, he shares his heart and secrets with us. We, in turn, intercede for those who need his help or who don't personally know him yet. God entrusts us with Jesus' name, his authority, so we will re-present him to the world that needs him. When we make a big deal over (glorify) Jesus, others will desire to gain the Biggest Deal offered, too!

Yada Time

Is praying in Jesus' name new to you? If not, has your definition of "in his name" changed at all? If so, how does it differ from before? What has God highlighted to you about asking in Jesus' name? In Jesus' name, ask the Father for what's on your heart. In faith, thank him for answering your prayer.

What do you appreciate most about carrying Jesus' name? What do you find the most difficult? In what ways do you misuse Jesus' name by your actions? Maybe you lack his patience or compassion toward others? Ask God to forgive you and help you to represent Jesus more genuinely to others.

Rejoice that God loves you as you are! Thank the Holy Spirit for continuing to make you more like Jesus.

Chapter 9
Rumpelstiltskin—Redeemed and Righteous
Questions for Reflection or Discussion

Day 1: Jeopardy

1. How had the Galatians "fallen away from grace"? (p. 152)

2. What Pharisee tendencies did you recognize in yourself?

3. What helped you recognize the weight of your sinfulness?

4. In what ways might we still measure God's acceptance of us by our actions? (p. 152)

5. What do we miss out on when we complete spiritual to-do lists from obligation? (p. 153)

Day 2: Let's Make a Deal

1. If you've ever made a deal with God when you were in trouble, share about it.

2. What is the cost of following Jesus? (p. 156)

3. What does it mean to carry your cross? (p. 156)

4. Why might we not make a trade? (p. 157)

5. Is there a trade you need to make?

Day 3: The Price is Right

1. Why didn't God accept Cain's offering? (p. 158)

2. How are we to approach God? (p. 159)

3. In what ways could you relate to having an orphan's heart? (p. 160)

4. Ephesians 3:12 tells us to approach God how? (p. 160)

5. How did Jesus reveal the Father? (p. 160)

Day 4: I've got a Secret

1. Why did God share his plans with Abraham? (p. 162)

2. How can we develop a deeper friendship with God? (p. 162)

3. Why did Jesus speak in parables? (p. 163)

4. Why does God hide things from us? (p. 163)

5. What should we do with the secrets God tells us? (p. 164)

6. List the qualities God looks for in a friend.

Day 5: Name that Tune

1. Why did Jesus refer to himself using "I Am" titles? (p. 165)

2. How can we know if a different religion worships the One True God? (p. 166)

3. What does Jesus' name mean? (p. 166)

4. What does it mean to ask in Jesus' name? (p. 167)

5. Besides using his name profanely, how might we misuse it? (p. 167)

6. How might we demonstrate his name appropriately? (p. 167)

7. Is there anything else in this chapter you want to discuss?

Share prayer requests and pray for each other. Let's approach God boldly through his Son, asking in Jesus' name.

Chapter 10
Snow White—Spotless Bride

Memory Verse:

"Come now, let us settle the matter," says the Lord.
"Though your sins are like scarlet, they shall be as white as snow;
though they are red as crimson, they shall be like wool."
Isaiah 1:18

Day 1: Mirror, Mirror

Snow White's name alludes to this beloved princess' innocence and virtue. In Disney's movie of the story, she's cheerful, childlike, kind-hearted, hardworking, optimistic, and perilously naïve. Her physical beauty surpasses all others. Today, we might compare her to Miss America, the title and crown many young girls dream of wearing. Snow White encompasses what most women long to be—beautiful inside and out. Yet, who would trade places with her?

After Snow White's mother died, her father married a raving beauty. This narcissistic woman acquired the well-deserved title of Evil Queen. Gazing into her magic mirror, the queen uttered these infamous words, "Mirror, Mirror, on the wall, who's the fairest one of all?" We know by now nothing good ever comes from asking a mirror for validation, magic or not.

For years, the mirror pronounced the queen the fairest in the land. But the mirror could not lie, and one day it answered that Snow White's beauty exceeded the Evil Queen's. The queen became enraged and ordered a woodsman to take her stepdaughter into the woods and kill her.

Jealousy can do that to a person. It caused Joseph's brothers to sell him as a slave. It also seduced Israel's first king, Saul, into trying to kill a young shepherd boy named David. King Saul began his reign humbly, hiding from the Israelites among the baggage at his coronation. Saul won the people's hearts as a valiant warrior. But his popularity waned when David, a ruddy young fellow, killed the giant Goliath who had been taunting Israel. Later, when David returned from another battle, the women turned their attention from Saul to David.

As the women danced, "this was their song: 'Saul has slain his thousands, and David his tens of thousands.' This made Saul very angry. 'What's this?' he said. 'They credit David with ten thousands and me with only thousands. Next they'll be making him their king!' So from that time on Saul kept a jealous eye on David" (1 Samuel 18:7–9, NLT).

One dictionary defines jealous as:

- Hostile toward a rival or one believed to enjoy an advantage
- Intolerant of rivalry or unfaithfulness
- Vigilant in guarding a possession[1]

Like the Evil Queen, who saw Snow White as a rival, King Saul saw David as a threat to his crown. I suspect we've all experienced jealousy at one time or another—and probably still do. We can become jealous when our best friend spends more time with someone other than us. Or losing the title of "best" at anything can cause a jealous fit. Jealousy can also arise when a spouse gazes too long at a person of the opposite sex.

God created us for himself, and he wants us to love and worship him above all others. When we're unfaithful to him, he gets jealous. Exodus 20:5 says, "You shall not bow down to [idols] or worship them; for I, the Lord your God, am a jealous God." Jealousy isn't always a sin. It's how we respond to jealousy that can lead to sin.

If something isn't ours to begin with, envy more accurately describes wanting what isn't ours. King Solomon wrote, "And I saw that all toil and all achievement spring from one person's envy of another" (Ecclesiastes 4:4). In modern slang, you might say we're trying to keep up with the Kardashians. Envy is a "painful or resentful awareness of an advantage enjoyed by another joined with a desire to possess the same advantage."[2]

Cain envied Abel's relationship with God, and it angered him enough to commit murder. Mark 15:9–10 tells us the Jews murdered Jesus from envy. "Pilate answered them, saying, 'Do you want me to release for you the King of the Jews?' For he was aware that the chief priests had handed Him over because of envy" (NASB).

Like envy, covetousness is "to desire wrongfully, inordinately, or without due regard for the rights of others."[3] Coveting made God's top-ten list of thou-shall-nots. But King Ahab didn't care. He coveted Naboth's vineyard located close to his palace. When Naboth wouldn't accept King Ahab's offer to trade vineyards, the king sulked until Jezebel, the most wicked queen ever, had Naboth killed (see 1 Kings 21:1–16).

Envy, jealousy, and covetousness often erupt involuntarily within us, but we can't let them rule us. We must heed God's warning to Cain: "sin is crouching at the door; and its desire is for you, but you must master it" (Genesis 4:7, NASB). We must rely on God's strength and refuse to put on any unwanted emotion. We should also strive to be content with who we are and with what we have. When we master contentment, sin won't have a fighting chance against us.

The Apostle Paul wrote, "I know what it is to be in need, and I know what it is to have plenty. I have learned the secret of being content in any and every situation, whether well fed or hungry, whether living in plenty or in want" (Philippians 4:12). Life experiences, both good and bad, provided opportunities for Paul to practice contentment. In the next verse, he shared his how-to secret: "I can do all this through [Christ] who gives me strength" (verse 13). God's strength will enable us to learn contentment and defeat the fleshly desires battling within us.

Envy, jealousy, and covetousness are acts of our sin nature. Paul tells the Corinthian believers: "for you are still fleshly. For since there is jealousy and strife among you, are you not fleshly, and are you not walking like mere men?" (1 Corinthians 3:3, NASB). If we were spiritually mature, would we desire what others have? Would we want to be like someone else?

Contentment is another process that involves renewing our minds. We must displace the lies we believe about us and agree with who God says we are. When we know full well (yada) that God created us fearfully and wonderfully, we'll be content with how he made us (see Psalm 139:14). We'll see ourselves as God sees us and not want to LAF (look, act, and feel) like someone else. By obtaining our identity in Christ, earthly crowns or titles won't matter.

Contentment's other side involves material possessions, power, and popularity. We reveal our discontentment when we covet what others have. We may possess something similar, such as a car, house, or job, yet we want what someone else has because it seems better. Maybe we desire a more successful career, or we want the popularity that a friend enjoys. Maybe we long to have more influence at work, church, or in our community. Discontentment isn't always wrong. It's how badly we want something, what we're willing to do to get it, and whether God wants us to have it that matter.

Discontentment can take many forms, but the 3-T approach to conquering it is the same: Turn, Thank, and Trust. Contentment begins by turning to God and not from him. Besides turning to gain his strength, we should turn to him to express how we're feeling. Unfortunately, too often in our discontentment, we choose not to talk to God. We may feel guilty or ashamed, or we might want to hang onto the negative emotions. This is all the more reason to talk to God. It's not as if he doesn't know how we feel. If we allow discontentment to grow, it can turn into a complaint against God. And it's better to complain to God than about him.

What if Eve had complained to God before taking that infamous first bite when she thought he was holding out on her? How do you think God would have responded? Is it possible we don't turn to God because we imagine him answering, "You can't because I said so"? God may have told Eve to trust him without explaining, but he may have responded differently. We'll never know because Eve never had that conversation. Maybe God would have explained his rules were for her protection. He might have reminded her that he created her in his image and she was perfect the way she was. God desires heartfelt conversations with us.

In the Book of Psalms, King David provided numerous examples of honest dialogue with God. His transparency encourages us to cry out to God. He wrote, "I pour out before [God] my complaint; before him I tell my trouble" (Psalm 142:2). David complained to God, not about him. Many of David's psalms end with his praising and thanking God. David's attitude didn't change because he'd gotten things off his chest; his encounter with God changed him.

Choosing to be thankful also displaces discontentment. Add praise to your thanksgiving soundtrack and contentment comes even faster. By thanking God for what we already have, we shift our focus from what we don't have. Our expectation increases as we reflect on the good things God provides. Then we'll expect his blessings to continue "immeasurably more than all we ask or imagine" (Ephesians 3:20).

We can trust God because he is faithful. He is for us, not against us. He will "never leave you nor forsake you" (Deuteronomy 31:6). Trusting God is at the heart of our walk with him. We can even trust God to change our desires. If our desires are from him, we can trust him to fulfill them—in his way and timing. The more we experience God, the more we'll trust him. The more we trust him, the more content we'll be to wait for him to supply all our needs.

In the first chapter, we learned one dictionary uses the word content to define happy. If we truly want to live happily ever after, we must learn not to put on envy, jealousy, and covetousness. We must learn to be content with who we are and with what we have. When we *turn* toward God and *thank* and *trust* him in every situation, happily ever after becomes our reality.

Yada Time

Do you often feel jealous or envious of others? Why do you think that is? If you don't know, turn to the Lord and ask him to show you the reason. Tell him how you feel and listen for his response. Allow him to heal any past hurt or bring truth to a lie. If you aren't content with how God made you, then ask him to help you experience how valuable you are and how much he loves you.

Thank God for what he's done for you and for what he's given you. Tell him about any need and desire you have. Now show him you trust him by thanking him in advance for answering your requests as he sees fit. If discontentment is an issue, ask God to help you learn contentment. Turn to him when discontentment surfaces and thank him for what you have. Trust him to work in you the ability to be content. Make him your heart's greatest desire.

Day 2: Wonder Woman

Had Snow White gotten stranded in the middle of our Minnesota woods in January, her story might not have ended so happily. At twenty below zero, she would have died from hypothermia. Thankfully, she happened upon a cozy cottage to take refuge.

Though our winters can be brutal, lightly falling snow can make them seem magical and wondrous, especially to children. Some of my fondest memories involve playing in the snow with my dad. Since he worked a full-time job besides farming, he had little time to play with us kids until winter.

One day, Dad plowed snow into a white mountain with the bucket attached to his John Deere tractor. Then he shoveled out a fort with multiple rooms so high my siblings and I could stand in them. Another time, after a fresh snowfall, he bundled us up and led us to an open field where he played Fox and Goose with us by moonlight.

Sledding, snow forts, and snowball fights create childhood memories that can last a lifetime, and it's a good thing they do. Like the snow, our playtimes melt away as we mature. Most adults view snow as a nuisance that needs removing from their driveways before going to work. To-do lists and other responsibilities also cut into our fun. Eventually, we take life so seriously we lose our childlike wonder. At least I did. When that happens, our happiness dramatically diminishes.

There's an old proverb: "all work and no play makes Jack a dull boy." Life shouldn't be only fun and games because all play and no work makes Jack a playboy—or, at best, childish. We've already looked at our need for maturity, so I'm not advocating anything less. Yet even the mature should keep a sense of playfulness and childlike wonder. If you've lost yours, you can regain it. Three adorable neighborhood girls helped me recapture mine.

It was 1999, and I had set out on a different quest. Harry Potter and Pokémon were capturing children's hearts around the world, including my two boys, then ages six and nine, and I wanted their affection toward God to increase, not their interest in hocus pocus. Hoping to provide a positive alternative, I invited our neighborhood children to join me in creating what I called a God Seekers' Club.

On Mondays after school and work, I opened our home to a dozen grade-school children and their preschool-aged siblings. I prepared weekly Bible story lessons and included a game, craft, and music. We played, prayed, and learned about God together in a safe, loving environment. Because we were neighbors, our interaction didn't stop there.

One Sunday afternoon, the three preschool-aged girls from the club knocked on our front door. When I answered, they asked, "Can you play?" I was overjoyed because they wanted to spend extra time with me; plus, little girls play differently than little boys. We colored, did crafts, and danced freely to Christian music. I made time to play and enjoy life again.

I had set out to teach children about our awesome God, never suspecting they'd teach me in return. Not only did they teach me, but they set me on the path to joy again. I'd been taking life too seriously for too long. I embraced becoming childlike and gained the ability to see the world with childlike wonder.

Then Jordan came home from school excited one day and told me his third-grade class was watching caterpillars transform into Monarch butterflies. I wanted in on that action. I knew these caterpillars liked to eat milkweed, so we drove to a nearby ditch and found a few caterpillars munching on the plants. We placed the caterpillars and their food supply in a gallon-size glass jar, and they chomped nonstop. Soon, the largest one spun itself into a chrysalis, and I got to watch it happen! Two weeks later, God granted me the honor of seeing it at the exact second it emerged as a magnificent Monarch butterfly. God is amazing, and so is his creation!

Jordan also became fascinated with the heavens, so we often took our sleeping bags outside to lie under the stars and locate the Big Dipper and other constellations. We became giddy when seeing a falling star, a lunar eclipse, or a meteor shower. So many things I'd once ignored or thought ordinary produced excitement in me. I became curious, creative, and as joyful as a child. I felt like Rip Van Winkle after he'd awakened from his twenty-year nap.

Recapturing your childlike wonder doesn't require you to spend time with children (or insects). Nor must you stargaze. But it requires you to slow down enough to enjoy the wonder-filled world around you. Children do this easily because the concept of time means little to them.

They are seldom in a hurry unless it's to run and play, and it's nearly impossible to rush them when they're in their "wonder mode" exploring the universe and discovering treasures.

We experience wonder in two important yet distinct ways. First, wonder happens when something spectacular surprises or amazes us. We may be filled with wonder at seeing a magnificent sunset or the Great Pyramid of Giza. This type of wonder often leads to wonder's second definition, which is to be curious, ask questions, or seek understanding.[4] Curiosity keeps us learning, ignites creativity, and instills critical thinking. Wonder makes life more wonder-full because it awakens our soul.

A life without wonder can seem boring or a drudgery. Consider King Solomon's life. He was the wisest, wealthiest, and most powerful king to reign over Israel, yet his writings in the book of Ecclesiastes seem as if he's the most depressed man ever to live. Solomon refers to everything as "vanity," "meaningless," or "a chasing after the wind." He wrote, "What has been will be again, what has been done will be done again; there is nothing new under the sun," (Ecclesiastes 1:9).

Could it be that Solomon had lost his childlike wonder? Maybe we would too if we were as smart as he was, but how many of us need to worry about that? However, we should be concerned if our attitude toward life becomes as pessimistic as Solomon's—or Winnie the Pooh's friend Eeyore. Can't you hear Eeyore saying, "It's a gloomy day, but 'there's nothing new under the sun' anyway?" We can guard against negativity by adding more wonder to our lives, which means we should pursue it.

We can't expect wonder to leap onto our laps. We must slow down enough to notice it. We must learn to live in the moment. Too often I'm thinking about what will happen next. When we worry about tomorrow or dwell on our past, we miss the magical moments in front of us. We won't recognize God's fingerprints in our surroundings or circumstances.

Children notice everything. They are constantly exploring and learning because so much appears as new to them. "Nothing new under the sun" seems untrue from a child's perspective, and it should from ours too because God is making all things new (see Revelation 21:5), including us. You are a wonder—a wonder woman. In Christ, you are a new creation (see 2 Corinthians 5:17). God's plan crescendos until he's made all things new.

We can experience more wonder in our lives by seeking the God of Wonders. First Corinthians 2:9–10 says, "But just as it is written, 'Things which eye has not seen and ear has not heard, and which have not entered the heart of man, all that God has prepared for those who love Him.' For to us God revealed them through the Spirit; for the Spirit searches all things, even the depths of God" (NASB). The Spirit has amazing things to share with us—and do through us—that will fill our lives with wonder.

We can have wonder-filled days when we go on adventures with God. As he directs our steps, we'll experience frequent surprises, divine appointments, unexpected conversations, and amazing miracles. We'll see his fingerprints in the tiniest details and be astonished. Those who live out of their comfort zones boldly will witness and perform the greatest wonders; they'll truly be Wonder Women.

God has called us to do the impossible—which isn't possible apart from him. When we do the good works he's prepared in advance for us; we'll live wonder-filled days without end. Life will never be the same as we witness all things being made new under the Son's radiance.

Yada Time

Have you ever had a question pop into your mind and soon afterward the answer appeared? That was God, surprising you with wonder. Stay alert to the questions you receive.

Do you need to learn how to play again? Schedule a playdate with a girlfriend, or go on an adventure with God. Recall the adventures you've experienced with him and ask for more. Be willing to drop what you're doing and follow him.

Practice staying in the moment. Slow down and see the wonder around you. Set aside time to admire God's handiwork. Experience the vast wonder found in our Creator. Enjoy his awesomeness. Come to your Daddy with childlike faith, and experience the wonder of being you.

Day 3: Community

Some mornings I wake up grumpy. Other mornings, I let him sleep in. It's an old joke, but I hope you at least smiled. Grumpy didn't. Not when he found Snow White sleeping across several of the Seven Dwarfs' beds. In the Disney movie, woodland animals led Snow White deep into the woods to the dwarfs' cottage while they were at work. When they returned home, personalities clashed as the dwarfs argued whether Snow White could stay.

Perhaps Snow White's beauty charmed them into giving her refuge, or maybe her desperate situation convinced them she could stay. The delicious aroma from the warm meal she'd prepared probably didn't hurt either. Communal living has its challenges, but it also has its advantages, such as sharing the workload.

While growing up in a household of seven, everyone had their chores. When Mom told us to set the table, we'd blurt out the task we wanted, often arguing over who'd said what first. Calling "silverware" was the least preferred option, unlike calling "plates and glasses." We learned to work, share, and care for each other. Sure, we also disagreed and often fought, but we always had each other's backs. Though we couldn't say it then, we loved each other and still do.

In the chapter on Chicken Little, we learned God created us to enjoy a relationship with him and others. As his children, he wants us to live as one big happy family because in a secure, loving environment we attain unity, maturity, and the fullness of Christ. Here we also bump into each other and knock off our rough edges, as The Princess and the Pea illustrated. Rapunzel taught us that walls keep us from experiencing community. And in Sleeping Beauty, we saw how fellowship with other believers creates a synergy that keeps us spiritually awake.

Throughout this book, I've told stories about the blessings gained from sharing life with other believers. I can't stress enough the importance of adhering to Hebrews 10:25, which tells us "not [to give] up meeting together, as some are in the habit of doing, but encouraging one another—and all the more as you see the Day approaching." Besides gaining the encouragement we all need, much more than that happens when believers gather in Jesus' name. Satan knows this, and that's why he tries to keep us apart.

Like the stock market, community has its risks. Most things yielding a high return do. Hosting a fellowship group may not seem risky to some, but I battled many fears before deciding. Our home would be one of several places the congregants could choose from. What if no one chose us? Everyone would see we had no friends if our sign-up sheet, displayed prominently each Sunday in the church's foyer, showed only our names. What if people did sign up, but no one got along? What if we disagreed in our beliefs? Fear and the endless what-if questions can muddle our thoughts and keep us from community, spiritual or otherwise.

Several brave souls gathered weekly at our home, and God blessed everyone beyond their expectations. However, the risks continued. That is probably why people quit attending or don't join groups to begin with. To truly connect with others, we must reveal our authentic selves in all our weaknesses, sins, and brokenness. It requires vulnerability and courage. Those who risk allowing others to get to know them will yield the highest return and become like family.

We don't know if the Seven Dwarfs were brothers or friends. But having lived together as adults, I imagine they considered themselves a family. Like most families, vast differences existed among the dwarfs, as their names suggest. God created each person to be unique. No two people are exactly alike, blood-related or not.

I'm reminded of this whenever the preschool children sing at the front of the church during a worship service. I love their diverseness and authenticity. Each child approaches the task differently, and not every child will sing. Some never open their mouths. Others sing only when the spirit moves them. One timid toddler usually cries. An ambitious tyke projects his voice so loudly he drowns out the rest. Several others bop to the music, bumping into those next to them. At least one child tires and sits down. Finding this unacceptable, his neighbor attempts to coax him to his feet. And there's always the little girl who waves and lifts her dress in an unladylike manner.

Before they begin, parents scurry to the empty front pew to take pictures or record their child's performance. Those in the audience shift in their seats to get a better view. Who doesn't love to watch children perform? Their personalities shine or become exposed under the spotlight. We applaud their courage, and we adore their lack of pretense. If only we could enjoy each other's uniqueness as much as we enjoy it in children.

As adults, our differences don't seem as endearing when personalities clash and perspectives differ. Yet, God created each person as unique on purpose, and for a purpose. Besides being a family, 1 Corinthians 12:27 says, "Now you are the body of Christ, and each one of you is a part of it." A body has many parts with differing functions, and each part must do what God designed it to do for the body to work properly. The Holy Spirit equips each person for what God has prepared for them to do.

Paul stated the same Holy Spirit gives different gifts, services, and workings for the body's common good (see 1 Corinthians 4–7). He gave the following examples in verses 8–10:

- Interpreting tongues
- Gifts of healing
- Speaking in tongues

- Knowledge
- Miraculous powers
- Distinguishing of spirits

- Faith
- Prophecy
- Wisdom

In Romans 12:6–8, Paul listed these additional gifts or services:

- Serving
- Showing mercy

- Teaching
- Leadership

- Encouraging
- Contributing to others' needs

Ephesians 4:11–13 includes the roles of apostles, prophets, evangelists, pastors, and teachers, which I referred to as the fivefold ministry in Chapter 7. These positions are "to equip his people for works of service, so that the body of Christ may be built up" (verse 12).

Paul encouraged the Corinthians to "follow the way of love and eagerly desire gifts of the Spirit, especially prophecy" (1 Corinthians 14:1), "[because] the one who prophesies speaks to people for their strengthening, encouraging and comfort" (verse 3). Giving practical application, Paul also said, "When you come together, each of you has a hymn, or a word of instruction, a revelation, a tongue or an interpretation. Everything must be done so that the church may be built up" (1 Corinthians 14:26).

God equips us to participate, not spectate, so we strengthen his body (us). But it seems the church gatherings in Paul's era were more interactive than ours today. That means we must plug into Christ's body outside the weekly hour we refer to as a worship service. We need additional outlets where we can use our gifts and serve others. We needn't choose one venue over another. Nor must we limit how often we meet. We can gather anywhere at any time to love and encourage each other.

The home-group setting I mentioned earlier provides a place where we can discover and use the gifts God has given us to encourage and build each other up. Attending classes or conferences addressing the various spiritual gifts can also be helpful. Some denominations promote using spiritual gifts at their gatherings, but many don't. How then will Christ's body mature without everyone doing their part?

Using our spiritual gifts can be as controversial as the Holy Spirit himself. At least it was in Paul's day, according to his letters to the Corinthians. Thus, Paul concluded his discourse on the various spiritual gifts in 1 Corinthians 12 by saying, "And yet I will show you the most excellent way" (verse 31). His answer: love. Its meaning and importance occupy the whole next chapter.

Because we often forget love's significance, I've included the first eight verses of chapter thirteen:

If I speak in the tongues of men and of angels, but have not love, I am only a resounding gong or a clanging cymbal. If I have the gift of prophecy and can fathom all mysteries and all knowledge, and if I have a faith that can move mountains, but do not have love, I am nothing. If I give all I possess to the poor and give over my body to hardship that I may boast, but do not have love, I gain nothing.

Love is patient, love is kind. It does not envy, it does not boast, it is not proud. It does not dishonor others, it is not self-seeking, it is not easily angered, it keeps no record of wrongs. Love does not delight in evil but rejoices with the truth. It always protects, always trusts, always hopes, always perseveres. Love never fails.

President Theodore Roosevelt said, "People don't care how much you know, until they know how much you care."[5] Likewise, our gifts, callings, services, etc. will mean nothing to others unless love accompanies them. Our highest calling is to love. You don't have to be gifted to love, but you need God's love to love the unlovable and to love sacrificially. When we love as God loves, we may discover our unique part in Christ's body by the direction God tugs at our heart.

Community works best when love is present. After all, we're a family. We must honor and embrace our differences, knowing each person's uniqueness contributes to a functioning body. Like pieces of a giant jigsaw puzzle, when we fit together perfectly, we reflect God's beautiful design. If we withhold our piece, the picture is incomplete. Christ's body won't function as God intended unless everyone does their part.

So, let us love and encourage one another, using our gifts and extending fellowship "until we all reach unity in the faith and in the knowledge of the Son of God and become mature, attaining to the whole measure of the fullness of Christ" (Ephesians 4:13).

Yada Time

Contemplate on how you fit into Christ's body. How are you using the gifts the Lord has given you? What direction is God stirring your heart right now? If you find it is difficult to love people, ask the Lord for his love toward others. When I did this, God poured his love into me so I had more to give.

When do you spend time with other believers outside your weekly church service? Would you like more fellowship? Share your heart's desire with the Lord. He may lead you to start or join a home fellowship group. You can glean much information about home groups from the internet. If you are reading this book alone, consider inviting others to read it with you so you can enjoy fellowship with others while discussing the questions as a group.

Seek God and stay alert and you will recognize the opportunities he provides.

Day 4: Spotless Bride

The Seven Dwarfs assumed the Evil Queen would try to kill Snow White again, so they warned her every day as they left for work not to answer the door. One day when the dwarfs were gone, the queen, disguised as an old peddler woman, appeared to Snow White. The queen engaged the princess in conversation, as the serpent did with Eve, and tempted her with a beautiful red apple. To gain Snow White's trust, the Evil Queen bit into the apple's non-poisoned half before handing it to the princess.

When the Seven Dwarfs came home, they found Snow White lying on the ground, presumably dead. Unwilling to part with their beloved princess, they placed her in a glass coffin so they could gaze upon her forever.

We know the story doesn't end there because it lacks a happily-ever-after ending. Snow White will awaken because she's destined to marry a prince—and so are we. Besides our collective role as Christ's body, the Bible also refers to us as Christ's bride. In Mark 2:19, Jesus calls himself the Bridegroom. Revelation 19:7 says, "Let us rejoice and be glad and give him glory! For the wedding of the Lamb [Jesus] has come, and his bride has made herself ready." Paul used the analogy of marriage when he said Christ died to "make her [the bride] holy … without stain or wrinkle or any other blemish, but holy and blameless" (Ephesians 5:26–27).

Though the Bible refers to us as Christ's bride, our current condition seems far from the holy and blameless bride he's returning for. It's hard to distinguish his bride from the rest of the world at times. However, our Prince is coming for us, and we will be as white as snow.

The Bible associates the color white with goodness, holiness, or purity. Daniel 7:9 describes the Ancient of Days: "His clothing was as white as snow; the hair of his head was white like wool." On the Mount of Transfiguration, Jesus' appearance "was like lightning, and his clothes were white as snow" (Matthew 28:3). Isaiah 1:18 declares our sins, when covered by Jesus' blood, are "as white as snow." This is positional holiness. We've discussed that God sees us in Christ as pure and holy because he took our sins on himself. However, many Bible verses also call us to demonstrate moral holiness.

First Peter 1:15 says, "But just as he who called you is holy, so be holy in all you do." The word holy in Greek is *hagos*. Besides meaning to be set apart, as in both the Greek and Hebrew, the Greek definition includes being morally pure and blameless.[6] Jesus clarified the holiness God expects when he addressed the sins of the heart. For example, he said, "But I tell you that anyone who looks at a woman lustfully has already committed adultery with her in his heart" (Matthew 5:28). He called the Pharisees hypocrites for cleaning the outside of ceremonial dishes when inside they were "full of greed and self-indulgence" (Matthew 23:25).

Jesus modeled the holiness God requires. Therefore, Jesus deserves nothing less than a pure and holy bride when he returns. Second Peter 3:9 says, "The Lord is not slow in keeping his promise [to return], as some understand slowness. Instead he is patient with you, not wanting anyone to perish, but everyone to come to repentance." Could it also be that he is waiting until "his bride has made herself ready" (Revelation 19:7)?

The Greek language has several words for ready. In this verse, the word is *hetoimazo*. It implies internal preparation, not external equipment.[7] Holiness, or getting ready for our Bridegroom, is an internal job. God has always been most concerned about our heart's condition. Jesus explained why when he said, "But the things that come out of a person's mouth come from the heart, and these defile them. For out of the heart come evil thoughts—murder, adultery, sexual immorality, theft, false testimony, slander" (Matthew 15:18–19).

In the Beginning Experience class where I met Chuck, we watched a video series based on John Powell's book *Happiness is an Inside Job*. As the title suggests and taught, we are responsible for our happiness. Likewise, we determine our moral holiness. We must choose to become who God says we are: pure and holy, no longer sinners.

When Moses called the Israelites to holiness, he said, "Circumcise your hearts, therefore, and do not be stiff-necked any longer" (Deuteronomy 10:16). While reading my Bible as a preteen, I asked my mom what circumcision meant. Our family rarely mentioned "private parts," and if we did, we never used their correct names. I can't remember my mom's answer, but I recall my embarrassment for having asked.

Circumcision removes the flesh. We first see its connection to holiness when God changed Abram's name to Abraham and said, "Walk before me faithfully and be blameless" (Genesis 17:1). God continued, "This is my covenant with you and your descendants after you … Every male among you shall be circumcised" (Genesis 17:10). Can you imagine Abraham's initial response? Had I been him, I might have stammered, "You want us to do what?"

Denying our sin nature and severing its hold on our heart can be as painful as physical circumcision was for Abraham. Colossians 2:11 says, "When you came to Christ, you were 'circumcised,' but not by a physical procedure. Christ performed a spiritual circumcision—the cutting away of your sinful nature" (NLT). We can't be holy apart from Christ, but we must deny our sin nature to become like him. This, too, is a process, and we'll progress more quickly when we cooperate with the Holy Spirit who searches our hearts, convicts us of sin, and reveals our hidden motives. Without his help, we are powerless to change, and blind to our sin.

My husband did the electrical wiring in the last house we built. While he strung the wires on the main floor one evening, I swept the debris on the second floor the workers had left behind. As the sun set and the house darkened, Chuck set up portable lamps to help him see. The lamps' light drifted up the open stairway and through the studs to the second floor where I continued sweeping.

The lighting seemed adequate, but I took extra precaution not to miss anything by sweeping in a systematic pattern. After Chuck finished, he came upstairs carrying a lamp. As he drew near, the nails, sawdust, and wood scraps came into view where I had already swept. I had missed almost as much as I had gotten. We often attempt to sweep ourselves clean without using a bright enough light or no light at all. Only God's light can expose the darkest areas and reveal our heart's true condition.

Though the Holy Spirit gently and lovingly shows us where we need cleaning, the process can hurt, such as when my employer reprimanded me. To help us stay clean, God allows transforming moments to be memorable: who can forget having food poisoning? I understand why God compares heartfelt change to circumcision. But humorous events can also leave a lasting impression, as this next story illustrates.

One spring day when I was still working as a mortgage loan officer, I sent flowering plants as thank-you gifts to the real estate agents who had referred clients to me. Several worked at the same company, and the beautiful plants brightened their desks throughout the office. I learned the plants caused the co-workers to mention my name frequently by asking who had given them the plants. My thank-you gifts had turned into an unintentional marketing tool.

Six months later at Christmastime, I sent Poinsettias to the same agents to thank them for their continued business. Secretly, I hoped they'd create as much office buzz about me as before. When I visited them, Poinsettias adorned all seventy-plus desks in their office—gifts from their boss. The ones I'd sent went unnoticed, and probably unappreciated. I sensed God laughing (with me), as he knew I had tried to hide my true motive.

I'm not saying God dislikes marketing, but he despises deceit. Therefore, our motives concern him the most. Proverbs 16:2 says, "People may be pure in their own eyes, but the Lord examines their motives" (NLT). We can never fool God. He knows whether we've done something with a pure heart or with a selfish motive, such as helping someone to gain praise.

When we give financially to a ministry that promises a miracle or blessing in exchange, both motives are wrong. We don't give to get; we get to give from the abundances we've received. Neither should we give out of fear that something bad will happen to us if we don't. Second Corinthians 9:7 says, "You must each decide in your heart how much to give. And don't give reluctantly or in response to pressure. 'For God loves a person who gives cheerfully'" (NLT).

Giving is just one example of how our selfish motives and sinful habits can elude us. David knew this when he wrote, "Search me, O God, and know my heart; test me and know my anxious thoughts. See if there is any offensive way in me, and lead me in the way of everlasting" (Psalm 139:23–24).

Only through God can we display moral holiness. When we seek to know and love him with our whole heart, he will illumine the darkness in us. When he does, we should rejoice. Every sin we conquer and every motive we purify brings us one step closer to living a holy—and happier—life. In this way, we will "make ourselves ready" to be the Bride of Christ.

Yada Time

Practice holiness in tangible ways. Speak the truth; don't lie or exaggerate. Keep your word and do what you say you will. Love others as you love yourself. Return things lent to you. If given incorrect change, give back what isn't yours.

Ask the Lord to shine his light and search your heart to reveal any area that needs deeper cleaning. Consider if your motives are pure. Work with the Lord to grow in moral holiness.

Day 5: Someday Our Prince Will Come

Days and weeks passed as Snow White lay in her glass coffin. One day, a prince and his entourage happened upon the Seven Dwarfs' cottage and the seemingly dead princess. Gazing at her beauty, the Prince fell instantly in love with Snow White. He begged the dwarfs to let him take the princess home with him, to watch over her. The dwarfs took pity on the love-smitten prince and agreed to his request. As the Prince's servants carried the glass coffin, they stumbled. The movement dislodged an apple piece stuck in the princess' throat. She lifted the coffin's lid and sat up. The Prince proposed to her immediately, and wedding plans commenced.

As young girls, many of us dreamt of our wedding day and of the "prince" we hoped to marry. We imagined ourselves walking down the aisle looking as beautiful as a princess. We made mental notes at the weddings we attended, planning our own. Fairy tales suggest the path to happily ever after begins here, at matrimony's altar. And, in a way, it does—but not as we imagined.

Romans 12:1 calls us to a sacrificial altar, "to offer your bodies as a living sacrifice, holy and pleasing to God—this is your true and proper worship." We will never find happiness until we live for God. He created us for his pleasure (see Revelation 4:11, KJV). However, he also wants us to experience the pleasure we bring him and the pleasure we gain by knowing and loving him. Christians should be the happiest people on earth, especially since the Father betrothed us to his Son.

Snow White's story ends where a believer's life in Christ begins: wed to the Prince of Peace, Jesus. When Love's first kiss awakened us to new life, we fell instantly in love and knew only he could complete us. So, we answered "Yes!" to his proposal and gave our lives to him. In biblical times, a couple's betrothal bound them to each other as legally as a marriage license does today. Therefore, Jesus is already our husband! The Apostle Paul wrote to the Corinthians, "For I am jealous for you with a godly jealousy; for I betrothed you to one husband, that to Christ I might present you as a pure virgin" (2 Corinthians 11:2, NASB).

Today's marriage process differs greatly from biblical times. The Old Testament tells us that a father determined when and whom his son would marry. Abraham sent his servant to a distant land to find a bride among Abraham's relatives for his son, Isaac. The master's servant brought gifts for the prospective bride and her family. If the father approved, he allowed his daughter to refuse or accept the servant's proposal (see Genesis 24).

Jewish marriage customs reflect God's beautiful love story with humankind. In the fullness of time, God the Father sent the Holy Spirit, the Helper, to find a bride for his Son, Jesus. Because God considers us of great worth, the Son paid the ultimate price with his life to obtain us as his bride. We, of course, are also given a choice to accept Jesus as our Bridegroom. When we do, the Holy Spirit lavishes us with gifts. In a binding agreement, we commit to stay pure and holy until our Bridegroom returns for us.

Preparing the disciples for his death, Jesus said, "My Father's house has many rooms; if that were not so, would I have told you that I am going there to prepare a place for you" (John 14:2). After a couple's betrothal, a groom spoke similar words to his bride before returning to his father's house. He then spent the next year or two adding a room to his family's home where he and his bride would live.[8]

The bride did not know the day or hour the groom would return for her—nor did the groom. After all the preparations had been made, the groom's father decided when the son could bring his bride home. Jesus said about his return, "But about that day or hour no one knows, not even the angels in heaven, nor the Son, but only the Father" (Mark 13:32).

A bride used the time between the betrothal and her groom's return to prepare herself for her husband. She didn't know when he would return, so she stayed alert and watchful, ready to meet him at a moment's notice. A groom often returned at night, and a shout from a groomsman heralded the groom's arrival.

The bride's attendants also had to stay alert, keeping oil in their lamps, as the parable of the twelve virgins indicated (see Matthew 25:1–13). In a torch-lit procession, the wedding party proceeded to the father's house for the wedding banquet.

First Thessalonians 4:16–17 describes Jesus' return for his bride:

> For the Lord himself will come down from heaven, with a loud command, with the voice of the archangel and with the trumpet call of God, and the dead in Christ will rise first. After that, we who are still alive and are left will be caught up together with them in the clouds to meet the Lord in the air. And so we will be with the Lord forever.

A glorious wedding feast awaits us, where one day we will see our Groom face to face! "Let us rejoice and be glad and give him glory! For the wedding of the Lamb has come, and his bride has made herself ready" (Revelation 19:7). How can we not be the happiest people on earth? God betrothed us to himself and promised to return for us. We live in the timeframe between our betrothal and the consummation of our union with Christ.

However, unlike an Old Testament bride who had to wait to begin married life with her husband, we can enjoy intimacy and companionship with our Beloved before he returns. God promised never to leave or forsake us (see Hebrews 13:5). He lives within us!

By turning our affection toward him—by seeking his FACE (faith, attributes, creation, or experience)—we can experience his presence. He's always with us, but he will not force himself on us. We must give ourselves to him, and nurture an intimate relationship with him as he relentlessly pursues us.

The romantic love between a bride and groom as found in the Song of Solomon (Song) describes God's passion toward us and what ours can be toward him:

The groom sings to his bride:

- You are altogether beautiful, my darling; there is no flaw in you. (Song 4:7)
- You have captured my heart, my treasure, my bride. You hold it hostage with one glance of your eyes, with a single jewel of your necklace. (Song 4:9, NLT)
- My dove, my perfect one, is unique. (Song 6:9)
- Who is this that appears like the dawn, fair as the moon, bright as the sun, majestic as the stars in procession? (Song 6:10)

The bride sings to her groom:

- I slept but my heart was awake. Listen! My beloved is knocking. (Song 5:2)
- My beloved is dazzling and ruddy, outstanding among ten thousand. (Song 5:10, NASB)
- His mouth is full of sweetness. And he is wholly desirable. This is my beloved and this is my friend. (Song 5:16, NASB)
- I belong to my beloved, and his desire is for me. (Song 7:10)

Love's yearning as expressed in the Song of Solomon is intoxicating, and it is how God feels about you! Isaiah 62:5 says, "As a bridegroom rejoices over his bride, so will your God rejoice over you." Doesn't that stir you to become the purest, most beautiful bride imaginable? Our Beloved deserves nothing less than our perfection.

Mike Bickle, director of the International House of Prayer of Kansas City, explains why he thinks Jesus saved the parable about the wedding feast until the last:

> I believe Jesus was enticing His people with a dynamic new emphasis on divine romance, knowing it would excite the human heart as nothing else would. He wanted to stir up a hot desire in each of us for extravagant "bridegroom love," with Jesus Himself as the Bridegroom, and we, His people, His church, the cherished bride.[9]

Nothing propels us more quickly toward happiness than passion for our Bridegroom. When we are lovesick, we will do anything to experience his LAFTER (love, adoration, favor, truth, and extravagant riches), and when we do, we will LAF (look, act, and feel) like daughters of the King and embrace our true identity as his beloved bride. We will stop living incognito and find courage to try on the shoes he's tailor-made for us.

Beware, our enemy will oppose us at every turn, but love for our Bridegroom will empower us to persevere and overcome. We fight from a place of victory because Jesus paid the price for everything we'll ever need. He pronounced covenant promises, his marriage vows, to us in his

Word. As he is faithful, we too should be faithful not to put on sin but to clothe ourselves with him.

We must run to our Bridegroom with our fears and problems because he is our strong tower. To find peace, we must gain his perspective and attitude while releasing our expectations to him. He alone can rescue us from our self-made walls of protection and demolish the enemy's stronghold. It might require we take a leap of faith, but his love will enable us to jump into his waiting arms. He will never let us fall.

His love awakened us to new life. We needn't strive for his acceptance; it's not based on our performance. He loves us unconditionally. We can find rest in him because he understands us better than we understand ourselves. He places his desires in our heart. Only our heavenly Bridegroom can fulfill all our wants and needs.

The romance never ends when God fills us with love's deep yearning. This overwhelming passion for our Bridegroom shifts our focus from ourselves and onto him. Here we realize happily ever after isn't our greatest desire. We want him, our Beloved. So we eagerly surrender ourselves completely to "this love that surpasses knowledge," yearning to be "filled to the measure of all the fullness of God" (Ephesians 3:19). We desire oneness with our Bridegroom more than anything else.

Our Prince has come, and someday he will return and we will be with him for all eternity. But we needn't wait to enjoy our union with him until then. Jesus lives in us. He came to give us abundant life. Betrothal to our Beloved surpasses anything we could ask for or imagine. As we abide in him, we experience love, joy, peace, patience, passion, pleasure, freedom, identity, fulfillment, acceptance, security, adventure, provision, a sense of worth, purpose, belonging, etc. He alone is our happily ever after.

Yada Time

While imagining yourself as Christ's spotless bride, bask in God's love for you. If you struggle to experience God's passion, ask him to romance you. Ask him to show you how much he loves you. Express your love and gratitude by turning your affection toward him. Fall in love with Jesus as never before and become a lovesick bride who desires to spend every second with her Bridegroom. "Amen. Come, Lord Jesus" (Revelation 22:20).

Chapter 10
Snow White—Spotless Bride
Questions for Reflection or Discussion

Day 1: Mirror, Mirror

1. Define jealousy. (p. 172) When do you get jealous?

2. When does God get jealous? Share examples. (p. 172)

3. How does envy differ from jealousy? (p. 172)

4. Which do you struggle with most: envy, jealousy, or coveting?

5. How did Paul obtain contentment? (Philippians 4:12–13, p. 172)

6. Discuss each step in the author's 3-T approach to conquering discontentment. (p. 173)

Day 2: Wonder Woman

1. Discuss the reasons we can lose our childlike wonder. (p. 174)

2. What are the different ways we can experience wonder? (p. 176)

3. What is the value of wonder? (p. 176)

4. How can we add more wonder to our lives? (p. 176)

5. Why can you claim to be a wonder woman? (p. 176)

Day 3: Community

1. Which "what if" worries keep you from enjoying community? (p. 178)

2. What must we risk or reveal to truly connect with others? (p. 178)

3. Of the children mentioned singing, which one best describes you as a child?

4. What gift or service do you possess for Christ's body? (p. 179)

5. When and where do you use your gift?

6. Why did Paul say we should desire the gift of prophecy? (1 Corinthians 14:3, p. 179)

7. What does God call us to do above all else? Why? (1 Corinthians 13, p. 179–180)

Day 4: A Spotless Bride

1. What is the difference between positional holiness and moral holiness? (p. 181)

2. What did Jesus say makes a man unclean? (p. 181)

3. What does it mean to circumcise our hearts? (p. 182)

4. Why must we depend on God to illumine the darkness in us? (p. 182)

5. How does holiness affect our happiness?

Day 5: Someday Our Prince Will Come

1. How is matrimony's altar like a sacrificial altar? (p. 184)

2. How binding is a biblical betrothal? (p. 184)

3. What does being betrothed to Christ mean to you?

4. Compare the Jewish wedding customs to God's love story with us. (pp. 184–185)

5. What marriage vows (promises) in the Bible do you cling to?

Share prayer requests and pray for each other. Let's rejoice together because we're betrothed to the Prince of Peace, Jesus, who will soon return for us.

Appendix A

God loves you more than you can imagine. In fact, "God so loved the world that he gave his one and only Son [Jesus], that whoever believes in him shall not perish but have eternal life" (John 3:16). Sin creates a barrier between us and God because God is holy. Because we are born with a sin nature, which we inherited from Adam and Eve, we all sin (see Romans 3:23). And the wages of sin is death (see Romans 6:23). Therefore, we are dead in our sins, separated from God, until we receive what Jesus did on our behalf.

Second Corinthians 5:21 says, "God made him [Jesus] who had no sin to be sin for us, so that in him we might become the righteousness of God." Jesus lived a perfect life. His sacrifice on the cross paid the penalty for our sins. Romans 6:23 says, "The wages of sin is death, but the gift of God is eternal life in Christ Jesus our Lord."

Salvation or eternal life is a gift.

Ephesians 10:8–9 says, "For it is by grace you have been saved, through faith—and this is not from yourselves, it is the gift of God—not by works, so that no one can boast."

Like any gift, we must believe the gift is ours and receive it. That's what "through faith" means: believe and receive. It's that simple. But it may take time for you to be *assured* of your salvation. It's normal to have doubts, but that doesn't mean you aren't saved.

I had a lot of questions when I first became a Christian. I feared I might lose my salvation if I sinned and forgot to confess something. (Don't worry, you won't.) I also wondered if I had truly made him Lord of my life. My life didn't always reflect Jesus being in control of every area. When I shared my concerns with a mature Christian, they provided answers from God's Word that assured me that I was saved. I encourage you to do the same. Assurance will come as you know (yada) God better and understand his truths.

Romans 10:9–10 says, "If you declare with your mouth, 'Jesus is Lord,' and believe in your heart that God raised him from the dead, you will be saved. For it is with your heart that you believe and are justified, and it is with your mouth that you profess your faith and are saved."

Once you've given your life to Christ, I encourage you to declare "Jesus is Lord" and tell someone about the commitment you've made.

There's no specific prayer or words you must say to be saved. It's a heart issue. You must repent (turn from) your sinful ways and accept God's forgiveness through Jesus Christ. You must surrender (give to God) your life and desire Jesus to live in and through you. Salvation is instantaneous. Colossians 1:13 says, "For he [God] has rescued us from the dominion of darkness and brought us into the kingdom of the Son he loves." But salvation is also an ongoing process in which we learn to reflect the light and resemble Jesus in our thoughts, words, and actions.

For those who would like a prayer to recite, I've provided the following:

Dear God,

I confess that I have sinned and cannot save myself. I could never be good enough to earn salvation. (Take a minute to confess specific sins that come to mind. Don't worry about remembering them all. You can confess more whenever the Holy Spirit reminds you.)

I believe Jesus is the Son of God, and that he died on the cross to pay the penalty for my sins. I ask you, Jesus, to come into my heart; be Lord of my life. I surrender my life to you.

I receive your gift of salvation, and I receive the gift of the Holy Spirit. I believe you live in me, and I desire to do your will.

Amen!

Now declare Galatians 2:20: "I have been crucified with Christ and I no longer live, but Christ lives in me. The life I now live in the body, I live by faith in the Son of God, who loved me and gave himself for me."

Welcome to God's family!

You are now a new creation in Christ Jesus. The old you is gone! (see 2 Corinthians 5:17). Share this good news with someone who will rejoice with you, and get plugged into the body of Christ. "Grow in the grace and knowledge of our Lord and Savior Jesus Christ. To him be glory both now and forever! Amen" (2 Peter 3:18).

Notes

Chapter 1

1. Coleridge, Samuel Taylor. http://www.phrases.org.uk/meanings/suspension-of-disbelief.html

2. "4100. pisteuo." From Biblesoft's *New Exhaustive Strong's Numbers and Concordance with Expanded Greek-Hebrew Dictionary*. Copyright © 1994, 2003, 2006 Biblesoft, Inc. and International Bible Translators, Inc.

3. Dobson, James. Adapted from *When God Doesn't Make Sense*. Tyndale House, 1993, pp. 120–121, used by permission.

4. Anderson, Neil T. *Victory over the Darkness—Realizing the power of your identity in Christ.* Regal Books, 1990, p. 110.

5. "3045. yada." From Biblesoft's *New Exhaustive Strong's Numbers and Concordance with Expanded Greek-Hebrew Dictionary*. Copyright © 1994, 2003, 2006 Biblesoft, Inc. and International Bible Translators, Inc.

6. "5287. hupostasis." From Biblesoft's *New Exhaustive Strong's Numbers and Concordance with Expanded Greek-Hebrew Dictionary*. Copyright © 1994, 2003, 2006 Biblesoft, Inc. and International Bible Translators, Inc.

7. Bullinger, E.W. *Great Cloud of Witnesses in Hebrews Eleven.* Kregel Classics an imprint of Kregel Publications, 1979, pp. 6–7.

8. "1411. dunamis." From Biblesoft's *New Exhaustive Strong's Numbers and Concordance with Expanded Greek-Hebrew Dictionary*. Copyright © 1994, 2003, 2006 Biblesoft, Inc. and International Bible Translators, Inc.

9. "Ecclesiastes 11:1" Study note on page 945 in the *NASB Study Bible*, Zondervan, 1995, editors Kenneth L. Barker, Donald W. Burdick, John H. Stek, Walter W. Wessel, Ronald F. Youngblood, Kenneth D. Boa.

10. "7965. shalom." From Biblesoft's *New Exhaustive Strong's Numbers and Concordance with Expanded Greek-Hebrew Dictionary*. Copyright © 1994, 2003, 2006 Biblesoft, Inc. and International Bible Translators, Inc.

11. Friesen, James G., and E. James Wilder, Anne M. Bierling, Rick Koepcke, and Maribeth Poole. *Living From the Heart Jesus Gave You, the Essentials of Christian Living*. Shepherd's House, Inc. 1999, p. 36.

12. Ibid, p. 46.

13. Hurnard, Hannah. *Hinds' Feet on High Places*. Living Books, 1904.

14. Wells, Orson. In "Orson Wells Quotes." BrainyQuote.com. https://www.brainyquote.com/quotes/quotes/o/orsonwelle162035.html

15. "5046. teleios." From Biblesoft's *New Exhaustive Strong's Numbers and Concordance with Expanded Greek-Hebrew Dictionary*. Copyright © 1994, 2003, 2006 Biblesoft, Inc. and International Bible Translators, Inc.

Chapter 2

1. "Movie Quotes from *Caddyshack*." Movie Quotes Database. http://www.moviequotedb.com/movies/caddyshack/quote_4832.html

2. "4991. soteria." From Biblesoft's *New Exhaustive Strong's Numbers and Concordance with Expanded Greek-Hebrew Dictionary*. Copyright © 1994, 2003, 2006 Biblesoft, Inc. and International Bible Translators, Inc.

3. "4982. sozo." From Biblesoft's *New Exhaustive Strong's Numbers and Concordance with Expanded Greek-Hebrew Dictionary*. Copyright © 1994, 2003, 2006 Biblesoft, Inc. and International Bible Translators, Inc.

4. "2716. katergazoma." From Biblesoft's *New Exhaustive Strong's Numbers and Concordance with Expanded Greek-Hebrew Dictionary*. Copyright © 1994, 2003, 2006 Biblesoft, Inc. and International Bible Translators, Inc.

5. Adams, Mark. "Whine or Shine." January 7, 2001. Redland Baptist Church. http://www.redlandbaptist.org/sermon/whine-or-shine/

6. Wilkinson, Bruce. *The Dream Giver.* Multnomah, 2003, p. 75.

7. Tozer, A. W. *The Pursuit of God.* Christian Publications, 1948, p. 120.

8. Johnson, Bill. In "Bill Johnson Quotes." AZQuotes.com. http://www.azquotes.com/quote/1318190

Chapter 3

1. "Commentary on 2 Corinthians 3:18." From *The Biblical Illustrator* Copyright © 2002, 2003, 2006 Ages Software, Inc. and Biblesoft, Inc.

2. "Commentary on Galatians 5:24." From *Bible Knowledge Commentary/Old Testament* Copyright © 1983, 2000 Cook Communications Ministries; Bible Knowledge Commentary/New Testament Copyright © 1983, 2000 Cook Communications Ministries. All rights reserved.

3. "7307. ruwach." From Biblesoft's *New Exhaustive Strong's Numbers and Concordance with Expanded Greek-Hebrew Dictionary.* Copyright © 1994, 2003, 2006 Biblesoft, Inc. and International Bible Translators, Inc.

4. Twain, Mark. In "Mark Twain Quotes." AZQuotes.com. http://www.azquotes.com/author/14883-Mark_Twain/tag/worry

5. "342. anakainosis." From Biblesoft's *New Exhaustive Strong's Numbers and Concordance with Expanded Greek-Hebrew Dictionary.* Copyright © 1994, 2003, 2006 Biblesoft, Inc. and International Bible Translators, Inc.

6. "O Be Careful Little Eyes What You See." Hymnary. http://www.hymnary.org/text/o_be_careful_little_eyes_what_you_see. Copyright 1956, Zondervan Music Publishers.

7. Lucado, Max. Taken from *You are Special.* Crossway, 1997. Used by permission of Crossway, a publishing ministry of Good News Publishers, Wheaton, IL 60187, www.crossway.org

8. Ibid, p. 29.

Chapter 4

1. Prince, Derek. *They Shall Expel Demons.* Chosen Books, 1998, p. 100.

2. Ibid, p. 110.

3. "Beauty." http://www.dictionary.com/browse/beauty?s=t

4. "Splendor." Merriam-Webster. https://www.merriam-webster.com/dictionary/splendor

5. "The Holy of Holies and the Veil." The Tabernacle Place. http://the-tabernacle-place.com/articles/what_is_the_tabernacle/tabernacle_holy_of_holies

6. "1567. ekzeteo." From Biblesoft's *New Exhaustive Strong's Numbers and Concordance with Expanded Greek-Hebrew Dictionary.* Copyright © 1994, 2003, 2006 Biblesoft, Inc. and International Bible Translators, Inc.

7. Tozer, A. W. *The Pursuit of God.* Christian Publications, Inc., 1982, p. 88.

8. Rich, Tracy R. "Shabbat." Judaism 101. http://www.jewfaq.org/shabbat.htm

9. Grant, Tobin. "The Great Decline: 60 Years of Religion in One Graph." Religion News Service. January 27, 2014. http://religionnews.com/2014/01/27/great-decline-religion-united-states-one-graph/

10. "The Shabbat Laws." Chabad.org. http://www.chabad.org/library/article_cdo/aid/95907/jewish/The-Shabbat-Laws.htm

11. Tozer, A. W. *The Pursuit of God.* Christian Publications, Inc., 1982, p. 105.

12. "4341. mak'ob." From Biblesoft's *New Exhaustive Strong's Numbers and Concordance with Expanded Greek-Hebrew Dictionary.* Copyright © 1994, 2003, 2006 Biblesoft, Inc. and International Bible Translators, Inc.

13. "3340. metanoeo." From Biblesoft's *New Exhaustive Strong's Numbers and Concordance with Expanded Greek-Hebrew Dictionary.* Copyright © 1994, 2003, 2006 Biblesoft, Inc. and International Bible Translators, Inc.

Chapter 5

1. Urist, Jacoba. "What the Marshmallow Test Really Teaches About Self-Control." The Atlantic. September 24, 2014. https://www.theatlantic.com/health/archive/2014/09/what-the-marshmallow-test-really-teaches-about-self-control/380673/

2. Ibid.

3. Clear, James. "40 Years of Stanford Research Found That People With This One Quality Are More Likely to Succeed." http://jamesclear.com/delayed-gratification

4. Westminster Assembly. Westminster Shorter Catechism. The Orthodox Presbyterian Church, 1646. https://www.opc.org/sc.html

5. Lloyd-Jones, Sally. *Thoughts to Make Your Heart Sing*, Zonderkidz, 2012.

6. Tverberg, Lois, and Bruce Okkema. *Listening to the Language of the Bible: Hearing It Through Jesus' Ears*. The En-Gedi Resource Center, 2004, 2006.

7. Warren, Rick. *The Purpose Driven Life*, Zondervan, 2002, p. 67.

8. "5293. hupotasso." From Biblesoft's *New Exhaustive Strong's Numbers and Concordance with Expanded Greek-Hebrew Dictionary*. Copyright © 1994, 2003, 2006 Biblesoft, Inc. and International Bible Translators, Inc.

9. Foster, Richard. *Celebration of Discipline*: *The Path to Spiritual Growth*. HarperCollins, 1978, 1988, 1998, p. 111.

10. Ibid, p. 112.

11. Ibid, p. 113.

12. *Hayah*. "Exodus 3:14." Marginal note on page 81 in the *NASB Study Bible*, Zondervan, 1995, editors Kenneth L. Barker, Donald W. Burdick, John H. Stek, Walter W. Wessel, Ronald F. Youngblood, Kenneth D. Boa.

Chapter 6

1. "Perspective." Merriam-Webster. https://www.merriam-webster.com/dictionary/perspective

2. Ibid.

3. Swindoll, Charles R. In "Charles R. Swindoll" quotes. AZQuotes.com. http://www.azquotes.com/author/14373-Charles_R_Swindoll

4. Story based on "Three Hairs." Spiritual Short Stories. http://www.spiritual-short-stories.com/spiritual-short-story-100-Three-Hairs/

Chapter 7

1. "Biblical Prophecies Fulfilled by Jesus." Christian Broadcasting Network. http://www1.cbn.com/biblestudy/biblical-prophecies-fulfilled-by-jesus

2. MacArthur, John. "What is Biblical Discernment and Why is it Important?" https://www.gty.org/library/questions/QA138/what-is-biblical-discernment-and-why-is-it-important

3. "1381. dokimazo." From Biblesoft's *New Exhaustive Strong's Numbers and Concordance with Expanded Greek-Hebrew Dictionary*. Copyright © 1994, 2003, 2006 Biblesoft, Inc. and International Bible Translators, Inc.

4. "Intuition." Merriam-Webster. https://www.merriam-webster.com/dictionary/intuition

5. "Understanding the Teen Brain." Health Encyclopedia. University of Rochester Medical Center. https://www.urmc.rochester.edu/encyclopedia/content.aspx?ContentTypeID=1&ContentID=3051

6. "Disciple." From Biblesoft's *New Exhaustive Strong's Numbers and Concordance with Expanded Greek-Hebrew Dictionary*. Copyright © 1994, 2003, 2006 Biblesoft, Inc. and International Bible Translators, Inc.

7. Friesen, James G., and E. James Wilder, Anne M. Bierling, Rick Koepcke, and Maribeth Poole. *Living From the Heart Jesus Gave You, the Essentials of Christian Living.* Shepherd's House, Inc. 1999.

8. "3619. oikodome." From Biblesoft's *New Exhaustive Strong's Numbers and Concordance with Expanded Greek-Hebrew Dictionary.* Copyright © 1994, 2003, 2006 Biblesoft, Inc. and International Bible Translators, Inc.

9. "2919. krino." From Biblesoft's *New Exhaustive Strong's Numbers and Concordance with Expanded Greek-Hebrew Dictionary.* Copyright © 1994, 2003, 2006 Biblesoft, Inc. and International Bible Translators, Inc.

10. Rhodan, Maya. "4 Times the World Came Close to 'Doomsday'." http://time.com/4193889/doomsday-clock-changed-2016/

11. Karacs, Sarah. "Doomsday Clock: Humanity might be edging closer to its end." http://www.cnn.com/2017/01/26/world/doomsday-clock-2017/

12. "5550. chronos." From Biblesoft's *New Exhaustive Strong's Numbers and Concordance with Expanded Greek-Hebrew Dictionary.* Copyright © 1994, 2003, 2006 Biblesoft, Inc. and International Bible Translators, Inc.

13. "2540. kairos." From Biblesoft's *New Exhaustive Strong's Numbers and Concordance with Expanded Greek-Hebrew Dictionary.* Copyright © 1994, 2003, 2006 Biblesoft, Inc. and International Bible Translators, Inc.

14. "2540. kairos." From *Thayer's Greek Lexicon*, Electronic Database. Copyright © 2000, 2003, 2006 by Biblesoft, Inc. All rights reserved.

Chapter 8

1. "What is an Inner Vow?" Hand of Jesus Ministries. https://handofjesus.org/healing/renouncing-inner-vows/

2. Godsey, Linda. *Origins: How the Choices of Your Ancestors Affect You Today.* Gateway Create Publishing, 2016, p. 66.

3. Hand of Jesus Ministries, *How to Renounce Inner Vows.* A publication of Hand of Jesus Ministries. https://handofjesus.org/wp-content/uploads/2015/02/HOJM-Inner-Vows-eBook.pdf

4. Rosenberg, Ross A. "Is Your Life Plagued by Loneliness? Tips to Overcome it." January 24, 2014. http://www.huffingtonpost.com/ross-a-rosenberg/loneliness_b_4648417.html

5. "The Anchor Holds." Metrolyrics. http://www.metrolyrics.com/the-anchor-holds-lyrics-ray-boltz.html. Published by Lyrics © Warner/Chappell Music, Inc.

6. "Praise the Lord." Metrolyrics. http://www.metrolyrics.com/praise-the-lord-lyrics-russ-taff.html. Published by Lyrics © Warner/Chappell Music, Inc.

7. "Blind faith." http://www.dictionary.com/browse/blind-faith?s=t

8. Frangipane, Francis. *The Stronghold of God.* Charisma House, 1998, p. 21.

9. Ibid.

Chapter 9

1. "Martin Luther, Passionate Reformer." Christianity Today. http://www.christianitytoday.com/history/people/theologians/martin-luther.html

2. Elliott, Jim. https://www.brainyquote.com/search_results.html?q=jim+elliott

3. Bonhoeffer, Dietrich. *The Cost of Discipleship.* The MacMillan Company; Tenth edition, 1968.

4. Ibid.

5. "7257. rabats." From Biblesoft's *New Exhaustive Strong's Numbers and Concordance with Expanded Greek-Hebrew Dictionary.* Copyright © 1994, 2003, 2006 Biblesoft, Inc. and International Bible Translators, Inc.

6. "8669. teshuwqah." From Biblesoft's *New Exhaustive Strong's Numbers and Concordance with Expanded Greek-Hebrew Dictionary.* Copyright © 1994, 2003, 2006 Biblesoft, Inc. and International Bible Translators, Inc.

7. "4910. mashal." From Biblesoft's *New Exhaustive Strong's Numbers and Concordance with Expanded Greek-Hebrew Dictionary*. Copyright © 1994, 2003, 2006 Biblesoft, Inc. and International Bible Translators, Inc.

8. Johnson, Bill. *Dreaming With God*. Destiny Image, 2006.

9. Rumpelstiltskin. https://en.wikipedia.org/wiki/Rumpelstiltskin

10. "Isaac." From *Easton's Bible Dictionary*, PC Study Bible formatted electronic database Copyright © 2003, 2006 Biblesoft, Inc. All rights reserved.

11. "Ben-oni." Ibid.

12. "Benjamin." Ibid.

13. "Abram/Abraham." Ibid.

14. Sumner, Paul. "'Elohim' in Biblical Context." http://www.hebrew-streams.org/works/hebrew/context-elohim.html

15. "El-Roi" From *International Standard Bible Encyclopaedia*, Electronic Database Copyright © 1996, 2003, 2006 by Biblesoft, Inc. All rights reserved.

16. "Yahweh." From *International Standard Bible Encyclopaedia*, Electronic Database Copyright © 1996, 2003, 2006 by Biblesoft, Inc. All rights reserved.

Chapter 10

1. "Jealous." Merriam-Webster. https://www.merriam-webster.com/dictionary/jealous

2. "Envy." Merriam-Webster. https://www.merriam-webster.com/dictionary/envy

3. "Covetous." http://www.dictionary.com/browse/covetousness?s=t

4. "Wonder." Merriam-Webster. https://www.merriam-webster.com/dictionary/wonder

5. Roosevelt, Theodore. https://www.brainyquote.com/quotes/quotes/t/theodorero140484.html

6. "40. hagos." From Biblesoft's *New Exhaustive Strong's Numbers and Concordance with Expanded Greek-Hebrew Dictionary*. Copyright © 1994, 2003, 2006 Biblesoft, Inc. and International Bible Translators, Inc.

7. "2090. hetoimazo." From Biblesoft's *New Exhaustive Strong's Numbers and Concordance with Expanded Greek-Hebrew Dictionary*. Copyright © 1994, 2003, 2006 Biblesoft, Inc. and International Bible Translators, Inc.

8. Valdivieso, Javier. "The Ancient Jewish Wedding: A Missing Link in Christianity." Triangle Association for the Science of Creation. October 2009. http://www.tasc-creationscience.org/content/ancient-jewish-wedding-missing-link-christianity

9. Bickle, Mike. "Called to be His Bride," from *Seeking the Savior*. Family Christian Stores, 2003, p. 9.

Special Thanks

To God the Father, Son, and Holy Spirit. I am eternally grateful for your unconditional love, acceptance, friendship, guidance, caring, encouragement, faithfulness, provision, etc. You are everything to me. Thank you for your continual work in my life and calling me to write.

To my best friend and husband, the love of my life: Chuck. You are God's "more than I could ask or imagine" gift. Thank you for loving and supporting me in so many ways.

To my parents: Joel and Janice Jensen. I am grateful for the faith you've lived and shared, your unconditional love, and for believing in me and always being there for me.

To my sons: Jordan and Jesse Doschadis. You've brought me more joy than I could have ever dreamed. Thank you for your love, support, and friendship. I am blessed to be your mom.

To my stepdaughter: Cindy Scherfenberg, and to her husband, Dave. Thank you for your love, friendship, and including me in your lives and the lives of your beautiful daughters Elle, Brooke, and Lacey. I am blessed to be a part of your wonderful family.

To my siblings: Scott Jensen, Terrie Ennis, Elicia Janning, and Jamie Trenberth. Thank you for your unconditional love, support, and endless hours of reminiscing and therapizing. You are more than siblings; you are great friends.

To Helen Allenson: You taught me grammar, punctuation, how *not* to split infinitives, and much more. I am grateful for your willingness to read and edit my work. You've helped me more than anyone could imagine (so let's keep that our secret). Thank you, dear friend!

To Pam Lagomarsino at *Above The Pages Editorial Service*. Thank you for your helpful guidance, encouragement, and instruction as you edited this book. Your expertise was invaluable and greatly appreciated.

To my first writing group: Cindy Hershberger, Dan McKay, Neil Frederickson, Renee Loehr, Shyla Thompson. Thank you for your friendship and constructive feedback. I will forever treasure the years we spent together.

To my first readers and study group participants: Donna Villiard, Judy Balluff, Karen Gemar, and Nancy Bradley. Thank you for your friendship and being my first test group. I am also grateful for your persistent encouragement to publish this book.

To Pam Haglund at *Living Well Women's Coaching*. Thank you for taking a chance on an unknown author and organizing and leading my second group. You're a great coach!

To the women who took part in Pam's group: Erin Enter, Teresa Hellerud, Dawn Rud, Gretchen Satterlund, Candi Schafer, Audrey Umbreit, and Janine Whited. Thank you for studying this book as a group and for your positive feedback.

To Marcie Lind and the participants in my third group: Joyce Newgard, Cathy Chresten, Evelyn Loraas. Thank you for studying this book and for your supportive feedback.

To my aunts and uncles: Donna Bruno, DeLoyce and Tom Anderson, Marilyn and Gus Bjorklund, and Sandra and Ken Dinse. Throughout the years, you've helped in ways too many to count. Thank you for being a caring, loving, and supportive family.

To my sister-in-law Carole Dahl and her husband, Gordon. Thank you for welcoming me into your family. You are truly kind, generous, and loving people. I am grateful for your friendship.

To my friends not previously mentioned, who encourage me in life: Becky Elert, Bev Fischer, Cheryl Abelmann, Cheryl Jordahl, Cindy Karlstrom, Gloria Springborg, Jane Dauffenbach, Jeanne Swick, Jodie Keck, Kathie Holoien, Kristie Fredrickson, Lori Salmon, Shelly Johnson, and Tami Hull. I could write a page on how much each of you mean to me. Thank you for your love and friendship.

In loving memory of my grandparents: Oscar and Eva Jensen; Donald and Peggy Bruno. You forged a trail that made my path easier. I'm grateful for your loving support and encouragement. I miss you and wish you were here to watch me follow in your footsteps.

About the Author

Kim A. Larson grew up in a Christian home and accepted Jesus as her Lord and Savior at age twelve. But it wasn't until she experienced the indescribable love for her sons that she began to grasp the extravagant love God has for his children. Then through an unwanted divorce, her journey to trust God for her every need deepened. Today, she is convinced of God's goodness and his ability "to do immeasurably more than all we ask or imagine" (Ephesians 3:20).

Kim has taught Sunday school, vacation Bible school, and led Bible studies and a single mom's ministry. It brings her great joy to share God's heart at Women's retreats, MOPs meetings, Mother-daughter programs or other Women's events. Kim is married to her best friend, Chuck, and has two grown sons, two stepchildren, twelve grandchildren, and three great-grandchildren.

REVIEW: If you enjoyed this book, please consider telling a friend and leaving a review online where you purchased this book.

FREE BOOK: If you'd like to read more from Kim, visit her website at KimALarson.com and subscribe to her newsletter. As a thank you, Kim will email you a FREE PDF copy of her first published work:

Love, Laughter,

and a few

Happily Ever Afters

A Collection of Short Stories and Poems

Made in the USA
Monee, IL
26 June 2020